Talcott Parsons and the
conceptual dilemma

International Library of Sociology

Founded by Karl Mannheim

Editor: John Rex, University of Aston in Birmingham

Arbor Scientiae
Arbor Vitae

A catalogue of the books available in the **International Library of Sociology** and other series of Social Science books published by Routledge & Kegan Paul will be found at the end of this volume.

Talcott Parsons and the conceptual dilemma

Hans P. M. Adriaansens

Routledge & Kegan Paul
London, Boston and Henley

First published in English in 1980
by Routledge & Kegan Paul Ltd,
39 Store Street,
London WC1E 7DD,
9 Park Street,
Boston, Mass. 02108, USA and
Broadway House,
Newtown Road,
Henley-on-Thames,
Oxon RG9 1EN.
Set in 10/11pt English Times Compugraphic
and printed in Great Britain by
Ebenezer Baylis & Son Ltd,
The Trinity Press, Worcester, and London
© Hans P. M. Adriaansens 1980
No part of this book may be reproduced in
any form without permission from the
publisher, except for the quotation of brief
passages in criticism.

British Library Cataloguing in Publication Data
Adriaansens, Hans P. M.
Talcott Parsons and the conceptual
dilemma. – (International library of
sociology).
1. Parsons, Talcott
2. Sociology
I. Title   II. Series
301'.01   HM22.U6P37   80-40056

ISBN 0 7100 0519 9

Contents

	Explanatory introduction	1
1	The general and analytical character of theory: Parsons's epistemological premise	9
	1 Introduction	9
	2 The concept of theory	10
	3 The general character of concept and theory	14
	4 The analytical character of concept and theory	20
	5 The theory of action, the theory of the social system and the theory of sociology	27
2	The voluntaristic pretension: Parsons's methodological premise	32
	1 Introduction: voluntarism as a methodological synthesis	32
	2 The methodological dimension of objectivist *versus* subjectivist *thought-patterns in historical perspective*	34
	3 The methodological dimension of social-nominalistic versus social-realistic patterns of thought in historical perspective	52
3	The structural-functional version of the action theory: the first attempt at conceptualization	58
	1 Introduction	58
	2 The frame of reference (1)	59
	3 The frame of reference (2)	61
	4 Analysis of action systems; structural-functionalism as 'second best mode of analysis'	65

*5 The combination of the voluntaristic frame of
　　reference with the structural-functional form
　　of analysis in a structural-functional theory
　　of action systems*   67
　　6 The structural-functional theory of social systems   72

4   The instability of the structural-functional version of
    the action theory   88
　　1 Introduction   88
　　*2 Inventorization of conceptual gaps in the
　　structural-functional version*   89
　　3 The conceptual dilemma: the clash of premises   93
　　*4 The instability of the structural-functional
　　version in the light of the conceptual dilemma*   96
　　*5 Reflections on the conceptual dilemma: the end
　　of the structural-functional version*   103
　　*6 The formulation of the new frame of reference:
　　the four-function paradigm*   107

5   The new voluntaristic action theory   116
　　*1 Introduction: the four-function paradigm and
　　the levels of the action theory*   116
　　2 The new theory of social systems   118
　　*3 The social system's symbolic media of interchange:
　　money, power, influence and value-commitment*   126
　　*4 Hierarchical relations between sub-systems and
　　media*   141
　　5 The general theory of action   143

6   Testing the theory against its premises   151
　　1 Introduction   151
　　2 The premises and the new theory   152
　　3 Average criticism and the conceptual dilemma   164

    Notes   177

    Bibliography   189

    Index   198

Figures

I.1	The plan of the book	6
2.1	The utilitarian dilemma	42
2.2	The voluntaristic theory of action	52
2.3	The voluntaristic thought-pattern as synthesis on two methodological dimensions	57
3.1	The orientation pole of the frame of reference	62
3.2	The situation pole of the frame of reference	64
4.1	The double bipolarity	101
4.2	Berting's diagram	102
4.3	The differentiation of action	110
4.4	Differentiation of the action system	113
4.5	Definition of action in 1937 and from *c.* 1953	114
5.1	The first level of the action theory	117
5.2	The inter-system relations of the economy	121
5.3	The primary interchange relations between the social systems	124
5.4	The primary and intermediary interchange between A and L	125
5.5	The interchange between the economy and the other sub-systems	125
5.6	The interchange paradigm with respect to media	141
5.7	The action theory and its differentiations	143
5.8	The general action system	144

Explanatory introduction

This publication is an attempt to interpret the prolific works of Talcott Parsons. Such an interpretation is necessary because of the mystification to which Parsons's work and the man himself have been subjected in sociological literature; the mention of his name and a number of his publications in the bibliography of a book is a guaranteed mark of distinction in the business of sociological dissertations. However, the reference is generally of a negative nature: in company with a distinguished predecessor whose views one 'whole-heartedly shares', one is surprised at the ambiguity of Parsons's language, the conservative one-sidedness of his premises, his theoretical metamorphoses and much more in this vein. At the same time, there is an impression that the interpretation of Parsons's work has become a process of reality-construction whereby the work itself plays a negligible part. Thus it would seem to be more important to know what others have said about Parsons than what Parsons himself has said and written.

That this publication makes no appeal to secondary literature may appear to be both pretentious and disrespectful since the views of so many eminent sociologists are thus ignored. Nevertheless, I feel it to be the best course – in this publication at least – to leave the flood of secondary literature for what it is. Only in this way is it possible to examine Parsons's work not piecemeal but in its original entirety. It gives the reader freedom to discover – perhaps after a deeper study of the original texts – that an unreasoning attachment to the opinions and interpretations of so-called 'great sociologists' may well offer repose, peace and standing, but gives no scientific satisfaction.

Any interpretation of an author's work must of necessity be carried out according to a particular plan. Our plan of interpretation consists of a simple differentiation of the concept of theory.

The most immediate meaning of the concept of theory – and in our plan it is the first aspect of theory – is in complete accordance with the aims of Parsons's scientific work and the instruments he regards as necessary aids to the achievement of those aims. It is the ultimate purpose of scientific work to gather 'dynamic knowledge' – i.e. knowledge of the relationships that exist simultaneously between a multiplicity of events. Such 'dynamic knowledge' must be the final result of the scientific procedure. In our plan of interpretation we call this result the *substantive aspect* of the concept of theory. However, the nucleus of Parsons's work lies not on this level of theory but on one which we call the *level of conceptual theory*. Parsons is trying to find a way to formulate a theory of action – i.e. a coherent system of concepts by which the analysis of action can be systematized. During the half-century occupied by Parsons's work this aspect of the concept of theory has been the central theme; therefore it is this conceptual aspect with which this book is mainly concerned. The formulation of a conceptual system is not, however, a thing apart; it implies certain starting-points. These starting-points are of a methodological nature in the widest sense of the word. They are centred on questions about the ways in which human action should be approached and the factors that play a part in determining such action. We put these questions too, under the heading of the concept of theory and refer to them as its *methodological aspect*.

Finally we distinguish a fourth aspect of the concept of theory, the *epistemological aspect*. Whereas the methodological aspect was concerned with questions about the approach to action and the 'patterns of thought' that are important to it, the epistemological aspect draws our attention to questions about the concept of theory itself: what is, for instance, the relationship between theory and reality, what is the logical status of concepts, etc?

In fact, this differentiation of the concept of theory reflects the plan of this publication. Since the nucleus of Parsons's work lies on the level of conceptual theory and this process of conceptualization rests on a basis of very specific epistemological and methodological premises, it is obvious that these premises must first be examined.

Therefore the first chapter consists of a discussion of Parsons's central epistemological premise, namely that of the 'general' and 'analytical' character of the concept of theory. As far as is possible these two aspects will be discussed separately. As we explain in section 3 the significance of the 'general' aspect of Parsons's epistemological premises lies in the dimension of individualizing *versus* generalizing conceptualization. What is meant by regarding a concept or theory as general or generalizing? What does a typical Parsonian expression like 'general(ized) theory of action' mean?

The following section of the same chapter (4) deals with the other analytical aspect of Parsons's epistemological premise. This option acquires significance on another fundamental dimension – one whose extremes are formed respectively by the so-called empiricist and by the analytical views of concept and theory. It refers to the *relationship* between concept and theory on the one hand and reality on the other. Is the concept a 'picture' of reality, does it reflect reality (empiricism) or are concept and theory logical forerunners to reality in the sense that they 'break it open', and in so doing construct a *perspective* on reality (analytical)? There is no doubt whatever that with regard to both points of the general and analytical character of concept and theory Parsons constantly refers back to his epistemological idol, Max Weber. That he does not follow Weber in every point is simply because he thought that Weber, in spite of his polemics, was still so much bound to the nineteenth-century historicist tradition that he was unable to follow the path towards a complete 'generalized analytical theory of action' right to the end. Nevertheless, Parsons takes a very firm stand behind Weber's epistemological premises.

The second chapter deals with the methodological starting-point which is at the root of Parsons's work and which we refer to by the general term 'voluntarism'. The methodological starting-point of voluntarism also consists of two different dimensions which must, as far as possible, be discussed separately. The first meaning of the word voluntarism becomes apparent in the dilemma of subjectivist versus objectivist approaches to action. Within the framework of this methodological dilemma Parsons concerns himself particularly with the implications of positivism and idealism. He develops the so-called convergence thesis, implying such a development of the social-scientific tradition that the one-sided objectivist view and the one-sided subjectivist view of the study of human nature converge. The second meaning of the voluntarism complex indicates Parsons's view of the dilemma of social realism *versus* social nominalism. At the root of this confrontation lies the question of whether society should be approached as simply 'a manner of speaking' (social nominalism) or rather as a 'reality of its own' (social realism). Here, too, Parsons's convergence thesis is significant in that he has tried to escape from this dilemma of nominalism versus realism.

Both aspects of the voluntarism complex are called *methodological* dilemmas. To avoid misunderstanding it must once more be established that the word 'methodological' is used in this publication to indicate the fundamental views which social scientists adopt in their study of social action and society. In this sense, 'methodological' refers especially to general methods of approach to mankind and society or, in the words of Zijderveld, to patterns of thought.[1] Thus, in adopting this terminology, we can say that chapter 2 is focused on the inception of Parsons's 'double' *voluntaristic pattern of thought*.

Chapter 3 concentrates on the third — and in Parsons's work the most important — aspect of theory: the conceptual aspect. This chapter deals with the way Parsons 'translates' the two premises already introduced in the foregoing chapters into a conceptual structure. The quality of the resulting conceptual structure, the so-called structural-functional version of the theory of action, suggests that the two aforementioned premises of epistemological and of methodological nature have not yet been sufficiently crystallized. In our interpretation this structural-functional version fulfils the function of a very temporary scheme whose chief merit is that it urges Parsons to reconsider the voluntaristic patterns of thought.

Such a reconsideration was necessary for bridging the discrepancy in the structural-functional version between voluntarism on the one hand and the general and analytical character of theory on the other. However this may be, in chapter 3 we try to explain the structural-functional version of the theory of action in a way that will clearly reveal its defects. Indeed, it is because this structural-functional version of the theory of action has been attacked on many counts and because the construction of it represents an important phase in the development of Parsons's theoretical work that we are giving it a great deal of attention. This does not mean, however, that Parsons has finished with the subject. Though it sometimes seems as if Parsons will be stamped for ever as a structural-functionalist, there are developments in his work which indicate that the characterization is no longer justified.

In our interpretation-diagram the new developments have their origin in the inadequate and even contradictory structural-functional translation of both the epistemological and the methodological premises. In chapter 4 we catalogue a number of points which lack clarity as a result of this defect and at the same time we discuss some new insights which give Parsons the opportunity to fit his central starting-point into a uniform, conceptual structure in a satisfactory way. We call this new conceptual theory the definitive version of the voluntaristic theory of action. The use of the word 'definitive' does not mean that Parsons has succeeded in a complete elaboration of this theory of action. There is a question of its being rounded off; a great many of the formulations are of a temporary nature and are therefore liable to be changed from time to time. Our meaning here of the word 'definitive' is that the gist of this new version of the theory of action represents an indisputable vindication of Parsons's starting-points and pretensions. An exposé of this final general voluntaristic theory of action follows in chapter 5.

In chapter 6 we pick out the most important conclusions from the line of interpretation we have followed. We confront our interpretation with a number of the most frequent criticisms of Parsons's work, and hope that in so doing we shall bring into greater relief the particular characteristics of our own argument. Parsons's contribution to the theory of action has undergone a clear development. Just as Parsons himself attributes the historic convergence towards voluntarism to the instability of a positivistic and idealistic position consequentially adhered to, so do we attribute the course of development of Parsons's theory of action to the instability of the structural-functional version, his first attempt at a conceptual translation of both starting-points. This instability first becomes apparent in a number of ambiguities and inconsistencies. On closer examination a number of reasons can be indicated to account for Parsons's inadequate translation of the premises.

From these introductory remarks it will be clear that this book describes the development of Parsons's continuous attempt to formulate an adequate general analytical and voluntaristic theory of action. The specific nature of this development can be explained by the interaction between Parsons's premises or pretensions on the one hand and his attempts to devise a consistent conceptual structure on the other hand. This undoubtedly raises the question whether we have not neglected a large part of Parsons's theory of action – namely the substantive aspect. Indeed the substantive aspect of Parsons's work is not discussed in this book except when it is directly related to the formulation of a conceptual paradigm. This means therefore that the book should by no means be regarded as a 'complete' Parsons exegesis. Since the 1920s, Parsons has been continuously occupied with an analysis of modern industrial society, thus continuing the work of the classical authors. In innumerable publications, from his Heidelberg dissertation to more recent books such as *The System of Modern Societies* (1971) and *The American University* (1973, with G. Platt), he has been systematically analysing many aspects of modern society.

From a quantitative point of view this latter 'substantive' type of publication is far greater. How then can the aforementioned limited conceptual orientation be explained? Has Parsons not already been sufficiently accused of a mania for concepts? The justification for this limitation is two-fold. In the first place, the construction of a conceptual paradigm is Parsons's most characteristic contribution to sociology and the social sciences in general.

Moreover, a knowledge of this paradigm is a *conditio sine qua non* for an understanding of his substantive contribution to sociological theory. It is this condition which is mainly responsible for the 'unreadability' for which Parsons's work has meanwhile become renowned: for the paradigm is the language that gives the story its meaning. Those who do not know the language cannot understand the story.

This brings us to a delineation of this book's pretensions. The reader will find in it neither a biographical portrait of a disputed sociologist nor a systematic summary of Parsons's analysis of modern society. What he will find, if our pretensions are justified, is:

(a) an introduction to the conceptual paradigm on which these analyses are based; an introduction – or 'language-course' –

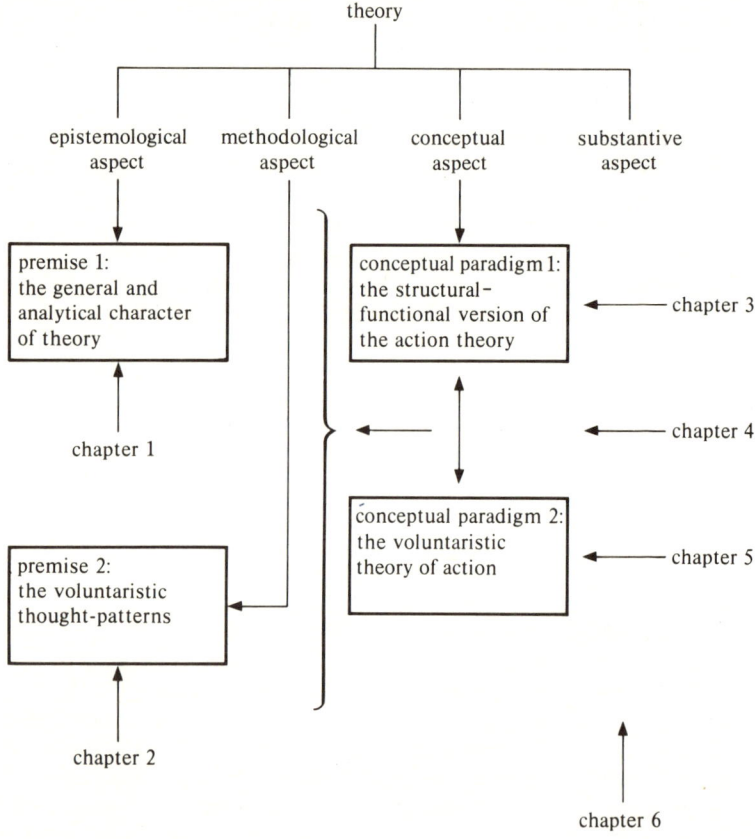

FIGURE 1.1 *The plan of the book*

which we hope will make Parsons's substantive analyses more accessible, and
(b) an analysis of the developments which this paradigm of the theory of action has undergone in the half-century of Parsons's work.

It was with these two pretensions in view that this book was written. With these two yardsticks we invite the reader to measure its contents.

Adapted from the Dutch (Van Loghum Slaterus, 1976). Translated by Mrs Van den Bergh-Marshall.

1 The general and analytical character of theory: Parsons's epistemological premise

1 Introduction

Sociology is one of the sciences of which Thomas Kuhn once said that they are still in a 'pre-paradigm' period. He meant that, unlike the natural sciences, these sciences have as yet no uniform conceptual framework or paradigm from which scientific research can take its lead and which would afford the possibility of working accumulatively. Instead of this, social science has been the battlefield of whole series of contending and sometimes contentious schools. There can be no revolutionary change − the theme of Kuhn's book *The Structure of Scientific Revolutions*[1] − in such a pluralistic science; all that happens is a periodical shift of the balance of power between the different schools.

Gordon Allport describes such a situation in the context of psychology. He says that although we scientists are acknowledged to be balanced and decent people, we have quite a number of peculiar whims. We have our own hoola-hoops, our own flying saucers and our own pole-squatting crazes. Normally speaking our scientific crazes last longer than these others, but none of them lives for more than a decennium. Thus there was McDougall's theory of instinct, followed by Watson's behaviourism which, in its turn, had to make way for Lewin's 'field theory'; after this all attention was turned to phenomenological psychology. There was, in short, a hit-parade of different 'movements'. Allport's description can be equally applied to sociology. Indeed, it may well be that accents in sociology shift even more quickly than they do in psychology. Be that as it may, we endorse without hesitation Allport's lament that 'we never seem to solve our problems or to exhaust our concepts; we only grow tired of them.'[2] Indeed, the sensitivity to fashion from which our science suffers has dire effects especially where concepts are concerned. Uncertainty about the exact meaning of social-scientific expressions makes a real scientific discussion impossible. Kenneth Boulding once said that physicists can only talk to other physicists and economists to economists. He omitted to say that sociologists often cannot even understand each other.[3]

There is no point in attributing the conceptual muddle in sociology to one particular sociologist or group of sociologists; the 'distinction' is a collective one. Of course there are one or two who, more than the average sociologist, have been held responsible for this confusion. Talcott Parsons is one of them. As has been pointed out so often by so many, his use of language is so full of neologisms that only a cryptogram enthusiast could find relaxation in the study of his publications.

Since this accusation of conceptual confusion has, indeed, been levelled at Parsons so often and by so many, there must undoubtedly be a hard core of truth in it. But here we come up against a strange paradox. For it is Parsons more than any other who has concerned himself with the conceptual fundaments of social science. How then can this concern, this care for the conceptual, have led to such conceptual chaos? In the following chapters we shall have ample opportunity to see how this paradox came about. We shall also see how it has been solved.

But first we, ourselves, must ensure that our publication is not marred by this same defect of conceptual confusion. In other words, we must take care that the concepts we use in our analysis of Parsons's work leave nothing to be desired in the matter of clarity. This means that central concepts will need to be defined. The following section is devoted to this preliminary task.

2 The concept of theory

It is characteristic of the above-mentioned conceptual muddle in sociology that the meaning of such a central concept as 'theory' cannot be taken as self-evident. Why it cannot will be obvious from the following example: Parsons is said by many to be an 'outstanding theoretician'; at the same time the word 'theory' is defined by many – often the same – scholars as 'a set of propositions concerning a particular field of research which have been or can be put to the test'. By putting these two together one might easily come to the conclusion that the most typical characteristic of Talcott Parsons's work is that it supplies information on all kinds of concrete fields of research. As we have already said in the Introduction, this idea is incorrect. But where then does the mistake lie? Obviously the first concept of theory ('Parsons as theoretician') is different in meaning from the second one.

The one-sided emphasis on the second concept of theory ('a set of propositions concerning a particular field of research which have been or can be put to the test') is characteristic of the empirical climate that determined the sociological weather in the 1950s and 1960s. This view of 'theory' is identical to the results of (quantitive) empirical research; 'theory' is then a resultant. The relation between theory and research, though always regarded as a life-size problem, can in this view be but a simple one; for theory follows from research, it is the result of it, and results which already exist (the existing theory) must not be forgotten when new research is being initiated.

Such a one-sided empiristic view of 'theory' is an understandable reaction to the speculative character of the great proto-sociological systems which determined the face of social science and sociology before the days of Weber and Durkheim. However, this laudable scepticism with regard to speculative procedures can easily extend to various other matters which are not, in fact, speculative at all. Thus, for example, there is a danger of neglecting all those theoretical decisions that logically precede the formulation of empirical or substantive theory; this scepticism, then, degenerates into an absolutism of 'facts'. With Parsons himself, but also in the reference to him as an 'outstanding theoretician', the emphasis lies precisely on activities which take place prior to the formulation of empirical theory. These activities also can be described as 'theoretical'. Here it is not a question of 'choosing' between the different meanings of the concept of theory. Nor is it necessary to make such a choice if we give the concept of theory a comprehensive meaning that embraces both the empirical or (substantive) theory and the activities that logically precede the formulation of such regularities. Of course, it is the aim of all scientific study to make (substantive) propositions about the object of its research and to combine these propositions in more comprehensive theories. This makes it possible to use the theory to explain or predict events other than those which gave rise to it. From the point of view of comprehensive meaning of the concept of theory this type of theory forms the so-called *'substantive aspect'*.

The *substantive aspect* of the concept of theory refers to substantive knowledge of relations between phenomena. This aspect of 'theory' is strongly emphasized in the aforementioned point of view. So we can be brief about it. However, it must be stressed that the construction we here place on this substantive aspect of theory is free from the one-sided reference to the quantitive opening-up of the reality of experience which is suggested nowadays by the word empiricism. Moreover, when we are concerned with a knowledge of relations between phenomena we include various types of relations in this aspect of theory. In other words, this 'substantive concept of theory' embraces not only functional and causal but also the so-called logico-meaningful relations.

However, the realization of such a substantive theory presupposes other theoretical activities and decisions besides. In the first place adequate means for constructing substantive theory must be available. The means or tools of a science are its concepts and the construction of substantive theory pre-supposes a language in which it can be formulated. We call this language the *conceptual aspect* of 'theory'. Activities aimed at systematizing the language of a science are called conceptual activities. They form an essential element in the construction of theory. It is with this conceptual aspect of theory that Parsons's work is chiefly concerned. Many of his publications are of a theoretical nature in this conceptual sense of the word theory and the characteristic theme of his theoretical sociology is the comparison and expansion of conceptual systems. First of all he turned his attention to the formulation of a frame of reference — 'the most general framework of categories in terms of which empirical scientific work "makes sense". Thus, in classical mechanics, three-dimensional rectilinear space-time, mass, location, motion are the essential elements of the frame of reference'.[4]

For instance, Parsons's central theme — a theory of action — is, in one of its most important aspects, such a frame of reference. It certainly does not formulate any empirical regularities that, in the substantive sense, merit the label 'theory'. As a frame of reference it provides a general formulation of what is meant by social action, what are the most important dimensions on which action takes place and, consequently, what concepts are needed in order to study and explain action. Such a theory formulates no knowledge that can be empirically verified, no empirical regularities, no 'substantive' theory but simply a perspective on the reality of action. It fulfils two functions at once for the construction of empirical regularities: in the first place it selects from the reality of experience those phenomena which are thought relevant to the science or group of sciences concerned. These relevant phenomena become the object of such a science or group of sciences while the non-relevant or non-selected phenomena form its 'data', 'givens' or 'parameters'; these latter phenomena become the objects of research for other sciences. Thus the theory of action leaves out of consideration all the strictly physical and chemical processes that accompany action. The man who jumps from a bridge, says Parsons, is interesting for the action-theory not because of the speed of his fall, the violence of the splash he causes or the physical-chemical processes that accompany his drowning; as far as the theory of action is concerned, none of these things is interesting, therefore none of them forms an object of research for the sciences that are based on this theory.[5] Theory as a frame of reference functions like a searchlight in the dark reality of experience; whatever the light does not reach is not seen and therefore not studied.

The frame of reference forms one aspect of the conceptual meaning of the concept of theory. Another aspect goes a step further. When once the phenomena to be studied, or some aspects of them, have been highlighted − in other words, when a clear frame of reference has been formulated − at the same time the apparatus must be available for naming, dissecting and classifying them.

In this context Parsons himself speaks of a 'categorial system', i.e. a system of synthesized concepts based on the frame of reference and forming an elaboration of it. Frame of reference and categorial system together make up the two most important elements of the conceptual aspect of the concept of theory.[6] It is indisputably these two conceptual elements that are at the heart of Parsons's theoretical activity. When Parsons calls himself an 'incurable theorist' he has these two levels of conceptualization in mind.[7]

But, of course, this conceptual interest does not stand alone. The nature and content of the frame of reference and categorial system − i.e. the conceptual aspect of theory − will no doubt vary with the nature of the methodological premises on which the scientist has based his study. This brings us to the third aspect of the concept of theory, the *methodological aspect*.

As we said in the Introduction, the word methodology as used in this book refers to fundamental views on human action and society. These views embrace the answers to such questions as: what sort of factors play the most important part in determining human action? Must the study of society be based on the actions of individuals or of the institutional structures by which they are governed? In other words methodology has to do with society and the actions of people within society.[8]

It is especially these general methodological options that are represented in the aforementioned frame of reference. This framework or paradigm forms the first conceptual translation of Parsons's methodological patterns of thought. Thus we see that this kind of methodological activity must logically take place before the conceptual and substantive levels of theory are approached. An adequate theory of action cannot dispense with these methodological considerations.

But this is not all that has to be done in preparation for the construction of a substantive theory. In constructing a conceptual system by which a substantive theory can be reached, the role of epistemological considerations should not be forgotten. This kind of consideration concerns attitudes to theory itself. It involves questions about the character of its concepts, the relation of those concepts to 'reality', and so on. These questions and the decisions that they bring about are called the *epistemological aspect* of the concept of theory.

Now we come to the core of this first chapter, Parsons's epistemological starting-point, to which the following sections will be devoted.

3 The general character of concept and theory

Parsons's epistemological starting-point is two-fold. It embraces both the general and the analytical character of concept and theory. In this section we concentrate on the *general* aspect of this epistemological aspect. This does not mean, however, that the two aspects can be considered as completely independent of each other. But, since there may be nuances in the categories of 'general' and 'analytical' we have thought it better to deal with each characteristic separately in order to give the clearest possible picture of Parsons's epistemological premise.

The general character of concept and theory achieves significance on the level of generalizing *versus* individualizing concept-forming. Parsons's position on that level is unmistakable; he takes the view that scientific theory and the concepts of which it is made up must be regarded as general or generalizing. The significance of this option stands out more clearly when seen against its historical background. The historical background of Parsons's view is to be found more especially in the discussions that took place in the nineteenth century in the German historicist tradition about the conflict between natural science and *Geisteswissenschaft*. The extreme, idealistic or historicist tradition in epistemology suggested that the two should be absolutely separated. Natural science and *Geisteswissenschaft,* they said, differ not only in respect of their material object but also in the formal method of attacking that object. According to this current of opinion the difference consisted of the nature of the concepts used, or available to be used, in the two different sciences.

Natural science makes use of general or generalizing concepts, that is to say concepts that transcend the particular and unique quality of the phenomenon, abstract precisely the general, the common, from a group of phenomena. These general concepts are rubrics with the help of which many concrete phenomena (examples) can be categorized. *Geisteswissenschaft* on the other hand – still according to this extreme, idealistic position in epistemology – approaches its object through individualizing concepts, that is to say through concepts which underline rather than abolish the uniqueness and particularity of the concrete phenomenon. Real *Geisteswissenschaft* must leave intact the most typical aspect of human action, namely the cultural aspect, and is therefore committed to concepts which respect the unique moment of subjective experience; hence the necessity for individualizing concept-forming. Thus from the extreme, idealistic or historicist epistemological position the material differentiation between natural science and *Geisteswissenschaft* coincides with an epistemological or formal differentiation: from that position it is the object towards which a science is directed that determines the possibilities for conceptualization and the nature of its theory. The nature of social-cultural reality cannot be expressed in generalizing concepts; whilst the nature of natural reality apparently lends itself to generalizing concept and theory forming, the cultural aspect of human behaviour remains such an impenetrable mystery that it can only be described in its uniqueness. As could be expected, there was no lack of response to this extreme, epistemological position with its typical consequences for the methodological, conceptual and substantive levels of theory. The most fundamental reactions came undoubtedly from within i.e. from epistemologists who had been brought up in this extreme belief. Foremost among them is Heinrich Rickert; he, too, differentiates between natural science and *Geisteswissenschaft* which he prefers to call cultural science. Rickert contests the idea that in this differentiation the material and the formal view coincide. In his opinion it is no longer the nature of the reality to be studied which leads to very specific theoretical − i.e. epistemological, methodological, conceptual and substantive − consequences. He considers it also possible, in principle, to apply the epistemological method of generalization in the field of the human spirit. On the other hand, he asserts, the historical − and therefore individualizing − method of cultural science can also be projected into the field of human nature.[9]

Although Rickert 'breaks open' the extreme position on a number of points (and he does this on the grounds of his strictly analytical view of concept and theory, thereby proving that our differentiation between the general and analytical character of concept and theory, is somewhat artificial) the idea persists in his work that, if a generalizing procedure is applied to action its cultural and subjective elements will be neglected and action will become 'Nature' or, in more modern terminology, 'behaviour'.

Max Weber's *Wissenschaftslehre* takes this aspect a step further. Parsons regards Weber's *Wissenschaftslehre* as one major attack on the historicist view that it is not possible, at least not desirable, to use general concepts in the field of the human spirit and culture.

As Parsons sees it, the whole of the *Wissenschaftslehre* revolves precisely around Weber's proposition that the particular and unique phenomenon can in no way be explained without the use of general concepts and without a 'nomological' knowledge or general theory.[10]

As far as Weber is concerned, the differentiation between natural and cultural science does not consist, as it does for Rickert, of the difference between generalizing and individualizing: every type of science, says Weber, is committed to the use of general concepts; without general concepts science would not be different from aesthetics. In Weber's view, the differentiation between natural and cultural science consists only of the way in which those general concepts are organized around cognitive interests. In natural science those interests are concerned mainly with the common and general, that which can be controlled, whereas cultural science uses the general concepts and the theory built up from them to explain the special and individual case.[11]

Here we have (in a nutshell) at the same time a characterization of the special nature of the types of concepts used by Weber, the ideal types. It is quite clear that 'ideal types' are generalizing concepts; by abstracting from one special case, they form a rubric that embraces a number of special cases. At the same time, however, it is the function of these 'ideal types' to clarify, or reveal, precisely the concrete and particular aspects of action. In Weber's terminology this concrete and particular is especially manifested in the irrational aspect of action; only by making use of general concepts in the form of rational 'ideal types' is cultural science able to interpret the special, unique or irrational aspect of action.

Since it was Parsons's greatest pretension to formulate a general theory of action which, in spite of its general status, would not degrade action to the level of 'behaviour' but would rather emphasize precisely the cultural, the symbolic and the subjective, it is natural that, in this aspect of epistemology, he follows Weber wholeheartedly. Parsons looks on Weber as the first social scientist to recognize not only the possibility but also the inevitability of using general concepts in cultural science. In Parsons's words: 'What Weber did was to take an enormous step in the direction of bridging the gap between the two types of science, and to make possible the treatment of social material in a systematic scientific manner rather than as an art.'[12] And yet, in Parsons's opinion, Weber did not go far enough: 'he failed to complete the process, and the nature of the half-way point at which he stopped helps to account for many of the difficulties of his position.'[13] In particular the generalizing character of Weber's concepts is not carried through to the construction of a general theory of action. The 'half-way point' of which Parsons speaks indicates precisely the impossibility of constructing a really systematic theory of action by using Weber's 'ideal types'.

That this is so is due to the nature of the 'ideal type' itself. Although this type of general concept, like every general concept, does not provide a formulation for a concrete and particular course of action, yet Weber – obviously under the influence of the tradition in which he was reared – tries nevertheless, *even in the very formulation of concepts,* to preserve something of that concrete and particular: his 'ideal types' point admittedly, not to concrete but to *hypothetically concrete actions*.[14] Thus the 'ideal type' provides a formulation for what may be imagined to be a concrete, particular phenomenon.[15] The word 'concrete' is used here in its literal sense: the concrete phenomenon is one that is 'rounded off' and 'composite'. This means that the 'ideal type' is, in principle, also a composite concept, in which a number of variable elements are brought together in a particular 'fixed' relation one to the other, whereby the logically possible variations in those variables remain unquestioned; this means, moreover, according to Parsons, that it is impossible to formulate a systematic general theory of action on the basis of this kind of general concept – the 'ideal types': theory constructed with the help of 'ideal types' tends to relapse into a 'mosaic theory' of reality.[16] It is almost impossible – and this is what Parsons means by that qualification – to get insight into the way the 'ideal types' overlap, are combined, fit together one with the other, etc. In other words, it is unlikely that the most important formal requirement of a general theory of action will ever be met in that way.

It is clear to Parsons that it is Weber's historical background that has allowed something of the concrete and particular, albeit in a 'hypothetical' 'imaginable' sense, to creep into the 'ideal type' itself. In this respect Weber has not been able to free himself entirely from the individualizing tendency in the idealistic scientific theory. Parsons sums up his view of Weber's 'ideal types' as follows: *'If analysis is confined to its use, certain possibilities of variation on other levels are arbitrarily excluded from consideration. This is not, of course, to say in any simple sense that it is "wrong", but only that it is limited in certain respects!'*[17]

How, then, does Parsons himself try to fill in the category of general or generalizing concepts? One thing is apparent at once: Parsons is going to differentiate the 'ideal type' in the elements or variables from which it was built up. For instance, he will try to split up 'ideal types' such as *Zweckrationales Handeln, Protestantische Ethik* and Tönnies's *Gemeinschaft* into their variable elements. Those elements in which such an 'ideal type' is differentiated are Parsons's general or generalizing concepts. *They do not describe concrete phenomena but abstract aspects of such concrete phenomena.* Just as in the science of classical mechanics such concepts as mass, velocity, movement etc. refer not to concrete events but to abstract, imaginable *aspects* of concrete events, neither do Parsons's general concepts refer to concrete or rounded-off phenomena. With the help of this type of general concept it is indeed possible to build up a systematic general theory of action: for the fixed relations within the 'ideal type' are 'broken open' and laid bare to analysis so that the possibility of conceptual overlapping is eliminated.

Parsons regards his pretension to the formulation of a systematic general theory of action by using general concepts as a logical continuation of the road that Weber was following. That Weber stopped half-way is attributed by Parsons to Weber's historicist background which made it impossible for him to realize that a completely generalized theoretical system need not necessarily conflict with the idea of individuality and subjectivity.[18] Parsons hopes to demonstrate this in his *general theory of action*.

His pretension to formulate a comprehensive general theory of action with the help of the general concepts described above has been the subject of frequent discussion in the history of sociology since the Second World War. The climax of the discussion so far was Robert Merton's famous suggestion that sociological theory should be regarded as being built up of 'theories of the middle range'.[19] Merton says that although the formulation of a general theory of action continues to be a scientific ideal, there is as yet no hope of success for such an operation. It should be observed that Merton's criticism of Parsons's pretension to a systematic general theory does not imply any principled scientific difference of opinion. It is rather that Merton is speaking from another viewpoint of theoretical strategy. He does not rule out the formulation of a systematic and general theory of sociology and sees no reason why it should not be held as an important scientific ideal. But an adequate fulfilment of that ideal presupposes a number of 'stepping-stones'; it is the 'middle range' theories which will serve this purpose and ensure that if ever the general theory reaches the realms of possibility it will not have become a monster completely removed from reality. He warns Parsons that[20]

> to concentrate solely on the master conceptual scheme for deriving all sociological theory is to run the risk of producing twentieth century equivalents of the large philosophical systems of the past, with all their suggestiveness, all their architectonic splendor and all their scientific sterility.

So Merton, like Weber, is apprehensive of the amount of abstraction involved in the construction of a general theory; he is afraid that such a theory would not do justice to the individuality of human action. In this respect there is no doubt that Merton's suggestion of 'middle range' theories runs parallel with Weber's 'ideal types': in spite of their general status, both kinds of concepts or groups of concepts try to keep as close as possible to concrete reality.

In this connection it is significant that Merton, as for instance in his famous essay on 'Puritanism, Pietism and Science', adheres to the typically Weberian procedure of formulating ideal types in order to get an insight into the *Wahlverwandtschaft* of the religious mentality in question on the one hand and the scientific attitude on the other.[21] That later on, Merton and his disciples (especially after their association at the Lazarsfeld research bureau) sometimes gave empiristic significance to this need to stay as close as possible to concrete reality should, in this light, be regarded as a slight change of position at the most. In spite of all their differences, both types of procedure have common ground in their respect for the concrete and particular.

That is why Parsons cannot avoid the impression that Merton's ideas easily lead to fragmentation and why he considers it quite legitimate to investigate the possibilities for such a systematic general theory from the foundations that were laid down by the classical sociologists. In the preface to his first major publication, *The Structure of Social Action* (1937), Parsons says:[22]

> it is a study in social theory, not theories. Its interest is not in the separate and discrete propositions to be found in the works of these men [i.e. Weber, Durkheim, Pareto and Marshall], but in a single body of systematic theoretical reasoning the development of which can be traced through a critical analysis of the writings of this group, and of certain of their predecessors.

This orientation on a general and systematic paradigm has been in the forefront of Parsons's work since the early 1930s. Here it must be added that Parsons was not concerned with 'just any' theoretical strategy that could be implemented or replaced by any other random strategy but with an inference from Max Weber's *Wissenschaftslehre* which shows the inevitability of using generalizing procedures to explain concrete action. This inevitability in science of forming general concepts is closely connected with the analytical character of such concepts. This relation is so close that it was difficult to speak of the general aspect of theory in this section without at the same time including its analytical character.

4 The analytical character of concept and theory

The second aspect of Parsons's epistemological premise is to be found in his analytical interpretation of concept and theory. This aspect refers to the question of how concept and theory relate to reality. At one extreme of this epistemological dimension is the empiricist view that concept and the theory derived from it are 'pictures' of reality; theory and concept are looked upon as objective representations, as photographs of an objective reality.[23] The other extremity of this dimension – the analytical interpretation – emphasizes that there is no question of such a direct photographic relation between theory and reality; in this interpretation, concept and theory are precisely subjective constructions of human understanding which can observe concrete reality only in optical distortions. In this interpretation, 'reality' is always understood to mean a 'reality of experience': theories are looked upon as 'perspectives' on this reality of experience.

Parsons's interpretation of the relation between concept and reality lies once more in the projection of Weber's epistemology. Since, in this respect also, Weber took up this position as a reaction to the extreme idealistic or historicist tradition already described, we can, in this paragraph, continue the structure of the foregoing one. We begin, therefore, with the implications of historicism for this epistemological dimension, continue with the reactions of Rickert and Weber and come finally to Parsons's position which we shall discuss first on the level of concepts and then on the level of theories or theoretical systems.

This historicist attempt to keep as close as possible to the concrete and particular in human reality, in other words, to register as precisely as possible the nature of that reality, is an example of an empiricist attitude. It is, in fact, an attempt to *create a picture* of reality. This empiricist tone is strengthened by the accentuation of a procedure which depends on 'feeling', on intuition. In the extreme historicist interpretation knowledge of cultural *Gestalten* can be acquired only through intuition or 'feeling'. Concepts have no other function here than that of *giving expression* to an 'immediate' experience. Concepts do not mediate in the process of acquiring knowledge; they only give expression to insight already gained, they give the clearest possible picture of reality.

Rickert was one of the first to oppose this 'intuitionism' and the picture theory and, in so doing, to create a so-called neo-Kantian tradition in the epistemology of the cultural sciences of which Weber is undoubtedly the best-known exponent. Weber's interpretation of the relation of theory to reality ties up to a large extent with Rickert's work. Weber's 'ideal types' form unmistakable analytical constructions that open a certain rational perspective on reality precisely in order to be able to explain the irrational or the particular. There can be no doubt that, in the epistemological dimension of the relation between concept and reality, Weber, too, is on the analytical side. But this is not all that can be said about Weber's position. For, considering the impossibility of *voraussetzungslose Abbildung* (i.e. presuppositionless copying of objective reality), the construction of concepts — in Weber's case, of 'ideal types' — threatens to become a rather random occupation. Would it not be possible to ascertain in advance the adequacy of the 'ideal type' constructions? From the point of view of the neo-Kantian school it would be impossible to guarantee anything in advance; that would conflict with the principle of *Voraussetzungslosigkeit*. But does this not mean that concept-forming can easily relapse into *Spielerei?* Is there no way to differentiate between serious and non-serious conceptualization? Weber clearly underlines his consequent neo-Kantian position by saying that the adequacy of concepts must be judged by the criterium of fruitfulness with regard to the cognitive interests on the basis of which the concepts were formed. That criterium is of a purely practical rather than of a logical nature; it implies no *a priori* judgment of the adequacy of concepts but an *a posteriori* judgment of their heuristic value.[24]

Although he completely agrees with Weber's analytical position on the empiricist-analytical dimension, here too Parsons has epistemological reservations. These reservations result in an epistemological position which diverges both from empiricist and from Weberian-analytical attitudes and which Parsons calls *'analytical realism'*. This paradoxical concept merits a separate discussion.

Let us first divide the expression 'analytical realism' into its two components. It is obvious that the first of these components (analytical) refers to the opposition to the empiricist interpretation of the relation of concept to reality. But what is the significance of the second component — 'realism'? Is not 'realism', as used to indicate the relation of concept or theory to reality, in flagrant conflict with the analytical nature of that relation? In other words, is not 'analytical realism' a contradiction in terms? Of course that would be the easiest conclusion to draw. But here again the easiest conclusion is not the best one. Parsons uses this epistemological formula to show the difference between his and Weber's analytical interpretation of the relation between concept and reality. The root of this difference is the distinction between 'ideal types' and 'elements' in the category of general concepts.

As we said earlier, Weber's 'ideal types' relate to *concrete reality* as *hypothetical constructions;* they formulate a course of action which, though logically pure is objectively possible. Thus these analytical constructions function as measures of concrete phenomena in reality. Since there can be no waterproof guarantees as to the quality of those measures nor, therefore, to the relation between the hypothetically concrete and the concrete, and their heuristic value can only be judged in retrospect, Parsons calls this variation of the analytical interpretation the 'useful fictions' variant. As far as Parsons is concerned, this is the only real neo-Kantian position on this epistemological dimension *given the use* of 'ideal types'. However, if in accordance with Parsons's suggestion, the category of general concepts is extended to include *analytical elements i.e. general concepts which refer not to concrete imaginable phenomena but to abstract aspects of such phenomena,* the relation between *type* and *concrete phenomenon* will become the relation between *analytical element* and *abstract aspect*. It is easy to guess that this latter relation is of a 'realistic' nature in the epistemological sense. For the analytical element indicates an abstract aspect of the concrete phenomenon so that the relation between element and aspect can be called 'direct'. This is why Parsons gives the name 'analytical realism' to his own variant of the analytical position.

Parsons is of the opinion – and in my view rightly so – that this epistemological formula for the relation between concept and reality represents a logical extension of the Weberian or neo-Kantian tradition. For this tradition is characterized by the idea that the concept must logically precede the reality, that the individual and concrete in human reality can be opened up with the help of general concepts and that there can be no guarantee beforehand of the adequacy of those concepts.

Weber was acutely aware of these consequences and was yet able to resist the temptation to add empiricist water to the analytical wine. Parsons pursues this line still further, with but one difference. He feels that Weber's 'ideal types' in themselves conceal some empiricist residue; his epistemological starting-point is analytical to such a degree that he tries to dispel this residue by formulating another kind of general concept, the analytical element. It goes without saying that the relation between the analytical element and the aspect to which it refers is realistic in the epistemological sense. More important is the fact that Parsons, like Weber, insists that the only test to which a concept can be subjected is that of fruitfulness. Thus Parsons will most certainly not be attracted to the attempts that have been – and are still being – made in sociology with the help of all kinds of different procedures to guarantee in advance the adequacy of concepts and particularly of Weber's 'ideal types'.

In this framework, Alfred Schutz's 'postulate of adequacy' has a particular bearing.[25] Starting from the idea that, according to Weber in spite of 'Wertbeziehung' and cognitive interests, a fairly random construction of 'ideal types' is in principle always possible, Schutz tries to design a sort of code within which the construction of types can be carried out:[26]

> Each term in a scientific model of human action must be constructed in such a way that a human act performed within the life-world by an individual actor in the way indicated by the typical construct would be understandable for the actor himself as well as for his fellow-men in terms of commonsense interpretations of everyday life.

Following Schutz's example, Zijderveld, too, tries to solve the question of the adequacy of types in a combination of neo-Kantianism and phenomenology. He suggests that Weber's analytical-deductive view should be amplified with the phenomenologically orientated doctrine of Schutz.[27]

No doubt Parsons considered this solution to the problem of adequacy too dangerous in that it was not sufficiently neo-Kantian. Like Rickert he saw analytical doctrines on the one hand and phenomenology on the other as two irreconcilable powers.[28]

Consequently, Parsons distinguishes three positions in the epistemological dimension discussed in this section. First there is the empiricist position. Second there is the[29]

> attitude toward scientific concepts and their relation to reality . . . that they are not reflections of reality, but 'useful fictions'. The principal example was Weber's own formulation of the status of his ideal-type concepts a formulation that was arrived at in conscious reaction against all . . . forms of empiricism. . . . There is, as has been shown, an element of truth in this view as applied to certain types of concepts, but, when applied, as Weber was inclined to apply it, to all general concepts of social or any other science, it also is untenable.

Third there is Parsons's own view of the concept-reality relation — a view in which the general and the analytical character of concept and theory are united in so-called analytical realism:[30]

> In opposition to all these untenable views may be set the epistemological position that seems to be implied throughout this study — analytical realism. As opposed to the fiction view it is maintained that at least some of the general concepts of science are not fictional but adequately 'grasp' *aspects* of the objective external world. This is true of the concepts here called analytical

elements. *Hence the position here taken is, in an epistemological sense, realistic.* At the same time it avoids the objectionable implications of an empiricist realism. These concepts correspond, not to concrete phenomena, but to elements in them which are analytically separable from other elements. *There is no implication that the value of any one such element, or even of all those included in one logically coherent system, is completely descriptive of any particular concrete thing or event. Hence it is necessary to qualify the term realism with 'analytical'.*

So far in this section, analytical realism has been mainly projected on to the character of *concepts*. *We can now go a step further and examine the consequences of this view to the concept of theory* as a totality of concepts, and to scientific discipline in general.

The best approach to the analytical-realistic interpretation of the concept of theory is provided by two of Parsons's earlier articles entitled 'Sociological Elements in Economic Thought'.[31] This title reflects Parsons's interest in the science of economics. In fact, it was through economics that he finally came to the study of social science and sociology. He had originally planned to study biology and, later on, medicine. It is not clear why these plans were abandoned, nor is it a matter of any importance. Parsons's Heidelberg dissertation on the concept of capitalism in German social-scientific literature[32] crosses and recrosses the dividing-line between economics and sociology in the same way that Weber's substantive theory also referred so often to that border-line. Parsons combines the neo-Kantian doctrine with his own substantive interest in the nature of modern industrial society into an epistemological criticism of the then current discipline of economics. This enables him to amplify some of the consequences of his analytical interpretation.

At this time, in the 1920s, the theory of economics was being contested by widely differing schools of thought. The argument centred on that inheritance from the past, the conflict between 'orthodox' and 'institutional' economics. Instead of throwing himself into the real conflict, Parsons questioned the epistemological premises which were at the root of it. This analysis made it possible for him to express for the first time his views on the relation between theory or theoretical system on the one hand and reality on the other.

At first sight it would appear that the conflict between 'orthodox' and 'institutional' economics is concerned exclusively with the question as to which factors ought and which ought not to be included in the frame of reference of economic theory. Whereas the orthodox school restricts the choice to one single factor, the theory of the institutionalists is of encyclopaedic amplitude. Though this representation of the conflict is true to some extent, nevertheless it disregards a number of important considerations. What these are will be obvious as soon as the expression 'orthodox theory of economics' has been defined. Under this heading Parsons gives pride of place to the view that the purpose of economics is to study those processes which provide individuals operating in society with the means to satisfy their needs. This view sees people as strictly rational, calculating beings who think and act only in terms of economic utility.

Parsons confronts this view with the question of how this economic theory relates to the reality of experience. Is it a reflection, a 'picture', or an analytical construction? The empiricist view of the relation theory – reality is that theory is a 'picture' of concrete economic reality and that there are certain phenomena which are *in themselves* of an economic nature. In the empiricist view the science of economics must study such 'economic' phenomena; in so doing it need refer to none but economic frames of reference.

It is not difficult to see that the *combination* of an 'orthodox' view of economics with an empiricist view of theory implies a far-reaching limitation of 'economic reality'. For if theory is really a reflection of a concrete piece of reality – the 'economic' part – then orthodoxy no longer holds water: its limited frame of reference ignores a large number of phenomena which, with equal justification, may be classed as 'economic' and thus it also denies that such phenomena exist. In short, the empiricist view of orthodox economics so 'reifies' its theory into reality that only a caricature of reality remains.

'Reification' of 'hypostasation' are terms that mean the often unconscious process of making theory independent of reality. A theory is said to become reified when it starts to take the place of concrete reality. It is exactly because, in the empiricist view of the concept of theory, theory itself is regarded as an adequate reflection of reality, that this 'fallacy of misplaced concreteness'[33] is inherent in empiricism. Parsons describes this empiricist process of reification as follows: 'The logically closed system of theory becomes, in an empiricist interpretation, an empirically closed system'.[34]

The caricatural reality that results from the combination of orthodoxy and empiricism – or from the reification of the orthodox economic theory – could not fail to provoke reactions. The most important is embodied in the 'institutionalist school'. This view does not accept a narrowing down of reality like the one described above and it allows the validity of factors in the science of economics other than the strictly (orthodox) economic one.

One of the best-known forerunners of the 'institutionalist' school is Thorstein Veblen. The subtitle of his most celebrated work *The Theory of the Leisure Class: an economic study of institutions* (1899) reflects the broad view he takes of the science of economics and explains why this doctrine of economic opinions is thus named. In Parsons's words, Veblen's economics have grown beyond themselves into 'a complete philosophy of history emphasizing everything in human life, ultimate ends . . . predation, technology, science, even institutions accounted for by habit, leaving out only the specifically economic element'.[35]

The institutionalists emphasize that economic action in the strictest sense of the word is interwoven with an enormous network of institutions, the study of which is essential for a comprehensive description and explanation of economic action. As Parsons says, the institutionalists' broad view of reality may be admirable but, just like the disciples of the orthodox school, they too, are the prisoners of empiricism from an epistemological point of view. The institutionalists react only to the consequences of orthodox-reifying thought and not to the reification (or empiricism) itself. Nevertheless, the reaction of the institutionalists to increase the number of explanatory factors − exposes the very same tendency to regard theory as a reflection of reality; this reality must be completely described and explained with the help of the amended theory of economics.

From the standpoint of the neo-Kantian doctrine the conflict between 'orthodox' and 'institutionalists' is relative and unimportant. For as Parsons says with regard to the relation between theory and reality they both lean toward the empiricist point of view. However, if the *analytical* view of theory is projected on to orthodox economics, the institutionalist reaction is entirely superfluous. For if orthodox theory − and more especially the frame of reference from which it is built, is no longer reified into economic reality, there are no grounds at all for the accusation that reality is not covered by economics. Then, surely, economics represents a perspective on reality, not a picture of it. This means that it can no longer be expected to present a complete description and explanation of the 'economic' part of reality but rather that it should select from the total reality of action, not a *concrete part* but an *abstract aspect* as object for study.

This differentiation between the two possible references of a theoretical system or discipline − 'concrete part' or 'abstract aspect' − is a repetition of the differentiation between the different possible reference of a single concept. A concept might refer to a concrete phenomenon which Parsons calls empiricism; but it might equally refer to an abstract aspect of a concrete phenomenon which would imply an analytical view of the relation between concept and reality.

The orthodox theory of economics can be seen as the study of a very specific aspect of human action; it also opens a very specific *perspective* on human action. In any case it is an outdated idea to think that orthodox economics, or any other kind of economics, can be regarded as reflections of a part of reality.

Parsons seized upon the discussion between the orthodox doctrinists and the institutionalists to mark his analytical view on theory and science. This kind of view requires that the different disciplines should be clearly classified in order for them to be attuned one to the other. It is therefore not surprising that Parsons has been continuously occupied with this question of categorization. Since it is not possible to interpret Parsons's work correctly without a clear insight into the way he distinguishes between sociology and other disciplines and the theory of action in general, the following pages will be devoted to a preliminary discussion of the question.

5 The theory of action, the theory of the social system and the theory of sociology

It was Parsons's most important aim to formulate a so-called theory of action. Such a general and analytical theory of action comprises a systematic unity of general concepts which opens one particular perspective on the sum total of events that take place around man. This perspective is aimed at a particular aspect of the totality of events, namely the aspect of *action*. No wonder that Parsons needed to spend so much thought on the the definition of this aspect for on it the whole complex of the theory of action had to be built (cf. chapter 2). Within the framework of this action-theory perspective Parsons distinguishes a number of 'secondary schemata' each of which in turn includes an analytically categorized aspect of action.

Until about 1951 there was no question of a completely systematic categorization of action disciplines in Parsons's work. This systematization was not achieved until a later phase. Up to then, Parsons's categorization of disciplines had to be altered from time to time because he had no uniform criteria on which to base it. Nevertheless, there are a few categorizations, even from this earlier phase that have withstood the test of time.

In differentiating the human sciences from the total theory of action Parsons reasoned thus: actions never occur independently of each other but can, by one means or another, always be organized into systems. When actions are organized around the pivot of individual personality, the result is a 'personality system'. It is, says Parsons, psychology which makes this analytical cut-out from the total action (or from the general action system). However, the same action can also be organized around the interaction between two or more individuals. Parsons gives the name of 'social system' to the cut-out from the general action system made in this way. Just like the personality system, the social system, too, is an analytical abstraction of concrete reality.

The view is often expressed that the social system is the subject of sociology. Parsons does not agree.[36]

> If a sphere for sociological theory as a distinctive conceptual schema is to be delineated, it must be either the theory of the social system as a whole, or some special aspect of the theory of the social system rather than the whole of it.
> The choice between the broader and the narrower views of the scope of sociological theory just stated . . . turns essentially on that of the status of economic theory. The broader view would treat economic theory as 'applied sociology' while the narrower would not. The narrower is the view taken here.

Both sociology and economics are concerned with the study of the social system. This raises the question as to how the distinction between these two disciplines can be formulated.

Like so many of his illustrious predecessors, Parsons arrived at the formulation of the sociological point of view through a critical examination of the theory of economics. We have already seen that an examination of the history of economics provided Parsons with the opportunity to formulate his epistemological position in the question of the theory-related relationship. The formulation of this premise of analytical realism implies that the orthodox economic explanatory method must be seen as an aspect approach to social action and that other aspects can also be distinguished. The most remarkable not strictly economic aspect is that of the *institutionalization of values*. The works of such classical authors as Durkheim, Weber and Pareto place a great deal of emphasis on the differentiation of this value element and Parsons agrees with them.

Referring to Emile Durkheim, Parsons says that although he was a layman in the field of strict economics, he made the greatest contribution to the delineation of sociology and economics. This is clearly to be seen in his study of the division of labour. The central theme of this study is the fierce controversy with methodological individualism which seeks to explain the economic order as a contract freely entered into. According to Durkheim, it is not possible to explain economic order and order in general simply by contractual relationships. He stresses that there must be 'something more' than the element of contracts freely entered into by autonomous individuals. For, the closing of a contract presupposes that the partners to it need to come to a mutual agreement. That need does not form an element of the contract itself but stems from a collective consciousness that is a logical preliminary to the contractual order. In other words, Durkheim emphasizes that the contractual order conceals another non-contractual order. It is this element, which Parsons calls 'a non-contractual element in contract', that sociology has to study.

Of what does this non-contractual element consist? Durkheim's answer leaves us in no doubt: it consists of a common value, a form of 'collective consciousness'. Without it there is chaos or anomie. The collective consciousness of modern society can be seen in collective appreciation of individual personality. It is for sociology to study these common values, these collective ways of acting, thinking and feeling. Indeed, Durkheim looks on sociology as the science of social facts or institutions. Like Durkheim, Weber and Pareto also made their contributions to the analytical differentiation between economics and sociology. In his famous study on the *Wahlverwandtschaft* (elective affinity) between Calvinist ethic and capitalist mentality, Weber tries to interpret the 'economic' phenomenon of 'capitalism' with the help of a non-economic factor; and, like Durkheim, he sees this non-economic factor in common and collective values, in a collective ethic.

Pareto, too, arrived at his differentiation between logical and non-logical action through confrontation with different current explanatory methods. We shall see that, according to Parsons's analysis, the category of non-logical action is full of the above-mentioned evaluations.

In the history of social-scientific thought we can therefore differentiate from the strictly rational point of view another, sociological, point of view which recognizes the collective, common evaluations that are the foundations of practical (e.g. economic) action.

Parsons's sociological definition completely follows the line of this classical tradition:[37]

> Sociological theory, then, is for us *that aspect of the theory of social systems which is concerned with the phenomena of the institutionalization of patterns of value-orientation in the social system,* with the conditions of that institutionalization, and of changes in the patterns, with conditions of conformity with and deviance from a set of such patterns and with motivational processes in so far as they are involved in all of these.

This is clear evidence, that, in Parsons's opinion, sociology is one of the disciplines engaged in studying the social system i.e. the organization of actions around the interaction between partners. The social system, in turn, itself forms an analytical-abstract aspect of the total or general action system. The exact relation between the general action system and the social system on the one hand and between the social system and the personality system on the other hand is not clear, even to Parsons himself, before he has developed uniform criteria for categorizing action into all kinds of systems and sub-systems. We shall return to this, also, in chapter 4.

Meanwhile it has become the custom to call Parsons a 'sociologist' and, of course, not entirely without justification. It is Parsons's substantive publications especially that are devoted to the border territory between order and rationality and are thus clearly aimed at the study of what Parsons regards as the typically sociological aspect of social action.

However, the publications which orientate more towards the conceptual and methodological aspect of theory overstep the boundary of sociology. This involves some of Parsons's publications in problems of general action theory, problems of the relation between disciplines of the social system on the one hand and those of the general action system on the other.

In other words, a large part of Parsons's work concerns an area which, according to his own definition, can hardly be called specifically sociological. In our opinion a more precise location of his work must surely lead to the conclusion that Parsons is, first and foremost, an action theorist who has specified that theory towards the theory of social systems. It should once more be remembered that, in Parsons's definition, the theory of social systems is not identical with the theory of sociology.

Of course it is possible to explain the view that Parsons was exclusively a sociologist. First, it is a fact that he is best known for *The Social System,* which deals mainly with the typically sociological aspect of the social system. This work is still regarded by many as Parsons's *magnum opus,* an opinion which, as we shall see later, ought now to be revised. A second reason why Parsons is regarded mainly as a sociologist is the fact that sociology is often defined in much wider terms than those used by Parsons himself. In many cases sociology is identified with what Parsons calls 'action theory'. In Parsons's scheme, as we shall see, 'social-behaviouristic sociology' in the tradition of Cooley, Mead and Thomas refers particularly to the level of action theory. This means that the practice of regarding this tradition as the opposite of 'Parsonianism' should certainly not be followed without discrimination, to say the least. After all, when Parsons finally returns to the most fundamental level of the action theory after his work on the systematization of the social system, it is particularly W. I. Thomas's conceptual scheme of the 'four wishes' that helps him to elaborate his general paradigm.

In all likelihood it is the confusion of action theory, social system theory and sociological theory, for which Parsons himself is perhaps to blame, that have led to misleading interpretations of his work. For instance, the persistent view that the 'social-behaviouristic' school represents an entirely different approach from that expressed in Parsons's writings finds its explanation mainly in the fact that the differentiation between the various levels of general action theory is ignored. It is certainly true that Parsons encouraged this kind of misunderstanding by failing for so long to define the criteria on which this differentiation is based. That by so doing he cast doubt on the general and analytical character of the first elaborated version of his action theory — the structural-functional theory of social systems — is one of the themes of our interpretation.

This concludes the discussion of the epistemological premise of Parsons's work. The second premise on which he bases his action theory is a methodological one. This premise — the voluntaristic pattern of thought — is the subject of the following chapter.

2 The voluntaristic pretension: Parsons's methodological premise

1 Introduction: voluntarism as a methodological synthesis

Parsons's epistemological confrontation with the German historicist school and, more especially with the neo-Kantian epistemology of Max Weber, strengthened his belief in the possibility of formulating a general and analytical action theory which would include the subjective and particular aspects of actor's orientation. This was the intellectual luggage that Parsons brought with him when he returned from Germany in the 1920s. However, back home in the United States he was immediately confronted with an entirely different scientific climate, that of behaviourism. Instead of concern for the individual and the subjective, now 'anyone who believed in the scientific validity of the interpretation of subjective states of mind was often held to be fatuously naive'.[1]

It was this behaviourism that led Parsons to the search for an action theory in the *methodological* sense i.e. a theory that would not involve a downgrading of action to 'behaviour'. In contrast to the formulation of his epistemological premise, his first reference this time is not to the German tradition of social science but to the behaviouristic tradition which took root in the United States in the first decades of this century. Parsons discovers the forerunners of behaviourism in a number of positivistic variants of the action theory. Therefore he starts his research into the methodological possibilities for a real action theory with a criticism of its positivistic variants. Parsons is going to show that the positivistic theory of action is characterized by instability and that developments in the work of 'positivistically inspired' classical authors are moving in a direction which tends to break open this positivism. He finds the same kind of development taking place in the idealistic variants of the action theory. Once again, he considers that it was Weber, above all, who found the methodological way to confute the extreme idealistic position.

According to Parsons, these developments from completely different points of departure converge on one and the same methodological premise (or the same thought-pattern). He calls this point of convergence *voluntarism*. Although the choice of this expression was undoubtedly influenced to a large extent by the (negative) reference to behaviourism, it would be wrong to suppose that voluntarism rests on a methodological premise that aims to explain human action mainly by means of the 'free will' factor. On the contrary, Parsons's voluntarism must not be defined in terms other than those of the abovementioned convergence tendency: it contains the promise to bridge the gap between the opposing ideas of positivistic and idealistic (or objectivistic and subjectivistic) traditions in social-scientific thought. For this reason, voluntarism can be formulated primarily as a *pretension:* a far-reaching pretension to provide a synthesis on a methodological level, on the level of thought-patterns, between hitherto irreconcilable currents of thought. What does Parsons consider to be the most important methodological antitheses between the two social-scientific traditions? What, in principle, are the methodological dimensions on which these traditions oppose one another? Parsons differentiates two such fundamental dimensions in *The Structure of Social Action* (1937). *First* and most important is the dimension which concerns the question − what type of factors lie at the root of action and of the society which results from that action? Are they factors which accentuate the objective physical environment of the actor or are they subjective orientations that emanate from the actor himself?

It is particularly on this dimension of objectivism versus subjectivism that the opposing methodological traditions of positivism and idealism acquire significance. The *second* dimension is the antithesis between social-nominalistic and social-realistic thought-patterns. Here the question concerns two fundamental views on the relation between the individual and society and the way in which social science must solve this problem at the methodological level. Should human action be studied from the viewpoint of the institutional structures to which the actor belongs or from that of the individual actions themselves?

As Parsons sees it these two dimensions are, in principle, independent of each other. But he tries to connect the latter as much as possible to the antithesis between positivistic and idealistic currents of opinion in social science. In respect of the second methodological dimension, that of social nominalism versus social realism, Parsons also thinks there are converging tendencies to be observed in the work of a number of classical authors. His concept of voluntarism is concerned with this convergence as well.

Thus the voluntaristic pretension is bipartite: not only does Parsons see voluntarism as a way to transcend the opposing ideas of extreme objectivist and extreme subjectivist currents of thought: he also thinks that his voluntaristic thought-pattern offers a solution to the conflict between social-nominalistic and social-realistic options. He himself formulates the pretensions of voluntarism as follows: 'It is hoped in transcending the old positivist-idealist dilemma, to show a way of transcending also the old individualism – social organism or, as it is often called, social nominalism – realism dilemma which has plagued social theory to little purpose for so long?'[2]

This description of the voluntaristic pretension was written in 1937. Since then, Parsons has been trying with varying degrees of success to fulfil this pretension. Before judging the quality of these attempts it is necessary first to examine his thesis of convergence more closely. Again – as in the foregoing chapter – we shall, as far as possible, give separate attention to the two dimensions that go to make up the voluntarism pretension.

2 The methodological dimension of objectivist *versus* subjectivist thought-patterns in historical perspective

Parsons uses the expressions 'positivism' and 'idealism' mainly to identify the two poles of the dimension of objectivist and subjectivist approaches. In so doing he gives the words a fairly specific meaning which necessitates a short explanation.

Parsons's concept of positivism

Parsons uses the concept of positivism mainly as a methodological instrument i.e. as an instrument for describing a complex of fundamental views on the forces and factors that lie behind society and action. In order to see how Parsons's concept of positivism differs from other versions we shall first try to sort out a number of the various accents placed on that concept.

Positivism in social science is a methodological position which appears at first sight to consist of a large number of accents that are more or less linked together. Obviously all these accents must have a common source in the history of social scientific thought. In that context positivism can be regarded as a continuation of the Enlightenment philosophy in which *reason* and *observation* became the new criteria for truth. The old criteria of revelation and tradition disappeared and, at the same time, such 'speculative' matters as religion, theology and methaphysics were rejected. In place of the invisible matters with which these attitudes of thought had been occupied, the accent now shifted very explicitly to observation of 'objective' facts. In contrast to the speculations of theology and methaphysics, science must now concentrate only on objectively perceptible elements. Those sciences which did not resort to godly and metaphysical causes to explain natural phenomena were called 'positive sciences'. It is obvious that the most *central meaning* of the word positivism has direct bearing on this. First and foremost, positivism signifies an attitude of thought which accepts nothing but the objectively perceptible, the so-called positive facts, (as opposed to 'speculative facts') as objects for study.

The multisignificance of the word positivism also has its origin in Enlightenment philosophy. For the enlightened thinkers not only emphasized that reason and observation would thenceforth be the criteria for truth; they fully expected it to result in Progress − the great salvation of mankind. No wonder that one of the most important connotations of the concept of positivism is closely linked to that belief in Progress. Both aspects, the 'objectively perceptible' and the 'world-improving, or moral' element, find expression in the positivism of Auguste Comte. There are unmistakable echoes of the emphasis on reason and observation in his view that the history of mankind can be divided into three phases − the religious, the metaphysical and the scientific − of which the scientific phase is the last and the highest. But closely linked to this in Comte's work is the element of world-improvement; Progress is identified with the construction of a new moral system, a new system of justice, a new religion, all of them to be cast in a scientific (i.e. a positive-scientific) mould.

The connection between these two meanings of the positivism concept is expressed, too, in the work of Emile Durkheim.[3] However, the relation between these different accents is not the end of the matter. It is precisely because the study of positive facts was believed to lead to a new moral system and because of the view that only a 'reasonable' study of objective facts could be *the single source* of that new moral system that positivism was and is sometimes referred to as 'scientism'. Positivism is here looked on as the only sensible attitude that man can assume towards reality. Thus it becomes 'total' thought; there can be no sense without the positivist attitude of thought. For this reason this third connotation of the concept of positivism is called the *pars pro toto* meaning.

In his use of the positivism concept Parsons is thinking mainly of the combination of the central meaning of the concept (objective observation of 'positive' facts) with this last *pars pro toto* meaning.

The moral or world-improving element plays no part in it whatsoever:[4]

> The peculiarity of the point of view under consideration now is that it involves explicitly (more the latter) the view that positive science constitutes man's sole possible significant cognitive relation to external (nonego), man as actor, that is. In so far as this inference is drawn or as the reasoning dealt with implies it as a premise the system of social theory in question may be called 'positivistic'.

According to this definition, positive science provides the only reasonable way for an actor to orientate to the reality that surrounds him. In other words, meaningful orientation of man to his environment can exist only through knowledge of objective and external relations between phenomena. We shall soon see how, according to Parsons, this positivistic position logically subsides into pure behaviourism.

The instability of positivism

In a very lengthy argument Parsons makes it clear that a positivistically defined theory of action becomes a prey to internal conflicts.[5] In particular, the subjective moment of actors' orientation, though inherent in the concept of action theory, gradually gets pushed into the background. This subjective factor in the shaping of action and society is under pressure in the abovementioned interpretation of positivism. The positivistic option that a positive scientific orientation of an actor to his environment is the only reasonable one results in a narrowing down of the actor's subjective orientation to objective rational science and thus deprives the theory of action of its most typical characteristic.

Parsons begins his criticism of the positivistic action theory with a criticism of utilitarianism.[6] It is not an easy matter to give a clear definition of the word 'utilitarianism'. Considered mainly as a general philosophical phenomenon, utilitarianism can best be understood as an attitude which 'seeks to determine the rightness and wrongness of action by reference to the goodness and badness of their consequences'.[7] In such an interpretation the ethical evaluation of actions is entirely dependent on its 'usefulness'. Actions are evaluated in terms of their usefulness, especially of their usefulness to the individual. The consequence of this utilitarian interpretation is that action becomes identified with the 'rational pursuit of self-interest', that is to say the most efficient possible attention to one's own strictly personal advantage.

There are two aspects of this 'doctrine of usefulness' which should be underlined in this context. The first is the emphasis which this interpretation places on the *individual*. The individual is the yardstick by which the usefulness of an action is measured. Everything revolves around the individual and individuality and nothing may be allowed to interfere with the independence of the individual. The second aspect of utilitarianism that interests us particularly is the emphasis it places on the strictly *rational* way of acting. The word 'rationality' is used here in its very narrow meaning of 'efficiency' or 'technical rationality'. According to this utilitarian theory of action, every individual, every actor will be influenced only by this norm of rationality. On the basis of this description, utilitarianism can be interpreted both as a form of action theory and as a variant of positivism. It is a theory of action because there is a place in its frame of reference for the subjective orientation of actors; it is a variant of positivism because it regards the individual actor as the most realistic kind of scientist who tries to achieve his ends as rationally as he can, that is to say by using his scientific knowledge. Thus, the utilitarian theory of action, with its characteristics of individuality and (technical) rationality, is *one* of the many possible positivistic theories of action; for this reason it is sometimes called *individual-positivistic* rather than utilitarian. In Parsons's view, this utilitarian or individual-positivistic theory of action represents an extremely shaky position of thought. The instability becomes apparent when the two characteristics of utilitarianism are combined. For how can a society be formed on a basis of the utilitarian premises of individuality and rationality? The combination of these two in 'the rational pursuit of self-interest' makes society in the sense of people living together an extremely doubtful possibility. The result of that 'rational pursuit of self-interest' is a society in which human existence can best be described in Hobbes's words as 'solitary, poor, nasty, brutish and short'.[8]

In principle when every individual is trying to satisfy his own desires and interests in a strictly rational way, all measures are admissible. The end is considered to justify the means because the norm of rationality does not, of itself, set a limit to the admissibility of those means: rationality implies the use of *all* means that will lead to success; from the utilitarian attitude the question of whether they are admissible or not can be neither asked nor answered. Force and fraud could, in principle, be regarded from this point of view as the most efficient and rational means to achieve particular ends.

No one has formulated this problem as sharply as Thomas Hobbes. According to utilitarian premises, Hobbes assumes that the most natural social relationship is war – war waged by all against all *(bellum omnium contra omnes)*. He asserts that man is ruled by a multitude of 'passions' the realization of which cannot be achieved without adequate means. To have the disposal of adequate means signifies 'power'. As soon as the struggle for the (scarce) adequate means begins, power becomes an end in itself; there is a struggle for power. In this struggle for power the 'rational' means of force and fraud play an important part.[9] Therefore, there is no normative regularity or *order* in a society built on strictly utilitarian premises; such premises can lead only to chaos, to normative chaos.

But such complete, normative chaos is not confirmed by the reality of our experience; (if it comes to that neither is complete, normative order). In other words, there is a discrepancy between the artificial utilitarian construction and the reality of experience. This discrepancy and, particularly, the fact that in the utilitarian tradition there is no complete, normative chaos either, raises the question which, since Hobbes, has been referred to as the *'problem or order': How is it that society is not in a chronic state of war waged by all against all and that violence and deception, though not unusual, are yet far from the general rule? How is it that people are even able to co-operate with each other?*

It is clear that even to pose this question is to betray the premises of utilitarianism: normative order appears as a 'surprise' which seems to be inexplicable in the framework of the theory. It might be expected, reasons Parsons, that this utilitarian theory, which allows such a 'surprise' to occur, will be short-lived. In any case it is obvious that the premises of a theory that is so far removed from reality must be re-examined.

How is it, asks Parsons next, that this utilitarian view, and with it the utilitarian theory of action, have been able to hold their own for so long? He finds the answer to his question in the nature of the 'solutions' to the problem of order which were provided by the utilitarian tradition. All of these solutions imply a modification of both the utilitarian premises; the wine is watered down, so to speak. This increases the reality-value of utilitarianism at the cost of its internal logical consistency.

What are we to think, for instance, of Hobbes's 'solution' to the problem of order? Of the aforementioned human passions which everyone strives to fulfil, he considers the passion for 'self-preservation' to be a very fundamental one. This care for self-preservation and safety leads man to 'reality': he relinquishes some of his individual autonomy to a sovereign authority, the Leviathan or the state which, in turn, guarantees him safety and protection. John Locke provides a similar solution but places less emphasis on the controlling function of the state. He looks on force and fraud as incidental problems and the state, which Hobbes regarded as a bitter necessity, he sees as an institution founded by intelligent people who are prepared to deal with any possible incidents. Locke places more emphasis on the positive aspects of personal association, something which is possible only on the grounds of a postulation which, says Parsons, is not devoid of wishful thinking – that of the 'natural identity of interests'. This postulation suggests the fact that the interests of different individuals can coincide.[10]

So what do we see? From strictly utilitarian premises Hobbes formulates the so-called problem or order. His own solution, the Leviathan, proves to be a construction that is difficult to place within those premises. The same is true of Locke's solution, the 'natural identity of interests' postulation. Neither of these solutions has sufficient regard for the premises of individuality and rationality. The freedom of the individual is curtailed and the original interpretation of rationality, of choice of means, is very difficult to reconcile with any form of co-operative 'reasonability'. This is the sort of solution which held up the discussion about utilitarian premises for a long time. This was why the utilitarian theory of action continued to exist long after the days of Hobbes and Locke.

Thus the instability of the individual-positivistic theory of action is most apparent in the so-called problem of order and in the fact that no solution can be found for this problem within the limitations of utilitarianism. Yet order and regularity do exist in society; without them social action and society itself would become impossibilities. This justifies the question which Parsons himself asked and which was the central theme in the development of modern sociology: 'How is it possible . . . to solve the Hobbesian problem of order and yet not make use of such an objectionable metaphysical prop as the doctrine of the "natural identity of interests?" '[11]

Various solutions to this problem have been put forward in the framework of the general positivistic tradition. In comparison with the doubtful utilitarian 'solutions' they have the advantage of undeniable logical consistency. However they have an enormous disadvantage; for every logically consistent, positivistic solution of the problem of order comes into conflict with the fundamental principle of the action theory, namely the subjective orientation of actors. This means that the positivistic solutions of the problem of order turn the theory of action into a sort of behaviourism.

We shall now give a summarized version of Parsons's view on these positivistic attempts to solve the Hobbesian problem.[12] The internal tension between the two utilitarian premises of individuality and rationality is reflected in a problem which is insoluble within those premises. Because the premise of rationality forms an essential element of the concept of positivism described above, the positivistic solution to the problem of order obviously implies that the premise of individuality – or subjectivity – is going to be modified.

In utilitarianism or individual-positivism the individual freedom of actors is 'rescued' as it were by allowing the category of ends – unlike the means – to remain outside the norm of strictly scientific rationality. In the 'choice' of means, actors are guided by considerations of scientific rationality but in the choice of ends they are entirely free. The only thing that can be said about these ends from the standpoint of the action theory is that they are completely random, not accessible for scientific analysis: the 'randomness of ends' postulation. It was inevitable that this postulation should be sharply criticized: the thought that the choice of ends is in no way influenced by any factors outside the individual is so alien to the truth as to give the impression that the expression 'individual freedom' has been misunderstood, to say the least.

Be this as it may, the important thing is the direction taken by the criticism of this untenable postulation. In practice, criticism is mostly confined to the framework of positivism with the result that not only the choice of means but also the choice of ends falls within the norm of rationality. The utilitarian action theory has to pay for its instability with a sliding descent into what Parsons calls a *radical-rationalistic positivism*. In this radically rationalistic positivism the choice of ends is decided by strictly positive-scientific criteria. But if the choice of ends is thus decided does not the actor then become simply a bystander? If the word 'choice' is interpreted to mean 'positive-scientific criteria' is there still such a thing as autonomic-individual choice? If the actor's subjective orientation is taken to mean positive-scientific knowledge how can the actor's orientation still be subjective? Does not that subjectivity become swallowed up by the 'objectivity' of positive science?

In short, the most important characteristic of the utilitarian *theory of action* – the actor's subjectivity – vanishes as soon as the doubtful postulation of the randomness of ends is criticized from a positivistic point of view. The choice of ends then becomes a matter of positive science whereby those objectives lose their independence and become simply part of the situation i.e. of the external objective conditions by which the actor's actions are determined. A strictly scientific choice of ends is no longer a real choice: it leads to a determinism in which there is no place for actors' subjective orientation.

Positivistic solutions to the problem of order lead inevitably to a one-sided accentuation of objective factors that are unrelated to the individual. They do provide a logical explanation, at least, for order in society. But these radical-positivistic offshoots of the utilitarian theory of action are no longer worthy of the name: by identifying actors' subjective orientation with pure scientism they have reduced action to behaviour.

That is why Parsons, underlining the instability of utilitarianism once again, speaks of the *utilitarian dilemma of the positivistic theory of action*. He formulates this dilemma as follows:[13]

> either the active agency of the actor in the choice of ends is an independent factor in action, and the end element must be random; or the objectionable implication of the randomness of ends is denied, but then their independence disappears and they are assimilated to the condition of the situation, that is to elements analyzable in terms of non-subjective categories.

The matter can be put more simply, thus: the utilitarian theory of action is a combination of 'positivism' and 'action theory': this combination presents great problems, especially the problem of order. Every effort to solve this problem involves breaking the combination: the positivistic solution leads to behaviourism in place of a theory of action: the action-theoretical solution leads to a rejection of the positivistic premises.

Parsons discusses an escape-route from the utilitarian dilemma other than that of radical rationalistic positivism. In emphasizing that action occurs on a rational-scientific basis, the utilitarian theory of action runs into difficulties as soon as actors do 'stupid things'. It is an inescapable fact of experience that actors do not always choose the best means to achieve their ends. The utilitarian action theory recognizes the existence of this piece of 'unsound' rationality and puts it down to ignorance and error. There is nothing more to be done with it and it, too, is looked on as one of the 'random' phenomena: the so-called postulation of 'the randomness of ignorance and error'.

This postulation, too, has been criticized: However, as long as the criticism keeps within the positivistic frame-work – as in practice it does – it means that the causes of 'ignorance and error' are not, in any event, to be found in actors' subjectivity (has this not already been identified with scientific rationality?) Therefore the causes are discovered in the objective conditions of actors' situations. These objective conditions vary from 'internal' factors like instincts, passions and other innate motive forces in human behaviour to 'external' factors like, for instance, climatological circumstances. Parsons calls this escape-route from the problem of utilitarianism: radical-anti-intellectualistic positivism.

The result of this escape-route leads equally to the utilitarian dilemma we have described above: *either* utilitarianism is a theory of action with a number of debatable postulations, *or* the postulations are criticized, in which case the status of action – theory disappears and we are left with only behaviourism.

To conclude this section we give a diagram (Figure 2.1) to illustrate the instability of the positivistic theory of action.

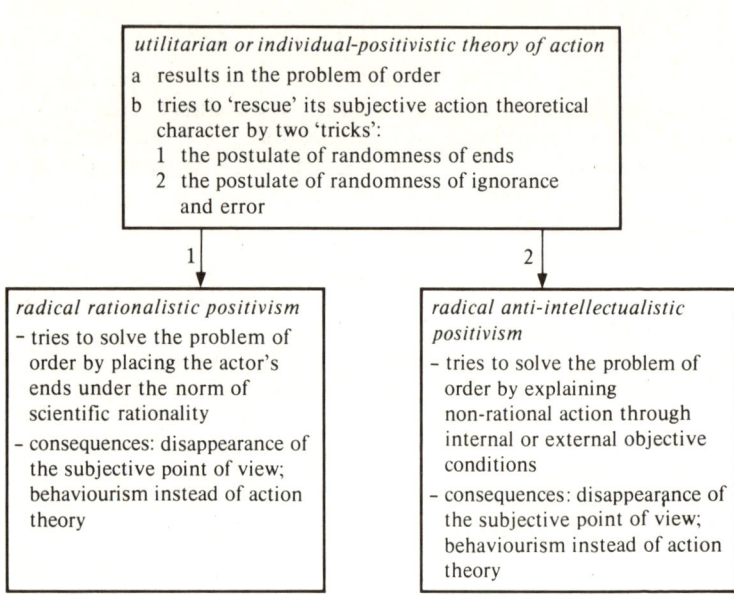

FIGURE 2.1 *The utilitarian dilemma*

From positivism to voluntarism

Apart from the radical-positivistic escape-routes from the instability of the utilitarian theory of action described in the foregoing paragraph, other developments are taking place in a different direction. These developments lead to a breakthrough in the positivistic framework in which the criticism of utilitarianism has so far been formulated. Absolute determinism, the result of radical-positivistic 'solutions', must give way very gradually to the view that there is also a subjective or active aspect of human action: the so-called *voluntaristic theory of action*.

It should be noted that the voluntaristic theory of action lays equal emphasis on the 'active' and on the 'passive' aspects of human action; human endeavours and human conditioning are both given a place in the voluntaristic theory of action. However, in contrast to the absolute supremacy of determinism in positivistic and behaviouristic doctrines, the essence of the voluntaristic theory of action is its 'active' aspect.

This voluntaristic tendency is to be found in the work of a number of classical authors of whom Parsons mentions Marshall, Pareto and Durkheim. In all these cases, he says, the starting-point of their activities lay in their attitude to the utilitarian or individual-positivistic theory of action. Moreover, in the sense of the central meaning of the concept of positivism indicated above, these authors can be described as 'positivists'. All of them strongly oppose speculative procedures in social science and prefer an objective method of approach to social action and social reality.

Nevertheless, some elements have crept into the ideas of these authors which are alien to the positivistic premise. It is these elements that give rise to the voluntaristic theory of action. In other words, these alien elements imply an answer to what Parsons considers to be the most central methodological question: How is it possible to safeguard the 'subjective' or orientation aspect in the solution to the question of order — and thus also in the general theory of action?' The answer is simply: *by transcending positivism.*

Marshall's contribution was a modern start to the development from positivism to voluntarism.[14] His background is strictly utilitarian and for him, too, action is nothing but the 'rational pursuit of self-interest'. On the basis of this idea he constructs economics as a 'utility theory'. This entangles him in typical utilitarian problems and there are passages in his work which suggest that he, too, tried to get round them by using the familiar radical-positivistic escape-routes.

But this is not all: there emerges from Marshall's scheme an element which cannot be interpreted either in utilitarian or in radical-positivistic terms — the element of 'activities'. In Marshall's definition these 'activities' are more or less isolated elements; they do not form the means to achieve more distant ends but are far more to be regarded as ends in themselves. To be energetic, to show initiative, to act rationally, to be resourceful — these are examples of such 'activities'. As objectives in themselves they are also *values* by which action can be appraised. In using these values or ethics, alongside the strictly orthodox-economic factors, to explain economic action, Marshall is extending economics from being 'a study of wealth' to being 'a part of the study of man'.

Thus these 'activities' can be regarded as immediate manifestations of social values. Marshall did not clearly realize that by introducing this factor he was breaking down the barriers of positivism. Occasionally he gives the impression of wanting to dress up this new conceptual element in a radical-positivistic guise; the remark that the above mentioned 'activities' have their origins in human 'character' is reminiscent of the anti-intellectualistic variant of radical-positivism. According to Parsons, Marshall was hardly aware of the methodological implications of introducing the concept of 'activities'; this, Parsons suspects, was because these 'activities' run completely parallel with 'rationality in the pursuit of self-interest'.

Pareto's contribution to the imminent development from positivism to voluntarism claims a great deal of Parsons's attention.[15] It is debatable whether, in view of his vehement reactions to the positivism of Comte, Pareto can be counted among the positivists. The source of this difference of opinion lies in our own differentiation between the meanings of the concept of positivism. Pareto's criticism of Comte is chiefly concerned with the moral or world-improving element of his positivism. Nevertheless, the central meaning of the concept of positivism (objectivistic approach) plays an important part in Pareto's conceptions. This is not surprising when it is realized that Pareto arrived at the study of sociology by the 'positivistic' paths of natural science and economics. Pareto distinguishes 'logical' and 'non-logical' action. Science is the prototype of 'logical action'; economic activity in the strict sense of the word also belongs to the same category. But Pareto digresses from radical positivism with the view that this category of 'logical action' by no means exhausts the forms of useful human orientation. 'Non-logical action' is not regarded by Pareto as a 'random' category unworthy of further attention; on the contrary, it is precisely this non-logical action that is allotted the most important place in Pareto's conceptual scheme and which Pareto subjects to further analysis.

How does Pareto analyse this non-logical action? When studying non-logical action he concentrates mainly on the non-logical theories that accompany such action either as a manifestation or as legitimation. These non-logical theories do not conform to the scientific standard; they are theories in which scientific rationality gives way to feelings or sentiment. These theories fall into two elements:[16]

> the theories c where sentiment plays a part, and which add something to experience, which are beyond experience . . . fall ( ) into a part a, consisting of the manifestation of certain sentiments, and a part b, consisting of logical reasoning, sophisms and also other manifestations of sentiments employed to draw deductions from a.

Thus, the element a is comparatively constant; it represents one and the same state of mind which can be concretized in various different ways. Pareto calls this constant element the 'residue': it is, as it were, the impulse that leads to concrete forms of action. Element *b* refers to the variable aspect of the non-logical theories; it represents the 'variations on a single theme'. Pareto calls this element the 'derivation'.

Parsons's analysis links up with this conceptual scheme made up of residues and derivations. He says the fact that Pareto's views on residues are often regarded as a sort of theory of instinct shows how much his (Pareto's) critics are committed to positivistic methods of interpretation. They think that Pareto is running away from utilitarian problems only to find himself caught up in radical-anti-intellectualistic positivism. Here action is explained by instincts, biological passions, 'external' conditions. It is often thought that in this way Pareto is putting forward a sociological variant of the psychological theory of instinct which was so popular at the time.

Parsons disagrees entirely with this interpretation. The key to his conflicting interpretation lies in the answer to the question: in what ways can non-logical action or non-logical theories deviate from the standard of scientific rationality? The study of Pareto's work makes it clear to Parsons that two ways may reasonably be indicated. In positivistic circles a great deal of emphasis is placed on the first of these ways, that of 'unscientificness'. This applies to theories that do not conform to the norm of scientific rationality; they are 'unscientific', based on 'ignorance and error'. But Pareto distinguishes another possibility for deviation from the standard of scientific rationality. Besides 'unscientific' theories there can also be 'non-scientific' theories. These non-scientific theories concern statements which do not lend themselves to scientific examination: they transcend the level of science and cannot be verified at that level. For instance, the statement that further emancipation of women is a socially-justifiable demand cannot be put to the logical-experimental test.

The non-scientific aspect of non-logical theories consists mainly of justification or legitimation of particular actions. These theories will no doubt contain unscientific aspects as well but, in essence, they are of a non-scientific nature. In other words, Parsons concludes that all these non-scientific theories are based on the same sentiment, viz. 'a sentiment that such and such is a desirable state of affairs'.[17] Thus there is a particular sort of residue which expresses this kind of sentiment. It is the special nature of this residue that it states the objectives of action; nor can these be regarded as 'intermediate objectives' but only as 'ultimate ends' or 'ends in themselves'. Another word for 'end in itself' is 'value'.

This shows clearly that in Pareto's scheme actors' evaluations occupy an important place. This emphasis on actors' evaluations introduces a subjective element which does not fit into the positivistic frame of reference. For the subjectivity of positivism is only a pseudo-subjectivity; it is either backed up with objective scientific knowledge or rescued by head-in-the-sand politics of postulations like that of the 'randomness of ends'.

Just as in his interpretation of Marshall's work, Parsons again concludes that the restrictions of positivism have been broken by the introduction of this new subjective element. Thus Pareto, too, has contributed to the formulation of a theory of action which does full justice to the most essential aspect of that theory — actors' subjective orientation. In this way Pareto escapes from the utilitarian dilemma of the positivistic theory of action: he solves the methodological problem that is inherent in the utilitarian theory of action by introducing a real subjective factor to explain order in society.

Durkheim is the third classical author of social-scientific studies who, in Parsons's interpretation, refers to the utilitarian problem of order and formulates solutions for it which at first are contained by and finally break out of the straitjacket of the positivistic framework.[18] Durkheim's most characteristic contribution to the criticism of the utilitarian theory of action is undoubtedly his sharp attack on the individualistic premises of its explanatory method. This is not the place to discuss this criticism; it is dealt with under the dilemma of social-nominalistic versus social-realistic thought-patterns (see 2.3). Suffice it for the moment to say that Durkheim replaces the strictly individualistic explanatory method of utilitarianism by one which is dominated by collective factors, i.e. factors that concern collective social facts. At this juncture we are only interested to see how these factors score on the dimension of subjectivism versus objectivism.

In this connection, we see that Durkheim, in his study *De la Division du travail social* (1893) points *via* the stages of 'moral' and 'material' density, to *population-growth* as an explanatory factor for the phenomenon of division of labour. This factor of population-growth is, for Parsons, clearly reminiscent of one of the two different forms of radical-positivism, anti-intellectualistic positivism. In using a 'biologically' objective factor to explain social reality, Durkheim is obviously unable to transcend the utilitarian dilemma. Parsons refers then to 'a breakdown of utilitarianism into radical positivism, in this case the 'biologizing' of social theory'.[19]

This is changed with the appearance of *Le Suicide* (1897). The anti-intellectualistic factor of 'population-growth' disappears from

Durkheim's frame of reference. Instead there is more emphasis on collective consciousness, a concept – the meaning of which at first seemed to refer to the phase of mechanical solidarity only and not to the organic phase. The characteristic of modern collective consciousness is a sacred respect for the personality of the individual and for his capacity to develop. Thus collective consciousness becomes more and more important in Durkheim's conceptual scheme; the central conceptual antithesis in his work – initially the antithesis between mechanical and organical solidarity – now becomes the antithesis between collective consciousness and anomie.

This development is apparent in his typology of the suicide phenomenon. The situation of 'normlessness', the absence of collective consciousness, leads to the type of suicide which Durkheim calls 'anomic'. This means that the other two types, 'egoistic' and 'altruistic', indicate situations where there is indeed collective consciousness: in this typology egoism and altruism apparently represent different kinds of collective consciousness.

The important question here concerns the factor of 'collective consciousness'. Should it be placed on the subjective or the objective side of our methodological dilemma?

This factor of collective consciousness as Durkheim's contribution to the solution of the problem of order has, for Parsons, two important aspects. To begin with, he says, Durkheim counted collective consciousness as one of the objective external conditions by which action is determined irrespective of the individual. Thus Durkheim stays within the framework of positivism.[20] He changes the individualistic factor of utilitarianism into a collective or 'sociologistic' factor; the objective and external character of that factor is upheld for the present. Therefore Parsons gives to Durkheim's variant of positivism the name of 'sociologistic positivism'.

However, Durkheim has gradually been renouncing this sociologistic positivism; he cannot for long maintain the view that human behaviour is determined by social factors in the same way as it is determined by physical factors. He discovers a difference between the working of a norm, a 'collective representation' on the one hand and the determination of a physical factor on the other hand. In his opinion the difference lies in the intervention of the *human will:* there is an automatic relation between 'not eating' and dying of starvation but the relation between committing a murder and execution by electric chair is dependent on human will in the collective sense.[21]

This development towards voluntarism is manifested particularly in the shift of meaning in Durkheim's interpretation of social facts. The social fact was initially characterized by 'exteriority' and 'constraint' indicating determination from outside. Now, however, 'constraint' as a characteristic of the social fact is interpreted as moral obligation. Thus the external determining power of Durkheim's positivist period has given way to a subjective, internal sense of duty. The normative element no longer belongs in the list of objective factors but is incorporated as a subjective factor in the conceptual scheme.

In the framework of the methodological dimension discussed here, Marshall's 'activities', Pareto's 'normative residues' and Durkheim's internalized 'moral duty' form, for Parsons, the most important milestones on the road from positivism to voluntarism. This constitutes one part of Parsons's thesis of convergence as far as the subjective-objective dimension is concerned. The other part, the opposite development from idealism to voluntarism, still has to be examined before there can be any talk of convergence.

From idealism to voluntarism

The foregoing chapter gave some idea of what Parsons means by 'a completely idealistic version of the theory of action'. In it, the version thus sketched functioned as a point of reference for Weber's neo-Kantian epistemology and Parsons's analytical realism. In this next section the extreme idealistic position has another function; though here too it serves as starting point for analysis, that analysis is now on the level of methodology and concerns the type and nature of the basic formative factors of society.

We saw in the previous chapter that the historicist epistemological interpretations were coloured to a great extent by the unique and exceptional quality of man and culture. It is natural that this idea of human uniqueness plays its part on the methodological theory-level as well. The objectivism and determinism of the positivistic variants of theory are replaced by pure subjectivism. Objective, external conditions are precluded from the 'explanation' of action. when the level of *wie es eigentlich gewesen ist* is transcended, these conditions are supplanted by accentuation of a subjective factor such as *Geist;* then concrete and individual action is regarded as a manifestation of that *Geist*. The accentuation of a *Geist* that is changeable according to time, place and people as a sort of basic mentality or basic pattern of culture makes for an excessive historicist relativism that is diametrically opposed to positivistic evolutionist thought. Concrete action is regarded exclusively as the expression of a mentality, a collective subjective fact. Conditioning environmental factors play no part in shaping the action and the social order that result from it:[22]

at the idealistic pole the role of the conditional elements disappears as corresponding at the positivistic pole that of the normative disappears. In an idealistic theory 'action' becomes a process of 'emanation' of 'self-expression' of ideal or normative factors. Spatiotemporal phenomena become related to action only as symbolic 'modes of expression' or 'embodiments of meanings'.

Disregard of the conditioning factor in favour of this subjectivism places this version of the theory of action in direct opposition to the various positivist versions. At the same time it leads to a completely different interpretation of the way social phenomena are interrelated; in place of causal relations it looks for meaningful relations and it regards society not as a causal order but as an order of meanings.

The methodological one-sidedness of the extreme idealistic position, as reflected in the one-sided view of the way social order is created, also stimulated reactions within the idealistic tradition itself. In those reactions the exclusive influence of the subjective factor in determining action was supplemented with a series of objective – or, in the style of the day, materialistic conditioning factors. Again Parsons considers that the most important of the reactions are to be found in the work of *Max Weber*. He regards Max Weber's work as an important contribution to the development of the voluntaristic pattern of thought. In his opinion, Weber arrives at the methodological point of convergence called voluntarism by a completely opposite path to that taken by Durkheim. In order to bring Weber's contribution to the voluntaristic pattern of thought into focus we must elaborate on part of his substantive theory.

Weber's substantive propositions, like those of Marx and Sombart, are centred on the development of the capitalist system. In the famous *Die Protestantische Ethik und der Geist des Kapitalismus*[23] he tries to relate two phenomena which at first sight are independent of each other. He starts with an ideal-typical description of the characteristics of capitalism. In its most general meaning this concept refers to a system of commercial undertakings all trying to make profit and all connected by market relations. The system is characterized by rationality, that is to say the pursuit of profit is regulated by a rational system; in modern bourgeois capitalism there is no question of unsystematic profiteering. The system is built up round a very specific kind of labour organization i.e. bureaucracy. This is a form of organization in which each 'member' has a clearly defined and specialized task. This allotment of tasks involves a certain hierarchical order:

authority appertains only to a particular function, not to the qualities of the person fulfilling the function. There are very clear moral connotations attached to the function (the special meaning of the German word *Beruf* has its equivalent only in the word 'calling' and in expressions like 'a clergyman's calling' and 'to call upon the service, kindness etc. of . . . '). In short, the discipline that is peculiar to capitalism is clearly illustrated by the system's bureaucratic form of organization.

The question of the character and background of this discipline inspires Weber to examine the fundamental values associated with modern capitalism. In other words, he tries to invent a formula to express the capitalist *mentality (Geist)*. That mentality consists of a system of attitudes with regard to economic activity. From this it is apparent that Weber regards economic activity as more than simply a means to achieve particular ends: to a large extent it is an end in itself. According to Weber there is no criterion for deciding that for the time being 'enough' money has been earned or profit made. Thus this view of economic activity as an ethical duty, as *Beruf*, results in a favourable evaluation of productive work. 'Work' is not regarded as a necessary evil but as a possibility to achieve high ethical aims: nobility in labour.

This capitalist mentality which is at the root of economic thought need not necessarily be regarded as an 'accidental' and independent phenomenon. Weber sees a certain parallel between the capitalist mentality on the one hand and the ethics of ascetic Protestantism, i.e. Calvinism, on the other. Calvinism combines a number of specifically Christian basic ideas in such a way as to impel human activity towards activism and asceticism: meekness and mysticism are repudiated. It is the doctrine of predestination, or rather a non-orthodox interpretation of this doctrine, by which activism is promoted. If it is believed that one's destiny is predetermined and unchangeable, the idea that the positive shape of that destiny is manifested in social success can be an inducement to untiring activity. Thus social success becomes a godly sign of having been chosen.

Weber shows that there is a large degree of congruence or consensus of meaning between the Calvinist ethics and capitalist mentality even though, at first sight, they seem to be independent spiritual attitudes. Weber refers here to the notion of *Wahlverwandtschaft* (elective affinity). A strictly idealistic theory of action would confine itself to the establishment of this *Sinnzusammenhang*. However, Weber goes further, says Parsons, and by doing so he progresses beyond the bounds of the idealistic theory of action: he tries to interpret 'timeless' congruence in a causal relation in which Calvinistic ethics are seen as 'stimulators' in the development of modern capitalism. This causal interpretation is borne out particularly in Weber's comparative sociology of religion. There too, the question as to the development of modern capitalism is pre-eminent, albeit in the 'negative' sense. Weber asks why, in spite of various forms of early capitalism in China and India, there is no modern capitalism in those countries as there is in the Western ones. He answers the question as follows: it is because in the West favourable *material conditions* receive an extra impulse from religious ethics; in China and India they receive no such impulse. The nature of religious ethics in China and India is such that it cannot apparently fulfil the stimulating function; this the ethics of Calvinism are apparently able to do.

This shows at the same time that on the methodological dimension of objectivism and subjectivism Weber dissociates himself from the scheme of a strictly idealistic theory of action. In fact, in constructing a relation between Calvinistic ethics and modern capitalism Weber is in no sense impelled by purely subjectivist pretensions. The subjective explanatory factors (ethics) are not the only ones to have played a part in the creation of modern capitalism. As is obvious from the foregoing section, Weber places importance on material conditions and especially on the interaction between material and idealistic factors. This is why Weber's approach to capitalism is not, like that of Sombart, unilaterally idealistic, but unquestionably reflects the importance of non-subjective factors in the explanation of human actions.

Thus, in the methodological sense, Weber's rejection of the strictly idealistic theory of action is manifested by the following:
(a) the explicit recognition of the influence of material objective factors on the shape of human action and of social order,
(b) the attempt to supplement *Sinnzusammenhangen* wherever possible with causal relations in which one particular factor is regarded as one of the causes or stimulators of a particular consequence.

To sum up, we can say that Parsons's voluntarism implies an answer to the question of order in society – an answer in which both conditioning objective factors and normative subjective factors alike play their part. Thus voluntarism is a synthesis of the objectivist one-sidedness of positivism and the subjective one-sidedness of idealism. Has Parsons in this way fulfilled his pretension of transcending the dilemma of positivism versus idealism? As long as it is emphasized that voluntarism transcends the one-sidedness of both the positivist and the idealistic theory of action, the answer is positive. It is negative if the question means that Parsons has also given an adequate picture of the mutual relation or *interaction between objective and subjective factors*. It is still a characteristic of voluntarism that it places subjective and objective factors next to each other; it is not clear in the first period of Parsons's work how they become intermingled and in our line of interpretation this will prove to be a stumbling-block in the way of a systematic conceptualization.

We shall close this section with a diagram of the convergence analysed by Parsons on the methodological dimension of subjectivism or objectivism which we have distinguished.

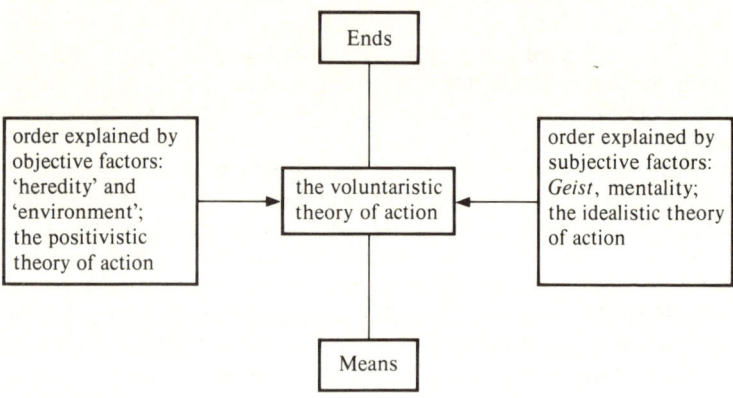

FIGURE 2.2 *The voluntaristic theory of action*

The vertical line in Figure 2.2 symbolizes the starting-point of Parsons's analysis – the individual rationality of the utilitarian means – ends scheme. In this context it can be called the dimension of rationality. This starting-point brings us to the problem of order. The two horizontal arrows together form the so-called dimension of order. At the end of the left-hand arrow is the objectivistic or positivistic solution to the problem of order. At the end of the right-hand arrow is the subjectivistic or idealistic explanation of social order. The direction in which the arrows point symbolizes the development to be traced in the work of the abovementioned classical authors from these two extreme positions. The voluntaristic theory of action unites both dimensions in one pattern of thought on man and society.

3 The methodological dimension of social-nominalistic versus social-realistic patterns of thought in historical perspective

We shall now discuss the second part of Parsons's voluntaristic pretension. It will be remembered that Parsons wanted to bridge at the same time both the abovementioned gap between objectivistic and subjectivistic explanations and that between social-realistic and social-nominalistic explanations; his voluntarism was to be a synthesis of these two opposing patterns of thought.

In Dutch sociological literature the author who has discussed this dilemma of thought-patterns most deeply is Zijderveld.[24] He confronts Durkheim's social-realistic thought-pattern with the social-nominalistic one of Weber. He shows that Durkheim looks at social action mainly from the standpoint of institutional structures – an attitude most markedly illustrated by the famous 'maxim' that social facts should be explained only by other social facts. This clearly demonstrates not only the *sui generis* nature of social facts but also Durkheim's dislike of individualistic explanatory methods. Weber, on the other hand, defines social action as meaningful action; he places far more emphasis than does Durkheim on the actor's subjective point of view. Weber looks from the individual, as it were up to the structures by which he is governed; following Theodor Geiger, Zijderveld calls this attitude (or thought-pattern) 'anascopic'. Durkheim looks down from the institutional structures to the individual and his behaviour; this attitude is called 'katascopic'. Zijderveld considers it necessary and possible to incorporate these two thought-patterns on the relation of the individual to society – the problem of institutionalization as he calls it – in a dialectic thought-pattern. This 'nominalism-realism dialectic' becomes significant when the Weberian and the Durkheimian accent are linked together:[25]

> when social reality as seen by Weber is phenomenologically interpreted as a cosmos purposefully constructed by individuals and when, following Durkheim, this constructed reality is described as an objective structure with sedimented meanings in the form of typifications which, though constructed by people, transcend and determine individual existence, then a dialectical approach to social reality and social action is possible. In the terminology of Sartre this approach is called the progressive-regressive (or synthetic-analytical), in the terminology of our study is is called the katascopic-anascopic (or realistic-nominalistic) method.

Thirty years earlier this same methodological dilemma of social science played a similar part in Parsons's *The Structure of Social Action*. Parsons's treatment of this methodological dilemma starts once again from the problem of order. For this problem of order is not completely solved by the introduction of a normative- or value element as subjective aspect. Those values – or 'ends in themselves' – can still be regarded as being quite independent of each other. If that happens, then the result is still a Hobbesian problem of order in which order can only be explained by a *deus ex machina*. Parsons's voluntaristic solution to this problem of order is essentially different. It proceeds from the assumption that the subjective and normative element (the values or ultimate ends) do not remain independent of each other but that to some extent they form a system common to various actors. At the same time this means that society can exist not only because of an exterior governing agent but because of the *common* systems of value that are inherent in that society. In Parsons's own words:[26]

> The other position is to suppose a significant degree of integration of ultimate ends into a common system . . . It opens the way to an interpretation of the basis of order in a society which is in a sense 'immanent', founded in the character of the society itself. Whether this element is to have empirical importance is essentially a question of fact and cannot be answered in terms of the present abstract analysis alone.

In Parsons's view, utilitarianism or individual-positivism is the prototype of a social-nominalistic approach to social reality. At the methodological level the characteristic of individual rationality results in 'methodological individualism' or 'atomism', i.e. a thought-pattern which reduces the social element to the individual element. The authors whom Parsons brings forward as representatives of the positivistic tradition (Marshall, Pareto and Durkheim) also broke away from the one-sidedness of utilitarianism on this methodological dimension.

The work of Marshall, especially his concept 'activities', represents a first cautious attack on this methodological individualism. Apart from the fact that 'activities' introduce a subjective value-element into the analysis of action, they point strongly to a certain sharedness of value-orientation. For Parsons, the introduction of the concept 'activities' in Marshall's work means the introduction of a collective orientation-moment in the explanation of social reality that overlies individual consciousness; in this respect, too, Marshall breaks out of the utilitarian straitjacket which considers as inadmissible any explanation that is not couched in terms of strictly individual satisfaction of wants.[27] Marshall's non-positivistic solution to the utilitarian problem of order is thus two-fold: besides cautiously introducing a subjective factor into his explanatory schema (see Figure 2.2), he also opens the possibility of interpreting that subjective factor not merely in an individualistic sense but in a collectivist sense as well.

Pareto's contribution to the breakthrough from the positivistic tradition of methodological individualism – and to the second aspect of the voluntaristic solution of the problem of order – is less pronounced. In a detailed analysis Parsons tries to show that the subjective or normative factor which, in Pareto's schema, appears in the form of a normative residue can also take the shape of a collective factor, above and beyond the individual.[28] This would mean that on this second methodological dimension too, Pareto passed beyond the boundaries of utilitarianism.

It would serve little purpose at this juncture to reconstruct Parsons's rather artificial interpretation of Pareto's work especially in view of the fact that this second aspect of the order problem is dealt with most pregnantly in the work of Emile Durkheim, Parsons's third 'positivist'. Initially, Durkheim's attack on utilitarianism concerned only the second aspect of the order problem, the methodological dilemma of social nominalism *versus* social realism. The other dilemma – objectivism *versus* subjectivism (see Figure 2.2) – does not become urgent for him till a later stage. From the very beginning of his sociological work Durkheim realizes that the order problem cannot be solved unless the basis of order is situated in *collective* ways of acting, thinking feeling and being. Durkheim's attack on utilitarianism is aimed chiefly at the methodological individualism of Spencer. He accuses utilitarianism, and Spencer in particular, of being imprisoned in the so-called 'anthropocentric postulate',[29] that is to say a premise which tolerates only those explanations of social reality which are based on attributes of the individual. Against this individualism Durkheim places a collective social factor, collective ideas, social facts or institutions. Where Spencer seeks to explain social order as resulting from contracts freely entered into by free individuals, Durkheim points to a factor, which forms the *basis* of such contracts. Whereas in Spencer's contracts the predominant factor is the utilitarian one of individual rationality, Durkheim points to a deeper sphere of common codes which logically precedes those contracts. In this context Parsons refers with great pertinence to the 'non-contractual element in contract' and to the 'institution of contract'.[30] Durkheim too, often uses the word 'institutions' in reference to this deeper order-creating sphere. He sees these institutions or social facts as 'collective ideas' or 'common value-patterns' which not only transcend individual consciousness but also provide a guarantee of social order.

Durkheim's *De la Division du travail social* (1893) is a discussion of the transition from the pre-industrial to the industrial type of social order.[31] In his view these two kinds of social order are the product of two quite different kinds of collective ideas. Pre-industrial order, consisting of a number of fairly autarchical and identical segments, is based on collective ideas of individuals with common aims and bound together by mutual ties into collective groups; individuality is not yet fully developed nor has it yet become emancipated as an individual consciousness from the restraints of collective consciousness. The social order that was based on these collective ideas, which Durkheim calls mechanical solidarity, is drastically undermined by the influence of the coming industrial development.

Does this mean that, with the undermining of this type of social order and the collective ideas on which it was founded social order itself will fall into chaos? No – says Durkheim – for it is evident that, in spite of all differences and conflicts, society continues to exist and social order is maintained. Consequently there must be a different type of social order based on different collective ideas. It is these collective ideas, the basis of the new industrialized social order as opposed to the old segmented order, which form the cement that holds society together. Durkheim sees these new ideas in the common or collective appreciation of man's individuality: thus the 'cult of the individual' is the institution which cements society together and in so doing is responsible for social order.

It is because, in criticizing utilitarianism, Durkheim at first limited himself to this dimension of social nominalism *versus* social realism and disregarded the other dimension (objectivism-subjectivism) that, as we saw in the previous paragraph, his thought-pattern at that time can be described as 'sociologistic positivism'. His change-over towards a voluntaristic attitude with regard to the other methodological dimension does not take place till later. Then the collective factor in explanations of social reality, the collective 'ideas', orientations or values lose their objective, conditioning character and can be seen as subjective, normative orientations (see Figure 2.2). Once Durkheim has got so far, he has also somewhat shaded out the rigid division between society and the individual for which his work has become famous and notorious. Now he, too, sees that society is no longer an objective power which determines the individual. The substratum of society is to be found in the actions of individuals and, on these the development of society depends. At the same time, individual action takes shape as a result of processes whereby the common collective values or orientations accepted by society or parts of society become internalized or institutionalized. This modification in Durkheim's attitude to the individual and society is paralleled by developments which have taken place on the idealistic side of this methodological spectrum concerning the same point of discussion.

The methodological argument between social nominalism and social realism is recognized also by followers of the idealistic tradition. Accentuation of the unique and special significance of human reality can be seen in an attitude which regards that reality as resulting fortuitously from the individual freedom of all participating actors. In this attitude (cultural) science is regarded as being entirely superfluous unless it is restricted to the purest possible registration of events.

However, accentuation of the unique and special can result in an attitude which regards a particular, changeable *Geist* or mentality as the source of social order. It is obvious that this mentality must be seen not only as a subjective but also as a collective 'factor' which transcends the individual. In Weber's work social-nominalistic and social-realistic thought-patterns are related one to the other. Just as he did in Durkheim's later work, Parsons sees in Weber a modified attitude to the relation between the individual and society. Of course Weber's *Kollektivgebilde* are based on meaningful actions by individual actors: they are continually confirmed or altered by those individual actions. However, at the same time, individual action is the expression and realization of a collective mentality such as, for instance, a capitalistic *Geist* or Protestant 'ethic'.

Therefore it is no wonder that on this methodological dimension as well Parsons thinks he has discovered a convergence between Durkheim's and Weber's work. It is this 'modified' attitude to the relation between the individual and society – or rather (to use Zijderveld's words) the nominalism-realism dialectic – that forms the second aspect of the thought-pattern which Parsons calls voluntaristic.

Has Parsons hereby fulfilled his second pretension – that of bridging the gap between social nominalism and social realism? This is another of the points about which we have our doubts. It is true that his intentions have become clearer but the major question as to how he intends to give a general theoretical shape to this as yet vague formulation remains unanswered for the time being. In the following chapters we shall see that his attempt met with varying degrees of success. To end this section we illustrate Parsons's voluntaristic pretension in Figure 2.3.

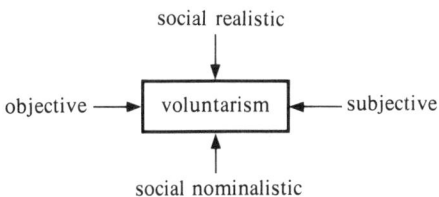

FIGURE 2.3 *The voluntaristic thought-pattern as synthesis on two methodological dimensions*

3 The structural-functional version of the action theory: the first attempt at conceptualization

1 Introduction

Now that the epistemological and methodological premises of Parsons's action theory have been introduced, it is time to consider how he moves on from these premises to the level of conceptual theory. In his early publications we find little more than the first beginnings in this direction; in *The Structure of Social Action,* for instance, there is as yet no question of a balanced frame of reference. In fact there is nothing but a formulation of the requirements which such a framework should fulfil.

These requirements can be summed up as follows:
1 The frame of reference must be the starting-point for a really general theory, i.e. a theory of action that will open an unequivocal, logically conclusive perspective on action.
2 Both the frame of reference and the categorial system based upon it must be built up of analytical elements, i.e. of concepts which select abstract aspects from the concrete reality of action rather than concrete parts.
3 Both the frame of reference and the categorial system based upon it must allow for the inclusion of the voluntaristic synthesis of objectivistic and subjectivistic ways of approach.
4 Both the frame of reference and the categorial system based upon it must give conceptual expression to the voluntaristic synthesis of social-nominalistic and social-realistic thought-patterns.

As we shall see, it is no easy matter to fulfil at one and the same time all these four requirements which Parsons himself laid down for the adequate formulation of an action theory. The structural-functional version of the action theory – the subject of this chapter – certainly falls short in this respect. However, this does not alter the fact that Parsons's structural-functional attempt was clearly aimed at transposing the epistemological and methodological premises already discussed to the level of conceptual theory; that this attempt did not succeed was due to very specific reasons which we shall examine in great detail. In order to demarcate as clearly as possible this first attempt at conceptualization on the one hand and, on the other hand, our own criticism of it, based on the aforementioned premises, this chapter will give an exposé of the frame of reference and the categorial system; the following chapter will concentrate on analysis and criticism.

2 The frame of reference (1)

Parsons's first cautious contributions to the construction of a frame of reference to the voluntaristic theory of action are concerned with a definition of 'the last unit of analysis'. This unit of analysis is the *principium differentiae* of the action theory, formulating as it does both the limits of the frame of reference and the aspects of reality that fall within its scope.

In *The Structure of Social Action* Parsons suggests the so-called *'unit act'* as the fundamental unit of analysis, the element from which conceptualization and analysis should proceed.[1]

> The first salient feature of the conceptual scheme to be dealt with lies in the character of the units . . .
> The basic unit may be called the 'unit act'. Just as the units of a mechanical system in the classical sense, particles, can be defined only in terms of their properties, mass, velocity, location in space, direction of motion, etc . . . , so the units of action systems also have certain basic properties without which it is not possible to conceive of the units as 'existing'.

All concrete phenomena built up of 'unit acts' belong to the field of the action theory. The 'unit act' is the utmost limit of the frame of reference; any further subdivision of action results in replacement of the action-theory frame of reference by another frame of reference and especially a cancelling out of the specific characteristics of action, particularly that of subjectivity. What, then are the fundamental characteristics of the 'unit act'? Parsons's formulation of them can be directly deduced from the two voluntaristic thought-patterns. Action may be said to occur as soon as and as long as the following four characteristics can be discerned:[2]
(a) *an aspect of ends:* for the purpose of the action theory an action is valid only when it is in some way directed towards the achievement of particular ends or, more generally, towards the realization of 'a future state of affairs';[3]
(b) *an aspect of means:* when certain parts of the situation in which

the action takes place are manipulated in order that above-mentioned ends should be achieved;

(c) *an aspect of objective conditioning:* when the action's orientation to particular ends is limited by parts of the situation which cannot be manipulated and have only a conditioning effect;

(d) *a subjective normative aspect:* when means and ends are not linked together purely at random but under the influence of internalized and institutionalized standards of value.

Both these two last aspects emphasize the system character of action. This is Parsons's way of getting round the antithesis between the individual and society conceptually; *in his definition, both individual orientation and institutional structures are action systems because as 'concrete' phenomena they are built up of 'units acts'.* In concreto, 'unit acts' never occur separately; they are always connected to other 'units acts' in one way or another. Because, naturally, the empirical reference of the action theory is to concrete phenomena concerned with individual and society, Parsons dares to state as early as 1937 that the action theory is, in principle, one of action systems and not of 'unit acts'. 'By a theory of action is here meant any theory the empirical reference of which is to a concrete system which may be considered to be composed of the units here referred to as "unit acts".'[4]

At this stage of his development Parsons is clearly dissociated from the fashionable controversy on a so-called 'action theory' as opposed to a so-called 'systems theory'. His 'action theory' is, *by definition,* a 'system theory'! There are innumerable ways in which actions can be linked together to form action systems; in other words, we can construct innumerable action systems from the total reality of experience. The individual and society form, as it were, the two poles of the dimension of action systems; they represent different levels. Every action system has a number of characteristics which are peculiar to the level on which it moves. These are the so-called *'emergent properties'* and they result from the interdependence of 'unit acts'. They cannot be converted directly to the characteristics of a single 'unit act' and would therefore disappear in an 'atomistic' or 'unit' analysis. Parsons gives the concept of 'economic rationality' as an example of such an 'emergent property'.[5] The economically rational action of an individual actor presupposes a rational consideration of many possible courses of action – both his own and those of other people. The characteristic of 'economic rationality' cannot be attributed to an isolated act – defined in terms of an end, a means, condition and a norm. When 'unit acts' can be combined at different levels into action systems, the field to be studied by the action theory becomes extremely complex and involved. How can it be put into some kind of order? 'As certain degrees of complexity are reached, there emerge other ways of describing the facts, the employment of which constitutes a convenient "shorthand" that is adequate for a large number of scientific purposes.'[6]

In this phase Parsons distinguishes two of these 'secondary descriptive schemes'.[7] The first is the 'social relation' schema or, in Parsons's later terminology, the theory of the 'social system'. Actions are 'organized' around the mutual interaction of individual actors. At that level, actions acquire their own 'emergent properties'. The same applies to a second type of 'shorthand', the scheme of individual personality. Here actions are organized around the individual and the 'emergent properties' are therefore of a different content from those of the social system. *The Structure of Social Action* (1937) falls short with regard to working out these starting-points. The frame of reference is not, in fact, elaborated till about 1950 with the publication of *Towards a General Theory of Action* and *The Social System*.[8] By then, as we shall see, there have also been changes in the content of the frame of reference itself.

3 The frame of reference (2)

The 'unit act', which was given pride of place in the above-mentioned first attempt to construct an action theoretical frame of reference, is superseded in the new plan by a new unit of analysis – the *'unit of action'*. At the time, Parsons himself attaches little importance to this change in unit of analysis. He makes only a passing remark about it – in a footnote – and justifies it by saying that the "unit act" is a special case of the unit of action.[9]

We are not, in this chapter, concerned to ask whether this change does indeed make a contribution to the generalization of the action theory. Our analysis in the following chapter will show that Parsons passes too easily over the significance of this change in unit of analysis.

Of what, then, does this new unit of analysis in the action frame of reference consist? The so-called 'unit of action' is formed by the actor-situation complex. Action is differentiated on the one hand in the actor's orientation and, on the other hand, in the situation to which he is oriented. This means that the division between subject and object is already allotted a place in the last unit of analysis. As a result, the action frame of reference falls into two poles: first, the elaboration of the subjective aspect, i.e. actor's orientation and, subsequently, that of the objective aspect, i.e., the meaning of the situation to which the actor is oriented. Parsons differentiates actors' orientation in a number of analytical aspects.[10] Since it concerns a large number of divisions we shall illustrate this analytical elaboration in diagrammatical form in Figure 3.1.

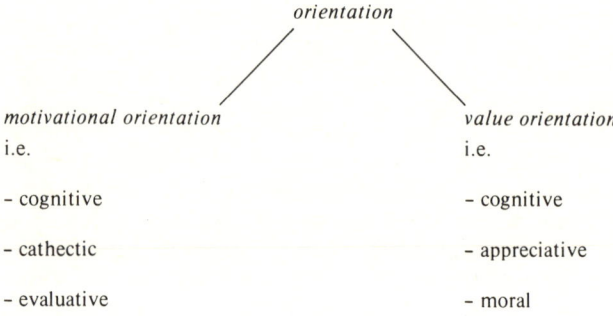

FIGURE 3.1 *The orientation pole of the frame of reference*

The first subdivision in the orientation concept is that of motivational orientation and value orientation. Motivational orientation refers to the use of 'energy' with the intention of satisfying particular needs. Here motivation is the cultural counterpart of the 'natural' energy concept. There are three aspects of this use of energy or motivational orientation. *The cognitive aspect* aims at determining and discriminating objects in relation to one another; in socio-psychological literature this aspect of motivational orientation is called 'cognitive mapping'.

The cathectic aspect of motivational orientation refers to the positive or negative attitude that can be assumed with regard to an object.[11] Cathexis implies a judgment as to whether or not the object in question contributes to the satisfaction of a need or the attainment of a goal. *The evaluative aspect* of motivational orientation indicates the energy used by the actor in choosing one course of action from many possibilities in order to optimize need-satisfaction. It concerns the way in which the actor 'organizes' his actions; he cannot use his energy or motivation in an endless number of different ways at the same time. Therefore he has to make a choice between a multitude of objectively possible ways of acting. The aspect of evaluative orientation must be regarded as such a choice; it is responsible for the co-ordination and system-character of action. In the history of social science this element of co-ordination has often been presented as a very positivistic phenomenon and is consequently sometimes identified with the concept of 'instinct'.[12]

As Figure 3.1 shows, the discussion of actor's orientation does not end here. For the motivational aspect of an actor's orientation is not an isolated phenomenon; the cognitive, cathectic and evaluative orientation aspects presuppose the existence of (collective) standards. These standards bring us to the other main aspect of orientation – *value-orientation*. 'Value-orientation refers to those aspects of the actors orientation which commit him to the observance of certain norms, standards, criteria of selection, whenever he is in a contingent situation which allows (and requires) him to make a choice.'[13]

In a manner parallel to the analytical subdivision of motivational orientation, value-orientation also can be divided into three different aspects. Like motivational orientation, value-orientation has a cognitive aspect: the process of 'cognitive mapping' presupposes the existence of *cognitive standards*. These cognitive standards provide the actor with a guarantee of the validity of the cognitive subdivisions that he has made. Cognitive standards may differ greatly between one culture and another. However, it is clear that in all the different cultures and all the different systems of knowledge, from magic to science, cognitive subdivisions (classifications) are based on a certain type of standards – the cognitive – and that those standards guarantee (or ought to guarantee) to the actors involved in that particular system of knowledge the validity of their cognitive judgments. The same thing applies to the standards on which the cathectic aspect of motivational orientation is based. Assessment of an object's significance to need-satisfaction (cathexis) equally presupposes the existence of standards on which such an assessment can be based. In this context Parsons refers to *appreciative standards;* they formulate rules by which actors decide whether or not objects already differentiated and classified are significant to the attainment of goals in the widest sense of the word, or whether some are more significant than others.

Last there is the type of standards which forms the basis of the evaluative aspect of motivational orientation. Here Parsons refers to *moral standards* by which he means the criteria which determine the way the actor 'organizes' his actions, which decide the direction the actions are going to take and which form 'the court of last appeal'. These standards integrate the actor's actions into a fairly stable action system.

The *situation* is the other component of the bipolar frame of reference.[14] Here, too, for the sake of clarity, we give a diagram of subdivisions (Figure 3.2).

A situation consists of objects. These objects may be of many different kinds and can be subdivided in different ways. In the first place we can differentiate between *social* and *non-social* objects. The class of social objects is made up of individuals and collec-

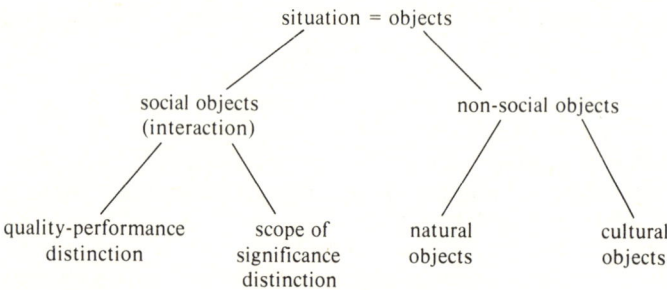

FIGURE 3.2 *The situation pole of the frame of reference*

tivities. There are two more criteria of classification that can be applied to these social objects, namely the dimension of quality-performance and the dimension of 'scope of significance'. The first of these subdivisions emphasizes that social objects may be important to the actor either because they possess certain qualities or because they carry out certain activities (performance). The second subdivision emphasizes that social objects may be of either general or specific importance to the actor; in the first instance we refer to a diffused significance of the objects to the actor, in the second instance to a specific significance i.e. one that is limited to a particular aspect of the object. The class of non-social objects falls into two categories – natural objects and cultural objects. Both have in common the fact that as orientation objects they themselves manifest no orientation on the actor; in other words, there is no question of interaction between actor and object. However, they differ from each other in a very specific way: cultural objects such as, for instance, laws, ideas and groups of ideas can be internalized and then form part of actor's orientation.[15]

This possibility of internalization does not, however, apply to natural objects: they can only be seen as orientation objects and not as an aspect of the orientation itself. Thus, action as illustrated by the frame of reference of the action theory moves between the two poles of orientation and situation. However, it is not always easy to draw a clear line between these poles because cultural objects may form both an aspect of orientation and part of the situation.

It is not only the bipolarity of orientation and situation, of subject and object, that occupies an important place in this 'second' frame of reference of the voluntaristic theory of action: the system character of action is also of focal significance just as it was in the first frame of reference.

It has already been briefly mentioned that the evaluative modus of motivational orientation is at the root of the system character of action. In the process of evaluative orientation the actor tries to attune and co-ordinate his actions, one to the other. This means that certain actions are connected with each other in a particular way and that particular relations exist between different actions. Because of the evaluative modus of orientation the succession of actions can be regarded not as a completely random series but as a more or less independent whole. In other words, the inclusion of the evaluative aspect of motivational orientation in the frame of reference of the action theory means that the phenomena to be studied (actor's orientation) do not form a random collection of separate and independent elements but are connected with each other in various ways. Thus the object of study disclosed by the frame reference may be regarded as a system and this object of study for the sciences based on this frame of reference can therefore be called 'the action system'.

The theory of action must not lose sight of this system character but must arrange its conceptual structure in such a way as to sustain the system aspect in the analysis. For Parsons, this means that certain very specific requirements have to be fulfilled at the conceptual level.

4 Analysis of action systems; structural-functionalism as 'second best mode of analysis'

The two frames of reference for a voluntaristic theory of action described above have in common the fact that they point to concrete actions as action systems and thus, in principle, they form the foundation for a theory of action systems. However, the total field of action is so indescribably complex that some preliminary arrangement and simplification is called for.

We have just discussed one aspect of such a simplification – Parsons's suggestion that, for certain system levels, 'secondary descriptive schemes' based on the frame of reference should be formulated. In the period between this suggestion (1937) and the two publications of 1951 Parsons makes yet another proposal for simplifying the analysis and conceptualization of the action systems.[16] Clearly under the influence of developments that were at that time taking place in other sciences like biology and psychology, Parsons put forward a method of analysis and strategy for conceptualization which, though not comparable to a 'real' dynamic analysis of systems, nevertheless represents the most feasible thus far for the action sciences: the *structural-functional form of analysis*. He, too, finds the structural-functional analysis a rather primitive form:[17]

Put a little differently, the essential feature of dynamic analysis in the fullest sense is the treatment of a body of *interdependent* phenomena simultaneously in the mathematical sense. The simplest case is the analysis of the effect of variation in one antecedent factor, but this ignores the reciprocal effect of these changes on this factor. The ideal solution is the possession of a logically complete system of dynamic generalizations which can state all the variables of the system. The ideal has, in the formal sense, been attained only in the systems of differential equations of analytical mechanics. All other sciences are limited to a more 'primitive' level of systematic theoretical analysis.

The sciences concerned with the study of the action system are bound to this kind of 'primitive' analysis; for does not the above form of dynamic analysis presuppose quantifiable information? Yet, according to Parsons, this kind of information need not necessarily be of prime importance in these sciences.

What is such a primitive method of analysis like? Since not all of the variables can be related to each other at the same time, a number have to be abstracted from the totality of processes and considered as constants. Those action processes which are taken to be constants form the *structure* of the action system.

Thus structure and process are very relative ideas; the structure concept is an analytical construction, a sort of experiment in thought that can serve as a departure platform for dynamic analysis.[18] The construction of such a structural platform is meant as a simplification of the problems attached to dynamic analysis. The simplification consists of representing as fairly constant a number of movements or processes. Thus, what is represented as structure consists of nothing but more or less regular action processes. The assumption of regularity is a pragmatic one dependent on the nature of the subject to be researched. There is nothing special about this kind of simplifying method as such; as Parsons says, differential equations in mechanics are also significant in the framework of such constants. The difference is that in mechanics those constants are placed outside the system while in the action sciences they are regarded as part of the action system itself.[19] This means that the structure as sketched takes its own place in the chosen explanatory schema and that care must be taken as to the way in which the structure is influenced by processes not included in it.

Once it has been established that the structure concept and with it the structure of the action system form an analytically constructed platform, the question arises as to how that structure should be linked to the remaining variable elements in the system. For the structure of an action system is its morphological aspect which, of itself, does not furnish the required dynamic knowledge. Parsons's idea is that the link between the structure and the dynamics of a system is formed by the function concept:[20]

> Its crucial role is to provide criteria of the *importance* of dynamic factors and processes within the system. They are important in so far as they have functional significance to the system, and their specific importance is understood in terms of the analysis of specific functional relations between the parts of the system and between it and its environment.

Parsons calls this peculiar form of analysing the action system *structural-functionalism*. The central characteristic of this structural-functionalism lies, not in the construction of a structure, but in the connection between the structure sketched and the motivational processes in the system: processes in the system are regarded in the light of their significance to the system as a whole. By linking the motivational processes to the problems of the system as a whole, Parsons hopes to preserve something of the ultimate aim of science, namely to establish the interdependence of different phenomena. The relation in this structural-functionalism between the concepts of 'structure', 'process' and 'function' is of a very specific nature. The structure concept constructs a number of relative constants out of the total variability. The function concept restricts the process concept in the sense that processes are considered only in the light of their implications for the total system. However, if useful conclusions are to be drawn about these implications they have to be related to a number of the system's characteristics. Parsons gives the name of *functional problems* to those characteristics or situations. Thus the structural-functional form of analysis makes use of a three-fold conceptual instrumentation: concepts of structure, concepts of function and concepts referring to functional problems.

5 The combination of the voluntaristic frame of reference with the structural-functional form of analysis in a structural-functional theory of action systems

Elaboration of a voluntaristic theory of action takes place within the conceptual requirements demanded by the specific form of the structural-functional analysis. A result of this is that the categorial system of the voluntaristic action theory under development is built around the three types of categories mentioned above: the concepts of structure, concepts of process and function and concepts referring to functional system problems.

The concepts of structure

The structural schema which occupies the most important place in this structural-functional phase of Parsons's work is that of *pattern variables*. Parsons claims that this scheme is directly deduced from the action frame of reference.[21] The pattern variables indicate a number of choice-problems an actor might have to deal with and they show how the actor can solve these problems. They refer back to the evaluative orientation mode of the action frame of reference in which both the choice and the system character of action are apparent. Only after the actor has chosen his 'solution' to all the problems presented by the schema is his 'orientation to the situation' defined: the 'pattern' of his attitude to the object world is set.

Therefore, the structure-describing schema of the pattern variables is moulded by the bipolarity of the frame of reference. For the structure of the action system can only be made up of patterns of 'orientation to the situation'. So orientation and situation, subject and object and their classification form the nucleus of the pattern variables schema.

The pattern variables that describe action chiefly from the actor's orientation are the variables of *affectivity* versus *affective neutrality, specificity* versus *diffuseness and self-orientation* versus *collectivity-orientation*.[22] The first of these variables formulates the 'choice' between an uncontrolled, direct and primary reaction to (aspects of) a situation on the one hand and, on the other hand, an attitude of well-considered, disciplined and calculated reaction. The 'engaged' member of an audience, the supporter or 'fan', will generally give very direct expression to his feelings towards his 'pop hero' and will not be restricted by any kind of rational consideration of alternative forms of behaviour. Therefore his action can be said to be 'affective'. In the case of the producer there is no such impulsiveness and his attitude is governed mainly by commercial considerations; thus, because of the attitude or orientation by which it is determined, his actions may be typified as 'affectively neutral'. The second pattern variable by which actor's orientation can be classified is that *of specificity* versus *diffuseness*.[23] An actor's attitude towards an object in a situation can be of a very specific kind; that is to say his interest in the object may be clearly limited. In a society divided according to occupation this specific attitude to (social) objects is of growing importance. A general attitude or orientation implies interest in the object in its totality; the interest that married couples or lovers have in each other is not generally restricted to clearly defined aspects but is of a more diffuse and general nature.

The third pattern variable that helps to define an actor's orientation is that of *self-orientation* versus *collectivity-orientation*.[24] The idea that Parsons wants to express by this variable is again that of different orientation possibilities. As he says, the actor can aim at achieving either his own interest or those of the collectivity. Particularly in his essay 'The Professions and Social Structure' (1935) Parsons uses these terms to compare the actions of professional workers and businessmen.[25]

The two pattern variables which concern the situation component of action formulate the way in which objects come to have significance for an actor. The starting-point here is not so much the actor's attitude or (motivational) orientation but the criteria on the basis of which the meaning of an object becomes apparent. To start with there is the pattern variable of *universalism* versus *particularism*. In a universalistic relation between actor and object the object acquires significance by belonging to a certain class of objects; in a particularistic relation between actor and object the significance of the object is linked directly to the relation itself. For example: the relation between teacher and student is or should be of a universalistic nature, i.e. the student is significant to the teacher as a member of a larger class of students and not as one of his friends or acquaintances. If the latter is the case, the relation is a particularistic one.

The last pattern variable, *quality versus performance,* also represents a criterion for attributing significance to an object.[26] The object may acquire significance to an actor as a complex of 'qualities', because it *is* something. In this case Parsons speaks of 'quality'. But the object might also be significant to an actor because of its activities; this is referred to as 'performance'. The example of the female driver committing traffic offences may help to explain. For the reactions of her (male) fellow-drivers might be influenced by her dangerous manoeuvres, regardless of her being a woman (performance) but they may (and usually will) be influenced by the fact that 'there goes another woman driver' (quality).[27]

Thus, the original scheme of pattern variables is as follows:
1 Affectivity *vs* affective neutrality;
problem of choice: direct, impulsive satisfaction of needs or indirect, disciplined action.
2 Specificity *vs* diffuseness;
problem of choice: orientation to aspects(s) of objects or to the complete object.
3 Self-orientation *vs* collectivity-orientation;

problem of choice: orientation to achievement of own interest or that of collectivity.

4 Universalism *vs* particularism;
problem of choice: whether the object derives its significance by belonging to a certain class of objects or from its relation to the actor.

5 Quality *vs* performance;
problem of choice: is the object's significance due to its qualities or to its activities or achievements.

Every case is concerned with a problem of actor's choice. Only when he has 'solved' these problems can there be any question of a relation between actor and object, orientation and situation. The pattern variables scheme classifies patterns in the relation between actor and object. When those patterns are regarded as fairly constant they form the structural basis of dynamic analysis.

The dynamic-functional categories; function, system, equilibrium and homeostasis

Concepts and classification schemes for describing the structure of a system acquire their real scientific significance only when they are linked to concepts that describe the dynamic processes taking place in that system;[28] orientations to a situation, are therefore considered only in the light of their functional significance to the system. As 'functions', these orientations are divided simply into two kinds, *mechanisms* – processes that stabilize the action system, and *tendencies* – processes that disturb the equilibrium of the system and lead to change.

Both of the function concepts of mechanism and tendencies are related to a certain condition of the action system called the state of equilibrium. The expression 'equilibrium' has its origin in mechanics; we speak of 'equilibrium' when an object situated in a certain place does not, of its own accord, move to another place. It does so only under external influence. The original equilibrium is then disturbed and is replaced by a new one. The new equilibrium is the result of a number of qualities possessed by the object itself and of influences or powers exercised upon it; the object will not move from the new place of its own accord. Thus, every equilibrium presupposes the interdependence of factors and every disturbance of equilibrium presupposes an external 'disturbance'.

Closely linked to this mechanical idea of equilibrium is Newton's so-called 'law of inertia', which formulates the idea of equilibrium from a more dynamic point of view. In mechanics, says Newton, we are interested not in the movement of objects as such but in *change* of movement. Movement itself can be seen as a constant and is not, of itself, of interest in the study of mechanics. Parsons takes this argument and projects it into the sphere of action systems: it is not the equilibrial 'regularity' of action processes with which the study of action is concerned but the processes that disturb this regularity and those which counteract such threatened disturbances: from this point of view, the action theory is applicable only when there is a question of (or possibility of) disturbed equilibrium.[29]

Parsons's interest in, and knowledge of, developments in the natural sciences, especially in biology, inspires him to extend what was originally a mechanistic concept of equilibrium in a more organistic direction. Impressed as he was by the work of Walter Cannon[30] in particular, he begins to lay emphasis on a very special kind of process, the so-called homeostatic mechanism. The concept of homeostasis complements that of equilibrium in a very special way. Just as the human organism, because of the interdependence of the organs from which it is built up, has the ability to remain itself in the face of external disturbance, so Parsons credits the action system with the same potentiality; external disturbances need not perforce entail a new equilibrium; as long as the disturbance is confined to certain limits it might possibly be 'absorbed' and the old equilibrium maintained or restored.[31]

Parsons tends to attribute focal significance to this homeostatic mechanism. Because of this, his attention is undoubtedly and strongly directed to processes that result in stabilization of the system; he has only a secondary interest in processes which break through the homeostatic barriers.

In this light the frequently expressed criticism of the structural-functional model's static implications is understandable. But on the grounds discussed above it might equally be quite possible in principle to cover processes of change with this method of analysis. The primary reason why Parsons at this period pushes questions about change into the background is one of *logic*:[32]

> For reasons which we must now try to make clear, the treatment of (change) comes in the present scheme *logically* last, and presupposes some level of theoretical solution of the other two (namely the structural and dynamic-functional level). This is true so far as the central point of reference is, as we have consistently attempted to make it, the concept of *system*.

From Parsons's point of view this is an understandable conclusion. However, the fact remains that it is the result of a theoretical assumption which emphasizes the homeostatic qualities of the action system.

The system problems

The structural categories create the platform from which the 'second-best' dynamic analysis can take off. The dynamic-functional categories indicate orientation of actors or groups of actors in so far as they are significant to the situation of the action system of which they form a part. If that significance is to be clearly determined, says Parsons, it is not sufficient to decide whether or not the system is going to continue. This continued existence needs more exact specification. To this end, Parsons introduces two system-problems that are to play a part in assessing the functionality of action; in order to ensure its continued existence, every system – including every action system – must find an adequate solution to the problem of *allocation* and the problem of *integration*. In other words, it must find a solution to the division of tasks, valued objects, resources, etc. (allocation) and it must match up and co-ordinate the different parts of a system to each other (integration).

We shall have to leave unanswered in this expository chapter the question as to how these dual system-problems arose, what is their logical background and how this system point of view can be reconciled to that of the actor. However, they are questions which cast doubt on the consistency of a categorial system thus constructed. Yet this is the basis of Parsons's first attempt at conceptualizing the voluntaristic theory of action. In the following section we shall discuss one of the possible subdivisions of the action system – the social system – as an example of this kind of categorial system.[33]

6 The structural-functional theory of social systems

As we have already emphasized, the complexity of action and action system necessitates a differentiation into sub-systems. For Parsons this means that points of contact have to be found on which to base this differentiation. At the start, he finds such points of contact on two levels – that of individual personality on the one hand and that of the relations between individual personalities on the other. In other words, he organizes the actions of the total action system round the 'point of contact' formed by the individual actor and in that way he constructs the 'personality system'. The 'social system' is a similar organization of actions around a particular pivot; in this case the pivot is not formed by the individual actor but by the interaction between actors, by the group. In the case of the social system, actions are organized round interaction.

The same actions can in this way be included in various sub-systems. The difference between a personality system and a social system arises not from the actions that form part of the system but from the way in which the same actions are, in principle, organized into sub-systems.[34] For Parsons this subdivision of the general action system into a personality system and a social system is parallel to the subdivision of a general science of action into sciences such as psychology on the one hand and the various social sciences on the other. Of this last category of sciences, sociology forms a part (see chapter 1), just like economics, political science, and cultural anthropology. They all study an aspect of the social system.

Parsons abstracts yet a third sub-system from the total action system and calls it the 'cultural system'. This, according to him, is a different type of abstraction and he refers somewhat hesitatingly to this third action sub-system: 'Neither systems of value-orientation nor systems of culture as a whole are action systems in the same sense as are personalities and social systems. This is because neither motivation nor action is directly attributable to them.'[35] However, because the cultural system can equally be said to represent a particular organization and selection of elements from the total action, it can still be seen as an action sub-system.

All in all, at this stage of his development Parsons does not seem very clear about the criteria on which to base the differentiation in the action system. The confusion as to what is and what is not a sub-system of action shows the lack of uniformity in the different criteria used. In fact, there is no question of real criteria; for this reason we spoke above of 'points of contact'. Only later did Parsons discover the criteria which made it possible to differentiate the action system in a systematic way.[36]

The cultural system consists of elements (ideas, values, norms, etc.) which are internalized by the individual actor and can be institutionalized in the pattern of relations between actors.

The confrontation between the action frame of reference and the structural-functional form of analysis reaches a climax in Parsons's theory of social systems as expressed in *The Social System* (1951). This publication follows the structural-functional train of thought and can therefore be divided into three parts. It starts with a general definition of the social system; then follows a very detailed description of the structure of such a system; the monograph ends with that coping-stone of structural-functional analysis – the dynamic processes.

We shall use the same arrangement in the following discussion of the theory of the social system.

The definition of the social system

In the concept of social system, actions or orientations are organized round the interaction of individuals. In the analysis of that interaction, therefore, the concept of system plays an important part:[37]

> The fundamental starting point is the concept of social systems of action. The *interaction* of individual actors, that is, takes place under such conditions that it is possible to treat such a process of interaction as a system in the scientific sense and subject it to the same order of theoretical analysis which has been successfully applied to other types in other sciences.

Social systems are abstractions of total action. These abstractions consist of the relations between a number of actors. The personality structure of the actors concerned is of no consequence here; it does not belong to the 'secondary descriptive schema' of the social system. It cannot be sufficiently emphasized that such a social system is only an aspect of the total action system. The sciences engaged in the study of this social system see human action in a particular perspective because of the definition of the object of their study. This specific perspective cannot be reduced or converted to the perspectives of other sciences on mankind and culture. Thus the perspective of the social system is theoretically independent.

The emphasis on the irreducibility of the social system's perspective, for instance to the theory of personality, is a constantly recurring theme in the social sciences, particularly in sociology. There is a danger that in the frequent discussions on this subject exaggerated attitudes will be adopted for the sake of 'clarity'; thus the differentiation between analytical independence and empirical independence is at risk of being lost from sight.

It goes without saying that the perspective of the social system can be regarded as independent only in the analytical sense. There can be no question of empirical independence: the 'reality' of the theory of the social system, just like the 'reality' of the theory of the personality system is an analytical abstraction of the reality of social action. There can be no doubt that reification of these theoretical constructions into concrete entities would be at complete variance with Parsons's intentions.

Analytical differentiation between the subsystems of action means that there must, of necessity, be relations between them. This means that the question must inevitably be asked as to the relations between social and personality system on the one hand and social and cultural system on the other. Parsons narrows down this question in a typically functionalistic way as follows: what must be the content of the relations with other action sub-systems if there is to be a stable social system? In other words, what are the functional conditions or requirements of the social system?

The problem of the functional conditions or requirements of a social system is not an easy one to solve. If formulation of functional requirements takes place at an abstract level it makes no contribution to knowledge and there is a danger of tautological reasoning; on the other hand, if formulation takes place at a very concrete and specific level there is no reason not to present it as the result of empirical research. Parsons chooses to formulate the functional requirements as a series of minimum conditions. From this it is, in any case, apparent that he regards interrelations between the perspectives of different systems as a problem; in spite of that he deals with it in a remarkably superficial way.

Thus he says that the functional condition for a social system deduced from its relation to the personality system 'is the need to secure adequate participation of a sufficient proportion of these actors in the social system, that is to motivate them adequately to the performances which may be necessary if the social system in question is to persist or to develop'.[38] The functional condition for a social system deduced from its relation to the cultural system is manifested in the assertion that 'a social system in the present sense is not possible without language and without certain other minimum patterns of culture, such as empirical knowledge necessary to cope with situational exigencies and sufficiently integrated patterns of expressive symbolism and value orientation'.[39]

As long as expressions like 'adequate' and 'sufficient' are not specified beforehand, the idea of functional conditions forms a very meagre implementation of the relations between the differentiated systems.

Parsons does not only narrow down the dynamic analysis of interaction in a structural-functional way. In the theory of social systems he gives a very special form to the unit of analysis of the action theory, the so-called 'unit of action' consisting of actor's orientation to the situation. 'For most analytical purposes, the most significant unit of social structures is not the person but the role. The role is that organized sector of an actor's orientation which constitutes and defines his participation in an interactive process.'[40] Thus the role is that part of an actor's orientation that concerns interaction with other individuals. The implications of this are important: in the first place, it looks as if a second criterion is now being introduced for differentiation of action systems without clear evidence of its relation to the abovementioned 'points of contact'. The role concept refers to an aspect of actor's orientation, and is considered to be a constituent of the social system concept.

Parallel to this role concept, Parsons distinguishes yet another aspect of actor's orientation, namely the pattern of need (the need disposition), which he regards as the unit of analysis for the personality system. It is not yet clear to what extent the unit of analysis of the cultural system – the normative pattern – should be interpreted as an orientation aspect.

The consequence of this new or second criterion of differentiation is, at least, that actions are not only organized and differentiated round a particular pivot (interaction, in the case of the social system), but also that differentiation is made in the action or orientation itself between the different aspects on which the subsystems in question are based. As a result, a social system is no longer made up of actions (which would be the case if the 'unit act' were used as last unit of analysis), nor of orientations (which it would be if the 'unit of action' were to be regarded as unit of analysis), but of roles. It is this regular shifting of the unit of analysis that makes Parsons's work complicated and difficult to read. The objections and causes that are attached to this shifting of unit of analysis will be discussed in the next chapter. Till then we can only regard the role as the unit from which the social system is built up and as Parsons's interpretation of the 'action' category to the social system level.

The structural paradigm

Because, in view of the last shift of the unit of analysis, the role is to be regarded as the unit from which the social system is built up, it is natural to suppose that the structural description of the social system will also be aimed particularly at this role concept. For Parsons, the structure of the social system is primarily a structure of roles.

In this context the scheme of pattern variables gives a classification of that part of actor's orientation to the situation that can be designated as a role: in the case of the social system, patterns of orientation to the situation are role patterns (in the personality system and the cultural system the pattern variables classify the other aspects of orientation, i.e. need-dispositions and normative patterns). In Parsons's structural examination, roles or role patterns indicate relatively constant ways of orientation between actor and object. From the point of view of the actor these ways of orientation are referred to as 'roles'; from the standpoint of the (social) object they are referred to as 'role expectations'. The schema of pattern variables has already been described in a previous paragraph so it will suffice here to give a short schematic indication of the analytical elements that can be distinguished in the role structure of the social system.

(a) *affectivity*
The expectation that the role player abandons himself directly to the object, untrammelled by evaluative considerations, e.g. the role of 'fan'.

affective neutrality
The expectation that the role player will be reserved towards the object, that his action depends on evaluative considerations, e.g. the role of therapist.

(b) *specificity*
Expectation that the role player's interest is directed at clearly defined aspects of the object, e.g. the role of employer or employee.

diffusion (generality)
Expectation that the role player's interest is directed at the total object, e.g. the role of husband or wife.

(c) *self-orientation*
Expectation that the role player's orientation is based on pursuit of self-interest, e.g. the role of the businessman.

collectivity orientation
Expectation that the role player's orientation is guided by the interest of the collectivity to which he belongs, e.g. the role of the doctor.

(d) *universalism*
Expectation that the role player determines the significance of the object by means of criteria which are independent of the relation of actor to object, e.g. the role of teacher in relation to student.

particularism
Expectation that the role player determines the significance of the object by means of criteria that are involved in his relation to the object, e.g. the role of husband and wife in relation to each other.

(e) *achievement* (performance)
Expectation that the role player connects the significance of the object to what the object *does,* e.g. the other is significant to the actor because of his achievements.

ascription (quality)
Expectation that the role player connects the significance of the object to what that object *is,* e.g. the other is significant to the actor for the sake of his attributes: man, woman, child, beautiful, ugly, etc.

With the help of the scheme of pattern variables the structure of the social system is described according to its orientation and situation aspects. Of course it would be possible to give a much more thorough description of the situation aspect in particular. Such a description would have to link up with the pattern variables in the 'situation set'. Thus the world of objects – including the actors – which are significant to the actor according to the two dimensions of universalism-particularism and achievement-ascription can be specified further according to the particular characteristic which give them their significance; characteristics like age, race, sex, biological position, personal qualities and capacities may give rise to the significance that one actor has to another. In *The Social System* a great deal of attention is given to the description of structures as a result of a fairly constant relation between orientation and situation. But this does not complete the paradigm for describing the structure of the social system. For up to now, only the elements of the social system, the roles, have been classified; for a complete description we must find out how, in such a system, the problems of allocation and integration can be 'solved'. We shall begin with the system's allocative structure: '*given* the role structure, we must analyze the processes of distribution of "movable" elements as between statuses and roles. This process of distribution of significant objects within the role-system will be called allocation.'[41]

What significant objects are to be allocated to the roles which make up the system? Parsons mentions three of them – persons, facilities and rewards. The manner in which allocation of persons to roles takes place in a particular social system is an important facet of the structure of social systems; for it is these regular processes which, from the system point of view, regulate the disposition of persons within the respective role structure.

In fact, this positioning of the individual in the role structure begins at the time of his birth. At that moment the most important criteria are mainly of an ascriptive nature: the newly born child is allocated a particular role according to its sex. In most societies these ascriptive criteria continue to play a predominant part in the process of allocation throughout the actor's life. In some other societies, achievement criteria are considered more important and the process of allocation occurs on a basis of appointment or competition. It is obvious that in general, but more especially in the case of competition, the way the process of allocation occurs in any particular society will raise problems of integration. The way these problems are solved forms the integrative structure of that society.

However, before we can discuss the integrative structure, we must first take a look at the other 'movable elements' of the allocation problem: facilities and rewards. According to Parsons, every social system has mechanisms that regulate the distribution of the facilities that are important to the achievements of ends. These facilities are naturally scarce and the possession of them is, of itself, a desirable matter. The question is then which facilities are to be allocated to which roles or clusters of roles? What actors are to have possession of (the right to) what facilities? In other words, the allocation of rights (and obligations), the allocation of facilities and, with it, the allocation of power are all interwoven with the role structure of a social system. Thus it is also clear that the phenomenon of 'power' has particular bearing on the way the terms of exchange are determined in the transaction between actors.[42] These terms of exchange form an important part of the structure of a social system in that they are of a fairly constant nature and not, therefore, redetermined for each new exchange.[43]

The institutionalized settlements of conditions of ownership which are expressed as legitimate rights and obligations form an important facet of the structure of the social system. The last aspect of the question of allocation that a detailed description of the system structure must take into account is the allocation of rewards. Parsons regards as a 'reward' any object which is valued not for its instrumental usefulness (as a facility) but for its expressive or symbolic significance. In the relation between actors rewards consist mainly of the loyal attitude assumed towards an actor. The big question is how the distribution of loyalty is regulated within a social system; this regulation, too, forms a part of the structure. Just as the allocation of facilities gives rise to a power structure, so the allocation of rewards leads to an order of rank, a social stratification within the social system.

The fairly constant processes that occur in a social system in connection with the problem of integration form the last of the constituents of the structural or descriptive paradigm on which Parsons places great emphasis. According to his reasoning, the allocation in the social system of persons, facilities and rewards always creates problems, even when that allocation is subject to a high degree of institutionalization. In the first place there is the problem as to how far self-interested orientation is permissible: measures have to be taken to keep role behaviour within its set bounds. These measures involve a whole network of sanctions. Besides this 'negative' form of integration, Parsons also distinguishes another, 'positive', form; this concerns the way in which certain processes in a social system contribute to the achievement of certain collective aims. In this context the significance of the institution of 'leadership' in the system does deserve to be considered. Thus, from the integrative problems of a social system, attention is drawn to a number of important and fairly constant processes, to an important facet of the structure of the social system.

Meanwhile, Parsons's structural paradigm is almost complete. This structural paradigm provides the researcher with a systematically developed checklist for the description of a social system.

The following is a synopsis of this paradigm – the essence of the first 'structural' part of *The Social System* – point by point; according to Parsons, structural description can be divided up as follows:[44]

1 Description of actors as social objects i.e. as objects of orientation; here the definition of their roles is of primary importance and it should be pointed out that the roles may be linked to both individual actor-objects and to collective actor-objects.

2 Description and classification of types of role-expectations and their distribution in the social system; here, too, we can discriminate between individual and collective actor subjects.

3 Description of the way in which instrumental facilities are distributed among the roles in the system; the organization of the power system.

4 Description of the ways in which expressive rewards are distributed among the roles in the system; organization of the reward system, social stratification.

5 Description of the ways in which cultural elements other than value-orientation are connected to the structure of the social system; we refer here to 'belief systems' and 'systems of expressive symbolism'.

6 Description of the ways in which problems of allocating facilities and rewards can be directed into the right channels; norms and sanctions; description of roles that make a 'positive contribution' to the achievement of collective aims: leadership etc.

This scheme or paradigm forms a checklist to ensure that the description of the structure of the social system is complete. Yet, however complete this structural description may be, it does not of itself, provide the dynamic knowledge required. A first step in this direction is the form of analysis which Parsons calls 'structural analysis'.

Structural analysis: framework for dynamic analysis

Elaboration of this structural paradigm might easily create the impression that there are innumerable possibilities for linking structural elements together. Indeed, the logical or theoretical possibilities are legion. Value-orientation, object-significance, allocative or integrative structures can be regarded as variables; a concrete structure, the structure of a particular social system, is then the specific combination of one 'value' of each variable. From the moment that Parsons begins to wonder whether all those innumerable, logically possible combinations can also exist in practice, his activities cease to be purely descriptive. Structural *description* starts to make way for structural *analysis*.[45]

Parsons gives a number of examples of specific combinations of structural elements, namely those of kinship, stratification, power and religion.[46] These four 'structures', irrespective of the system to which they belong, represent a fairly constant cluster of structural elements. Kinship, for instance, is a universal social phenomenon built up round a number of ascriptive characteristics like sex, age and biological position. Kinship is also an important social phenomenon: social prestige, sexual and erotic relations as well as important facets of the process of socialization are more or less bound up with kinship in every society. In this connection it is important to note that 'kinship units' — in spite of a certain degree of variability — always belong to a type of structure that can be very accurately defined and which embraces only a fraction of the total of structural possibilities.

With the help of the pattern variables and irrespective of the actual variations, the 'kinship unit' can be described as a structure in which diffuse orientation predominates and particularism plays an important part. Why, asks Parsons, is the arrangement of sexual relations in the 'kinship unit' so universally bound up with the care of children? Why is not the care of children and the responsibility for socialization given a place outside the 'kinship unit' in the same way as education? Why do not 'kinship units' show the same orientation pattern as do industrial organizations? Parsons's answer to these questions reflects the restricting and conditioning effect exercised by the environment on whatever system is involved. The reason why only a limited number of all possible structural combinations actually occur he finds in 'that societies are subjected to certain functional exigencies'.[47] These 'functional exigencies' can be divided into two kinds. On the one hand there are the functional conditions already mentioned which Parsons calls, in this context, 'universal imperatives'. Whenever these imperatives are not fulfilled, the existence of the social system is threatened. On the other hand, Parsons mentions the so-called 'compatibility imperatives'. These reduce the chance that different structural elements will be combined.[48] For Parsons, there are two sides to this system-theoretical idea of compatibility. In the first place it answers the question as to why the reality of experience reveals only a fraction of the logically possible structural combinations. The answer lies in the irreconcilability of structural elements, i.e. of roles and the standards of value on which they are based. Accordingly, the idea of compatibility can also be used in another way; thus it can happen that completely consistent implementation of a particular dominant value gives rise to a variety of emotional tensions. This consistent implementation of such a value-pattern (e.g. universalism or achievement) is then irreconcilable with the adequate fulfilment of the functional considerations which the system has to take into account. In that case, says Parsons, it is likely that patterns will become institutionalized which, though they may deviate from predominating value-patterns, therefore fulfil a conflict- and tension-regulating function; here Parsons speaks of 'adaptive structures'.[49]

From this it is already obvious that this form of structural analysis does not, of itself, explain anything; it only suggests possible explanations. If one were to regard this structural analysis as a really dynamic analysis of social action – which Parsons definitely does not – then it would become a thing of magic by which everything could be 'explained'; certain structural components that do not fit in with a particular dominant value-orientation could simply be regarded as 'adaptive structures' so that they would still fulfil the requirement of compatibility.

For Parsons this means two things: in the first place, that the instrument of structural analysis must be used with discretion; second, that a form of analysis such as this acquires significance only when it is implemented with a study of the orientations or motivations of the actors or group of actors underlying these relations of compatibility.

As far as Parsons is concerned, structural analysis is nothing more than a mental experiment analogous to the way in which Weber's analysis represents a form of (cultural) sociological speculation in terms of 'ideal types' and *Wahlverwandtschaft* or congruence.[50] Structural analysis is really a 'short-circuit' analysis. The two instruments of functional requisites and compatibility together form an abbreviated version of the processes of orientation that take place among groups of actors. Structural analysis is a kind of stenography by which the real dynamic processes are condensed into two system-theoretical instruments. Therefore, in Parsons's view, structural analysis can never be the ultimate aim of science. As we have already seen, that ultimate aim is dynamic knowledge i.e. knowledge of the motivational processes that operate in interaction between individuals. Structural analysis does not supply this knowledge. At the most, it offers a framework in which to place dynamic analysis.

The kind of dynamic analysis which Parsons envisages is the

structural-functional one. This will be discussed in the following section.

The motivational paradigm:[51] *the connecting link in the structural-functional theory*

The structural experiment in ideas as described above, becomes significant only when the motivational processes are filled in. Unless this happens, the explanatory or predictive power of this form of analysis is very doubtful. Therefore Parsons's structural-functional theory is not complete until the apparatus is available for dealing with the motivational processes as such. As soon as the structural apparatus is there a start can be made on the analysis of motivational processes. After all, it is this analysis of motivational processes with which Parsons is concerned; this is what will provide the dynamic knowledge he seeks. The structural-functional theory of social systems begins with a few important theoretical, non-empirical assumptions. The first of these concerns the state of equilibrium of the system in question. As we have already seen, equilibrium presupposes that a system does not, of itself, instigate processes of change; thus every change in the arrangement or structure of the system's elements is caused by a factor external to the system. Projecting this idea of equilibrium on to the social system, we see that stable social systems can only be said to exist when the integration between patterns of role-expectation, their complementarity and reciprocity are at a maximum. As Parsons sees it, there can be equilibrium in a social system only when all actors know exactly and are satisfied with what they mean to each other. Such an[52]

> established state of a social system is a process of complementary interaction of two or more individual actors in which each conforms with the expectations of the other(s) in such a way that alter's reactions to ego's actions are positive sanctions which serve to reinforce his given need-dispositions and thus to fulfill his given expectations.

In this connection Parsons speaks of complete *institutional integration*. This completely institutionalized system of equilibrium forms the starting-point for the dynamic aspect of the theory of social systems. Here, the 'first law of social process' in analogy to Newton's law of inertia, asserts that the continued existence of such a completely institutionalized social system presents no problem to the theory of the social system.[53] Therefore the theory need not concern itself with the academic question as to how a social system once stabilized can continue to exist independent of its environment. The crucial problem of such a structural-functional theory concerns the mechanisms that contribute to the stabilization of the system in the face of certain destabilizing tendencies.

It really should not be possible for social scientists to give such a childish interpretation of this 'first law of social process' as some of them have, in fact, done.[54] However embarrassing the following remarks may be, they are obviously not entirely superfluous: this 'first law' does not mean that, in Parsons's view, concrete social systems are completely institutionalized and stabilized. On the contrary, this kind of equilibrium does not occur in the reality of experience; as Parsons says, complete harmony 'should be regarded as a limiting case like the famous frictionless machine'.[55] Neither does this theoretical assumption mean that concrete systems will always tend towards a maximum of institutional integration; they vary between the two extremes of institutional integration – harmony and anomie – both of which are non-existent in their absolutely pure form. Their position on the dimension of institutional integration is an empirical question which cannot be answered on grounds of theoretical assumptions.

Parsons's structural-functional theory of social systems tries to conceptualize the dynamics of action in terms of the idea of stability. In so doing, it takes a version of a social system which, in an absolutely pure form is non-existent, and promotes it to the model against which concrete social systems are to be compared and analysed. This strictly theoretical construction of a balanced and stable social system forms the starting-point for the conceptual elaboration of the dynamic aspect of the theory of social systems. The functions which, in the structural-functional form of analysis, represent the dynamic orientational or motivational aspect of action thus become significant only when the balance in the social-system model is disturbed. This means that the general tendencies to disturb the social system must first be conceptualized and then the functions or mechanisms must be defined. Parsons brings all these dynamic processes of a motivational or orientational nature together in his so-called motivational paradigm.

The tendencies and mechanisms that can be placed around the model of completely institutionalized social systems can both be divided into two parts. In the first place, there is an obviously disturbing tendency in the fact that actors entering a social system are not automatically imbued with their own role orientations. Society, seen as the most inclusive social system, is inundated, as it were, with factors that threaten its state of equilibrium, were it only by the birth of new actors. This 'barbarous invasion' is a threat to the complementarity of interaction and would undoubtedly lead to large-scale alterations in the social structure if its disturbing effect were not absorbed by homeostatic mechanisms i.e. kinds of action which restore or maintain equilibrium in the face of disturbances or possible disturbances. Parsons gives the name of socializing processes to the processes in the social system which serve this purpose. Thus, from the point of view of its function in the system, socialization is a mechanism for promoting the stability of the process of interaction.[56]

However, the problem of 'barbarous invasion' is not the only threat to the stability of the ideal-type of social system. The equilibrium can also be affected by autonomic changes in the environment surrounding it. Some of these changes will no doubt be absorbed by a kind of prolonged process of socialization which will resolve new situations into that of the existing standards of value. But it might be that such changes disturb the complementarity of interaction by giving rise to processes of deviant behaviour. Actors who are very well acquainted with the content of the existing patterns of role expectations may thus be liable to relinquish those standards. Particularly when – as is always the case in concrete social systems – the structure of the personality is no longer absolutely parallel to the structure of the social system, when there is a diminishing degree of institutional integration, deviant behaviour presents an obvious disturbance of the equilibrium.

For this kind of disturbance, too, Parsons conceptualizes an appurtenant mechanism which – again to a certain extent – can absorb and redress the effects of such processes. And of course this mechanism in turn consists of nothing but (collective) motivational processes; Parsons calls them the mechanisms of social control.[57]

In this way both kinds of mechanisms are, in a conceptual sense, deduced directly from the 'unreal' theoretical construction of a completely stable social system. Parsons's motivational paradigm consists mainly of an elaboration of these mechanisms.

The elaboration of the motivational process of deviance and social control is linked to the possible discrepancies between the needs of individual actors and role expectations based on standards of value. The deviance schema is based on the ambivalent motivational structure that is activated in the personality by disturbances of the interactive balance: on the one hand, the actor has need of an non-conflictory relation with the other; on the other hand he has so internalized the normative patterns which are flouted by the other that he wants to conform to them. These two poles of the dimension 'conformative-alienative behaviour', combined with a second dimension of 'active *vs* passive attitude', result in four types of deviant behaviour to which Parsons refers with the expressions:

compulsive performance, compulsive acceptance, rebellion and *withdrawal.*

According to the theoretical model these four types of deviance, which can of course be further specified with the help of many other dimensions, will escalate unless they are in some way or another and to a certain extent absorbed by differently oriented motivational processes, the so-called controlled mechanisms. Parsons classifies these controlling mechanisms in three categories as follows:[58]

(a) Those, which tend to 'nip in the bud' tendencies to development of compulsively deviant motivation before they reach the vicious circle stage,
(b) Those, which insulate the bearers of such motivation from influence on others and
(c) The 'secondary defenses' which are able, to varying degrees, to reverse the vicious circle processes.

The mechanisms of category (a) are those of normal daily contact. They are the mechanisms which tactfully dissipate small irritations in human interaction and they vary from humour to a diplomatic use of language, from tact to demonstrative silence. The mechanisms of category (b) restrict the consequences of deviant behaviour. Through them the various non-compatible institutions are so well separated that latent grounds for conflict are subdued. The deviant and his associates are set apart, as it were, so that there is no longer any risk of confrontation. Last there are mechanisms which can not only break the vicious circle but can also re-direct it. The difference between these latter types of mechanism can best be illustrated with the help of the aspects of controlling mechanisms distinguished by Parsons.

Starting with the example of psychotherapeutic control, he distinguishes four aspects that may carry different weight per mechanism. They are 'support', 'permissiveness', 'restriction of reciprocation' and 'conditional manipulation of rewards and sanctions'.[59]

'Support' refers to the loyal attitude that is assumed towards a deviant: the relation with the deviant does not cease now that he has gone beyond certain normative expectations. This gives him the reassurance of 'still belonging' and diminishes the chance of aggressive or defensive behaviour and the creation of a vicious circle of deviance. This loyal attitude implies a certain degree of 'permissiveness'. It is obvious that in some situations transgression of patterns of expectation can be tolerated with comparative ease. For instance, more tolerance is shown towards the deviant behaviour of people who are under great emotional strain. There is an attitude of forgiveness and indulgence. The mechanisms in (b) are characterized by both these elements.

But loyalty and the spirit of forgiveness are not quite the same as 'co-operation'. Is it because the deviant is more or less set apart that no new complementarity of interaction ensues; the other does not co-operate and this makes it harder for the deviant to persist in his behaviour. When, in that case, the other has at his disposal a whole battery of punishments and rewards, there is every chance that the deviant behaviour will be reversed.

The mechanisms listed under (c) incorporate particularly these two elements ('restriction of reciprocation' and 'conditional manipulation of rewards and sanctions') of the social process.

We shall not here attempt further elaboration of Parsons's motivational paradigm. For the purpose of our interpretation the important point is that, because the conceptualization of the process aspect of social systems refers so strongly to the level of personality, the theoretical dividing-line between the two action systems threatens to become problematical. This is only one of the possible questions concerning the structural-functional theory of social system. Of all the very wide range of questions that may be raised about this theory there is a limited number in which we are interested; these are the ones which can give us an answer to the other question – why is it that in this first attempt at conceptualization Parsons seems gradually to lose sight of his epistemological and methodological premises?

This means that in the following chapter we shall have to confront our description thus far with those premises and, where premises and elaboration do not agree, we must try to find the reason for the discrepancy. When we have found that reason, it will perhaps be easier to regard Parsons's more recent publications as a new and better attempt at conceptual interpretation of his epistemological and methodological premises.

4 The instability of the structural-functional version of the action theory

1 Introduction

The structural-functional theory of social systems must be seen as the first elaborated attempt at an action theory. No doubt it represented Parsons's efforts to translate both his epistemological premises on the general and analytical character of theory and the methodological premises of voluntarism to the conceptual level of theory as well as he possibly could.

So far, we have not questioned the success of his attempt for fear of confusing the issue and adding to the complexity of the foregoing chapter. This chapter will be devoted to this aspect. The question of whether the structural-functional translation of the action theory's premises is adequate or not, does not stand alone. Whatever many of the critics seem to think, a negative answer does not imply total disqualification of Parsons's work. In fact, the structural-functional phase in the construction of the action theory represents a very specific period which ended soon after the publication in 1951 of *The Social System*. It is obvious, even to Parsons himself, that the conceptual form of the structural-functional version was not the be-all and end-all of conceptual wisdom.

In the total period of Parsons's activities it is apparent that the structural-functional theory of social systems is no more than a very temporary version of the action theory, as evidenced by the large number of ambiguities and inconsistencies it contains. On the other hand, it was exactly these conceptual gaps that inspired Parsons to reconsider his epistemological and methodological premises and started him off on a new phase of conceptualization.

Yet *The Social System* — the publication which above all others is an exposé of the structural-functional theory — is often regarded as Parsons's *magnum opus*. This, to say the least, carries the suggestion that the conceptual structure it describes is the model on which Parsons based his action theory and its translation to the level of social systems. Moreover, it gives the impression that Parsons's concern with the construction of theory reached its final conclusion in *The Social System*. Examples of this erroneous idea are to be found in publications such as *The Social Theories of Talcott Parsons* edited by Max Black (1961),[1] Alvin Gouldner's *The Coming Crisis of Western Sociology* 1971 (1970)[2] and Walter Buckley's *Sociology and Modern Systems Theory* (1967).[3] Among other things, these show that the new conceptual developments which were beginning to appear in the early 1950s were not generally recognized as such but were taken to be minor alterations in what was actually a structural-functional theory. Parsons himself encouraged this completely wrong attitude by naming an article he published in 1964 'Recent Trends in Structural-Functional Theory'.[4] Those who have not read further than the misleading title have missed an opportunity to see for themselves that there is no longer any question in this article of structural-functionalism in the sense referred to above.

Clearly, this chapter will have to find an answer to two related questions. The first concerns the quality of the structural-functional version of the action theory as measured up to Parsons's own pretensions; the second concerns the function which this version fulfilled in the totality of Parsons's theoretical development.

The considerations which both answers must take into account are so closely connected that they can be included in one and the same discussion. To start with we shall make an inventory of the conceptual gaps in the structural-functional version (section 2). Next we shall try to find the fundamental reason for the inadequacy of this version (section 3). Then we shall relate this fundamental reason directly to the inexactitudes already mentioned; in other words, we shall try, by a process of 'backward reasoning', to 'predict' these inconsistencies (section 4). Finally, we shall show how Parsons himself — though he was not aware of it — removed that fundamental reason and thus created the possibility to transfer his premises to the conceptual level (section 5).

2 Inventorization of conceptual gaps in the structural-functional version

One only has to make a comparison between some of Parsons's structural-functional publications to realize the practical impossibility of distilling from them a completely consistent picture. This is partly due to the continual process of development that was taking place during the writing of all Parsons's publications. However, this does not alter the fact that even the most sympathetic interpretation of the structural-functional action theory results in an ambiguous whole and is therefore vulnerable to many and varied accusations. Because of this, the expression 'structural-functionalism', like 'Parsonianism', has acquired a clearly deprecatory meaning.

In pointing out here some of the conceptual inexactitudes we have in mind, we shall refer to the exposé given in the previous chapter. It will not be possible to examine all the criticisms of the structural-functional model that have appeared in the last two decades. So we shall concentrate mainly on those conceptual ambiguities which resulted from an altering of definitions, explicitly or otherwise. In this way we hope to get more insight into the reason for the instability of the structural-functional version of the action theory.

Foremost in Parsons's systematic elaboration of the action theory's frame of reference is the so-called bipolarity of the actor's orientation on the one hand and his environmental situation on the other. At first sight, this approach appears to harmonize completely with the fundamental ideas expressed in *The Structure of Social Action*. The actor's subjective orientation was one of the central themes of this book and was, moreover, one which was being contradicted in all the positivist action theories. In this light it is understandable that, in Parsons's own elaboration of the action theory, conceptualization proceeds partly from this subjective orientation.

In short, there is no doubt at all that Parsons was at pains to include the results of *The Structure of Social Action* in his schema. Nevertheless, this concern resulted in divisions that are not as clear as they appear at first sight. The differentiation between actor's orientation on the one hand and the situation on the other is Parsons's conceptual translation of the voluntaristic way of thinking with regard to the subjective-objective dimension; it is true that both the subjective and the objective aspect have a place in the scheme but the relation between the subjective moment of orientation and the objective situation aspect remains unclear.[5] A good example of this is the pattern-variable of specificity versus diffuseness. At the beginning, this variable is supposed to describe an aspect of the situation (i.e. the 'scope of significance' dimension); later, however, it is seen to belong to the so-called 'orientation set' and mainly to describe an aspect of the actor's motivational orientation.[6]

In another place Parsons asserts that the pattern variables in the 'orientation set' (affectivity *versus* neutrality and specificity *versus* diffuseness) are mostly useful for describing the personality system, whereas the variables in the 'situation set' (universalism *versus* particularism and quality *versus* performance) are useful chiefly on the level of the social system.[7] Could this mean that the bipolarity of the frame of reference is 'divided' between the theory of the personality system and that of the social system? In other words, does the theory of the personality system start out mainly from the actor's orientation and the theory of the social system mainly from the situational aspect of action? And, if this is the case, does the category of value-orientation belong to the actor's orientation or to the situation? In such cases of conceptual ambiguity it is Parsons's custom to make a virtue of necessity by giving the abovementioned relation between the two sets of pattern variables the impressive designation of 'symmetrical asymmetry'.[8] But this does not make the position any clearer.

A second ambiguous theme in the structural-functional version of the action theory is the one that refers to the other voluntaristic way of thinking, the so-called nominalism-realism dialectic. As soon as the frame of reference is based on the bipolarity of orientation and situation, the question arises as to the relation between orientation of the individual and the more inclusive point of view of society and the social system. Parsons claims to have overcome the contradiction between these two points of view at the conceptual level and decides therefore to include them both in his theory. This leads him to make constructions in which the objective characteristics and requirements of the system are connected to the subjective and individual orientation of the actor. The link between the two aspects is formed by the concept of 'function' which places the individual modes or orientation in the framework of the system's objective requirements. But here, too, clarity is entirely lacking: for surely such a representation of the case assumes that individual orientations and system characteristics are mutually independent aspects? And is this not in complete conflict with Parsons's more articulated attitude to the relation between the individual and society?

A third theme of ambiguity follows directly on from this and concerns the nature of system definition. In Parsons's original formulation, an action system was a network of actions, of 'unit acts'. However, now that the frame of reference of the action theory is based on a different unit of analysis – the 'unit of action' it is natural to suppose that the action system will henceforth be regarded as a network of orientations, whereas the definition of personality and social system must make it clear that they organize those orientations in a particular way. But since, as Parsons himself said, the cultural system cannot be regarded as a way of organizing actors' orientations, he has to change his tack somewhat and explain that the cultural system is not an action system in the 'real' sense.[9] It is hard to see then why the cultural system is placed side by side with the other two and regarded, like them, as a sub-system of action. It is obvious that at this stage in his work Parsons himself is not clear about the relation between an action system and action sub-systems.

The ambiguity is only increased when Parsons suddenly introduces a new criterion for differentiating between action sub-systems.[10] The category of actors' orientation is divided into need-patterns and roles. (In view of the above it is not at all clear how far the third category, i.e. the normative pattern, can be called an aspect of orientation). A personality system consists then of a network of need-patterns whereas the social system represents a network of roles. This further specification of the unit of analysis creates the impression that, as far as the unit of analysis is concerned, the theory of the personality system and that of the social system differ one from the other. This implies an alteration of the original view that both systems or sub-systems were to be differentiated not according to the unit of analysis but solely according to the pivot around which the unit of analysis was organized into a system.

Moreover, this shift of position gives a certain degree of independence to the action sub-systems in question. Just like the personality system, the social system also has its own internal structure; combined with the tendency to attribute the motivational aspect of orientation to the theory of the personality system and value-orientation to the theory of social systems, this produces the impression that both theories restrict themselves to separate aspects of orientation. The relation between these theories remains as obscure as ever.

This tendency to separate or mark out the area of action sub-systems receives an extra impulse from the projection of the homeostasis analogy on to the field of the action sciences.[11] The independence of the system with regard to its environment is strongly emphasized by the stress that is laid on the processes which protect the system from threatened infringement. It seems as though the theory of the social system is no longer a 'secondary descriptive scheme' and that it need call on no other discipline in order to *explain* social action. It is questionable whether this can be reconciled with the way actors' subjective motivation is linked to the requirements of the system in the structural-functional theory.

The emphasis on the internal structure of the different systems and with it the suggestion that they may be independent of each other is very closely connected to another theme of conceptual

ambiguity in the structural-functional version of the action theory, i.e. the extremely careless conceptualization of the relations *between* the different systems. It is not surprising that the conception of inter-systems relations also suffers from misapprehensions of the idea of system. Very little attention is given to inter-system relations in the structural-functional version; they are conceptualized as 'functional conditions'. Thus the conditions requisite to the functioning of the social system are:
(a) 'adequate' motivation of the actors in the system
(b) a 'certain' level of cultural consensus.[12]
The first of these functional conditions refers to the relation with the personality system; the second to the relation with the cultural system. Such formal statements have little meaning. They only illustrate the point that Parsons's structural-functionalism is unable to deal with inter-system relations.

All these are questions which, as far as the present writer is concerned, remain unanswered, even after regularly repeated readings of Parsons's publications on the subject. Of course, a lot more questions might be put to the structural-functional version of the action theory about the system of pattern variables, the formulation of two system problems or functional requirements, about the danger of tautological methods of argument, about possible conservative implications of such a theory etc. A great deal has been published on these questions,[13] and it need not all be reproduced here, especially since the 'themes of conceptual ambiguity' which we have mentioned play a bigger part in the *development* of Parsons's formulation of the action theory.

To end this section we give a list of the kinds of ambiguity described above:
(a) ambiguities that are directly connected with the differentiation between orientation and situation
(b) ambiguities directly connected with the relation between actor and system
(c) ambiguities concerned with system definitions
(d) ambiguities concerning the differentiation of systems
(e) ambiguities concerning the independence of subsystems
(f) ambiguities concerning the conceptualization of intersystem relations.

3 The conceptual dilemma: the clash of premises

Since there are so many conceptual gaps or ambiguities in the structural-functional version of the action theory, it is most unlikely that they can be attributed entirely to the scientific carelessness of its author. This is even more unlikely because in his scrupulous analyses of the 'classics' Parsons showed himself to be anything but careless and his pretension to formulate a general action theory seems to have been founded on a strongly felt need for schematic precision. The contrast between this need and the actual lack of precision in the conceptual scheme suggests that there may be other causes more important than carelessness. In other words, if we assume that the conceptual ambiguity of the structural-functional version of the action theory is due to a deeper cause than that of pure carelessness, we shall have to look for that cause in the *way* in which Parsons gives conceptual expression to his epistemological and methodological premises. This brings us back to the four requirements which, according to his own premises, a conceptual system has to fulfil and which we summed up in the previous chapter. Without further comment we suggested that these four requirements (of generality, of the analytical character of the theory, of the synthesis between subjective and objective factors and of the dialectical relation between the individual and society) would not be easy to fulfil in combination with each other. We shall now enlarge on that statement.

As we said in chapter 2, Parsons tries to steer his own voluntaristic course on two methodological dimensions between the Scylla of positivism and the Charybdis of idealism. These two aspects of the voluntaristic way of thought form a synthesis of extremes; on the one hand they imply interaction between the subjective and objective moment of action; on the other hand they imply a dialectic of social-nominalistic and social-realistic views on the nature of society.

On the methodological level of thought-patterns this voluntaristic attitude presents no problems. On the contrary, it can be seen as an important contribution to the development of social science. *The problems start, however when such a voluntaristic pattern of thought has to be translated to the conceptual level in an unambiguous general theory.* Is it, in any case, possible to fit a 'dialectical' way of thinking into one systematic and general conceptual scheme? Is it not true that however articulated the attitude towards e.g. the individual and society may be, the requirement of generality will of necessity mean that conceptualization and analysis must start from one or other of them — the individual or society?

In his discussion of this methodological dilemma of social science, Zijderveld,[14] too, comes up against the problem of translating a pattern of thought to the level of conceptual theory. He has this to say about it:[15]

> Here we must immediately ask a question which we shall

THE INSTABILITY OF THE STRUCTURAL-FUNCTIONAL VERSION

deliberately omit to answer. In the previous paragraphs we made a plea for a dialectical approach in the social sciences as an adequate way to describe the process of institutionalization. The question now is whether this dialectic does not turn into *complementarity* when such a dialectical theory is empirically tested. For, if one verifies the katascopic-anascopic theory empirically it will probably be impossible to avoid separating the katascopic from the anascopic elements so that, at the moment when the katascopic element is being tested the anascopic element will be pushed to the background; conversely, the katascopic element will disappear whenever the anascopic element is being tested.

Zijderveld is not concerned about a solution to this problem because his study is aimed at trying out the possibilities for a dialectic thought-pattern with regard to the individual and society and is therefore restricted to the methodological theory-level.

Parsons, of course, does feel the need to translate methodological thought-patterns into one conceptual action theory. Zijderveld's suggestion — that the dialectic thought-pattern with regard to the individual and society on the conceptual level of theory lapses into complementarity of its own accord — clearly shows that Parsons is in a very difficult position. Such a form of complementarity — differently orientated conceptual systems behind or side by side with one another — is in total conflict with Parsons's pretension of generality. For, to Parsons, the requirement of generality means that one conceptual system has to be formulated from a strictly unambiguous point of view; to settle for complementarity would be tantamount to abandoning the pretension of generality. Parsons is certainly not prepared to do that. But what then?

In 1937 and for many years after that, Parsons failed to realize that he was caught in a dilemma.

There are in principle two 'impossible' solutions for this *conceptual dilemma of the voluntaristic action theory*. On the one hand, it might be possible to construct a really *general* action theory with the danger that the voluntaristic thought-pattern might then fall apart into one-sidedness. On the other hand one could translate the voluntaristic thought-patterns to the conceptual level; but then the theory would lose its general character and lapse into complementarity.

This conceptual dilemma reveals a possible discrepancy between Parsons's epistemological and methodological premises which arises *whenever these latter are translated to an unambiguous conceptual structure.*

It is this conceptual dilemma which, in our interpretation, forms the most important explanatory factor for the instability in the structural-functional version of the action theory as shown by the abovementioned conceptual ambiguities.

Before going deeper into this interpretation we should like to point out the parallel between Parsons's explanation of the instability of positivism and the explanation we suggest for the instability of the structural-functional version of the action theory. In *The Structure of Social Action* Parsons developed an argument in which both the instability of the individual-positivistic or utilitarian theory as well as the developments which started from that unstable basis were explained through the so-called 'utilitarian dilemma of the positivistic action theory'.[16]

Our 'conceptual dilemma of the voluntaristic action theory' answers the same purpose, albeit on the conceptual rather than methodological level of theory. The common characteristic of both dilemmas is that in principle they always result in inconsistencies and one-sidedness. There were two 'impossible' solutions to the utilitarian dilemma; either the action theoretical character could be defended by two unsubstantial postulations, or a radical positivism could come into being which would argue the actor's subjectivity out of existence. The conceptual dilemma also has two such impossible solutions: either to construct a general theory in which the voluntaristic thought-patterns lapse into one-sidedness or to uphold voluntarism with the resulting loss of the theory's general nature and a dissolution into complementary points of view.

The methodological dilemma of the positivistic action theory was not solved until the spell of positivism had been broken. The conceptual dilemma of the voluntaristic action theory can also be solved under certain conditions. These will be discussed in section 5. This is the start of an entirely new phase in the *conceptualization* of the voluntaristic action theory just as the solution of the utilitarian dilemma was the start of a new methodological development in that theory.

However, we must first find out whether the instability of the structural-functional theory of action does indeed have its origins in this conceptual dilemma. To this end, the manifestations of instability as listed in the previous section will have to be interpreted in the light of this dilemma.

4 The instability of the structural-functional version in the light of the conceptual dilemma

If we are able to find a direct connection between the aforementioned conceptual gaps and the conceptual dilemma of the voluntaristic action theory, then we can be certain that the developments in Parsons's work which often appear so contradictory do not have their origins in inexplicable 'theoretical metamorphoses',[17] but should rather be compared to the corrective movements of a rope dancer in danger of losing his balance. The surest test of a direct relationship which we assume to exist between the ambiguities mentioned in section 2 and the conceptual dilemma is obtained by a process of backward reasoning: by trying, after the event from the position of the conceptual dilemma to 'predict' a number of the aforementioned inconsistencies.

The conceptual translation of the first voluntaristic thought-pattern (the methodological subjective − objective dimension)

After a first preliminary attempt to formulate a frame of reference in terms of the 'unit act', Parsons bases his systematically elaborated frame of reference on a different unit of analysis − the 'unit of action.' Here the theory is built, not round the action itself, but round the actor's orientation to the situation. This 'unit of action' is actually a composite category in which both the subjective and the objective aspects of action are represented. It is, in itself, the translation of the first voluntaristic pattern of thought to the conceptual level of the frame of reference.

As we have seen, Parsons places great confidence in this conceptual translation of the voluntaristic pattern of thought, particularly when he compares it to the old 'unit act'.[18] In view of his pretensions, we do not consider this attitude to be justified. To divide action into a subjective aspect and an objective aspect, orientation and situation, is to reduce the voluntaristic thought-pattern on the conceptual level to complementarity and to conflict with the pretension of generality. Unless the frame of reference is able to differentiate clearly between the subjective and the objective aspect and to show explicitly the relation between the two aspects, the theory remains caught up in the conceptual dilemma: either there must be two complementary theories so that each pillar of this voluntaristic thought-pattern can be included in a separate theory, or there must be a general theory which, of necessity, emphasizes one of the two points of view.

Parsons tries to find a way between these two different possibilities. But he cannot avoid the fact that his attempt to reconcile the irreconcilable raises questions about both the general and the voluntaristic character of his structural-functional theory. As regards the pretension of generality there are plenty of problems. In this connection Parsons himself speaks of two *'points of view'* − the subjective point of view of the actor and the objective point of view of the 'neutral' observer.[19] There is various evidence of these two points of view in the elaborated frame of reference and the categorial system: in the first place they can be seen in the bipolarity of the framework but also in practically all the classification-schemes to be found in the structural-functional version. However, the most fundamental characteristic of a general theory is that it must be defined from one single point of view. It is only possible to admit different points of view behind one another or side by side when their mutual relationship is exactly defined. Again, this implies that the two points of view have to be united in one overall point of view. Unless this is the case, there is a great danger of undetectable overlappings and redundancies.

It was exactly these conceptual overlappings and redundancies which struck us in the structural-functional action theory. To start with there was the vague demarcation between orientation and situation. In particular, there was no clear distinction between the concept of value-orientation and that of situation so that it was possible, for instance, for the pattern variable of 'universalism-particularism' to represent an aspect of the actor's value-orientation and yet at the same time to belong to the so-called 'situation set'.[20]

This problem of demarcation can also be seen in the changeover of the pattern variable 'specificity-generality' from the 'situation set' to the 'orientation set'.[21] In principle, there are three ways in which Parsons can organize the repairs thus necessitated by the conceptual dilemma. In the first place he can try to have his cake and eat it by reconciling voluntarism as far as possible with the generality claim. The ambiguities referred to above are examples of the conceptual compromises to which this can lead. A second way to tackle the conceptual dilemma is to emphasize the voluntaristic thought-pattern at the expense of the pretension of generality. In Parsons's idea of the 'symmetric asymmetry' of the pattern variables there is a strong suggestion that the theory of the personality system is concerned with subjective or motivational factors, whereas the theory of the social system is orientated more to objective or situational factors. It is apparent that a lot of people regard this tendency as the 'normal' form of Parsons's theory of the social system: how otherwise could someone like Homans quite seriously try to show, in his famous pamphlet 'Bringing Men Back In', that as soon as Parsons wants to *explain* something he has to call on motivational or psychological processes![22]

A third way of dealing with the conceptual dilemma is to place extra emphasis on the theory's pretension of generality and to avoid dividing it into complementary theories. It would be natural to suppose that the voluntaristic thought-pattern would then be translated inadequately and one-sidedly to the level of conceptual theory. Apparently some authors have got this impression from Parsons's theory of social systems; an author like Don Martindale would not otherwise have described the development of voluntarism to the theory of social systems as a 'theoretical metamorphosis' in which the original social-behaviouristic idea of voluntarism has to give way to a strictly normative determinism or objectivism.[23]

In conclusion, the least we can say is that all the three aspects of the voluntaristic action theory's conceptual dilemma described above are to be found in Parsons's theory of social systems. This does not explain all the inconsistencies of the structural-functional version. To complete the picture we must try to find out how the second voluntaristic thought-pattern also became caught up in the conceptual dilemma in its translation to the conceptual level of theory.

The conceptual translation of the second voluntaristic thought-pattern (the methodological dimension of social nominalism-social realism)

In the structural-functional version of the action theory the bipolarity of orientation and situation gives way to another kind of bipolarity i.e. that of actor and system. When he first started work on the voluntaristic frame of reference it looked as though Parsons would manage to avoid this opposition between actor and system but now that the unit of analysis is no longer the 'unit act' but the 'unit of action', the social system is no more to be regarded as a network of actions but as a network of actors.[24]

At first sight, this bipolarity of actor and system appears to fit in well with Parsons's voluntaristic thought-pattern. However, it is obvious from the idea of the conceptual dilemma that the action theory's pretension of generality is once more being contravened. And once again there is a danger that this voluntaristic thought-pattern will be irreconcilable with the epistemological requirements which Parsons himself thought the action theory ought to fulfil.

Here again, there are three possible reactions to this aspect of the conceptual dilemma. First one might try to reconcile the two premises as far as possible. And this is obviously the course of action Parsons would have preferred. In fact, to our way of thinking, the most typical characteristic of the structural-functional theory is the curious connection between actors' individual orientations or motivations and the overlying characteristics of the social system. It is particularly the concept of function that plays an important part in this connection. But here too, the same objection applies as to the first voluntaristic thought-pattern: not until the characteristics of the system can be defined independently of the characteristics of individual actors, not until the demarcation problem has been solved, will the structural-functional version of the action theory be anything but a careless mixing of two more or less complementary points of view in a so-called 'general' theory.

This theory's pretension to generality can only be supported at the price of an increasing number of inconsistencies. In fact Parsons himself admits the existence of two different theoretical points of view when he says, for instance, that the 'allocation of persons' concept has the same significance from the system point of view as the 'socialization' concept has from the motivational point of view.[25] The overlappings and redundancies that result from this bipolarity make the theory of social systems difficult to read and literally incomprehensible.

A second way of dealing with the instability caused by the conceptual dilemma lays such stress on the voluntaristic thought-pattern as it concerns the relation of the individual to society that the pretension of generality has to be relinquished altogether. Although in some places Parsons opposes the theory of personality with that of social systems in a sort of actor-system relationship this is not a typical Parsonian reaction;[26] on the contrary, the average criticism of this facet of his structural-functional version concerns precisely the way he maintains the pretence of generality *at the expense of* the voluntaristic thought-pattern (i.e. the third possible reaction). Martindale emphasizes that, in Parsons's scheme, individual motivation has to give way to the destructive force of a social system 'sui generis'.[27] Dennis Wrong refers to the 'oversocialized conception of man'[28] and Ralf Dahrendorf sees Parsons's social system as a sort of Utopia where nothing ever changes because perfect harmony exists between the individual and society.[29] Martindale and Dahrendorf try to back up what they regard as Parsons's one-sided theory with another, complementary, theory which lays particular stress on the active, creative and antagonistic aspect of action; but here again, they remain enmeshed in the voluntaristic action theory's conceptual dilemma.

So once more the consequences of the conceptual dilemma reach out in different directions. To start with there is the danger that a different meaning will be attributed to this most crucial concept of system. The social system is no longer regarded as a network of actions as the first attempt at a frame of reference suggested; is has now become an association of individual actors. Moreover, action systems are now differentiated according to different criteria at the same time; under the influence of the biological homeostasis model, the internal structure of the subsystems that finally emerge is considered to be more important than their relations with other subsystems.

Bit by bit, Parsons is even running the risk of allowing this 'self-reliant' view of the social system to conflict with his second epistemological premise i.e. the analytical character of concept and theory. The social system tends to become a limited group of actors in concrete reality rather than an analytical aspect of action.

The double bipolarity of the structural-functional version of the action theory

In the foregoing sections we have tried to show the impossibility of combining in a single general theory all the four pretensions on which Parsons's voluntaristic action theory is based: in any case the result would be utter confusion. We do not dispute that Parsons suggests other ways of dealing with this conceptual dilemma but he concentrates chiefly on trying to reconcile the pretension of generality with the voluntaristic thought-patterns at the conceptual level in a bipolar structural-functional theory. The structural-functional theory forms a sort of federative link between four complementary points of view.

This double bipolarity is illustrated in Figure 4.1.

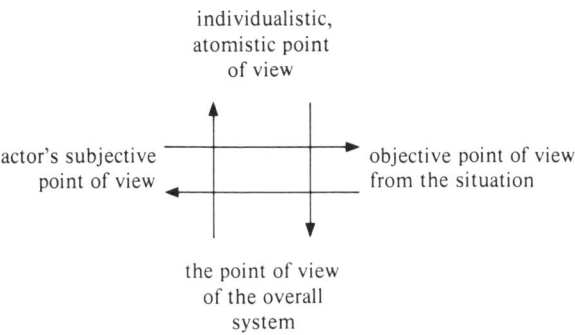

FIGURE 4.1 *The double bipolarity*

Thus the same actions can be conceptualized and analysed from completely different angles. Since the most fundamental requirement of a general theory is that it should represent a single 'point of view', it was only to be expected that the structural-functional action theory would eventually collapse under the burden of its own inconsistencies.

If one considers the theoretical state of affairs in modern

sociology it looks as though the federative system of Parsons's structural-functional theory is ever more clearly being replaced by a set of unequivocally formulated and mutually complementary 'currents'.

Quite recently, Berting made a diagram of these currents constructed on the basis of the same two dimensions as our diagram of the double bipolarity of the structural-functional theory. In fact Berting's diagram produces a cross-section of the present situation in sociological theory in which multiple perspectivism in the form of many complementary theories occupies an important place (Figure 4.2)

Berting puts functionalism in cell A together with what he calls the collectivistic theory of exchange. If he were to include Parsons's structural-functionalism in this category, it would indicate that, in Berting's interpretation, the objective and collectivistic implications of this theory are predominant.

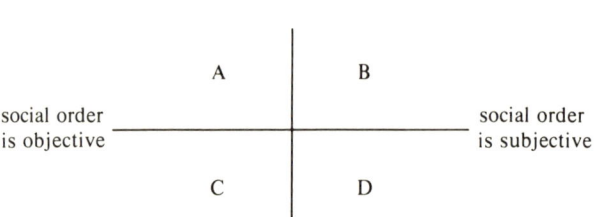

FIGURE 4.2 *Berting's diagram*

In cell B he puts currents such as Croce's neo-idealistic view of history, Winch, and the Frankfurt School. Cell C is occupied by Homans's and Blau's individualistic theory of exchange while the position in cell D is taken up by symbolic interactionism.[30] If we had to fit the structural-functional theory of action which we have described into this schema we should no doubt place it at the intersection of the two lines, since the four currents distinguished by Berting have all been in one way or another a 'point of view' in Parsons's structural-functional theory.

Of course, from a purely historical point of view, all these currents date back further than the 1940s and 1950s – the years when Parsons's structural-functionalism came into being. But the recent revival of these different currents, after a period in which structural-functionalism predominated, may be regarded unreservedly as a logical extension of the structural-functional theory's double bipolarity.

If we accept that Berting's description gives a reasonable picture of the internal differences in sociological theory – and considering the chapter headings of most modern text books this seems a fair assumption – it means that Parsons's attempt to formulate a general voluntaristic theory of action resulted in the opposite, namely a set of different theoretical points of view in which voluntaristic ideas are chopped up into conceptual pieces. If, on top of all this, the protagonists of these different theoretical points of view regard their one-sidedness as the be-all and end-all or as of general validity – which is fortunately becoming less and less the case – then the conceptual dilemma of the voluntaristic action theory has the theory of sociology firmly in its power.

But in spite of the obvious bankruptcy of the structural-functional version of the action theory Parsons does not lose heart; he keeps making new attempts to formulate his voluntaristic premises in a really general theory.

These attempts are a pure waste of energy *until Parsons has found a way to overcome the conceptual dilemma in its entirety.* In other words as long as he is unaware of the conceptual dilemma, he cannot escape from its restricting influence. *Only when he starts to think about the circumstances which have brought about this dilemma does he consider a completely new attempt at conceptualization.*

5 Reflections on the conceptual dilemma: the end of the structural-functional version

To sum up our arguments in the foregoing section we conclude that Parsons's translation of the voluntaristic thought-pattern into conceptual theory falls short of the requirements which a general theory must fulfil.

Assuming that the formulation of a general theory is still possible and desirable, it is natural to seek the solution to this problem in a different conceptual translation of the voluntaristic thought-pattern. This was the conclusion which Parsons reached soon after the publication of *The Social System*. Apparently he, too, had the feeling that the excess of conceptual subdivisions called for a re-examination of the fundaments of the conceptual theory. He described this re-examination in *Working Papers in the Theory of Action*.[31] This publication is one of the most salient examples of the 'thinking aloud' which occupies such an important place in Parsons's work: his ideas are in a continuous state of flux and, especially in his attempts to formulate a general theory with a voluntaristic foundation, nearly every new publication is more or less contradicted by the next. In *Working Papers* the new ideas follow each other in quick succession. This sequence of ideas revolves round a new conceptual translation of the voluntaristic thought-pattern. We shall describe this new development as it concerns the two voluntaristic premises.

The first of these, the intermingling of subjective and objective factors in the determination of human action, is conceptualized in the structural-functional version as *orientation* and *situation*. Parsons regards the actor's subjective orientation as the crux of his contribution to social-scientific theory; it is this accentuation of the actor's subjective orientation that distinguishes Parsons's action theory from positivism and behaviourism and it is understandable, if only because of his controversial attitude to these two currents of social-scientific thought, that this same subjective orientation turned up again in the conceptual schema. This means, however, that the pluri-perspectivism of the thought-patterns becomes wrapped up in a conceptual theory based on the pretension of generality and consistency. The resulting conflict can only be solved by removing the perspectivism aspect from the conceptual theory.

This means, in reality, that the frame of reference of the voluntaristic theory as elaborated in the 1951 publications will have to be cast in a different form for that frame of reference was based on the bipolarity of orientation and situation and thus created the conditions of conceptual constraint from which the structural-functional version and its off-shoots have never been able to escape.

But if the bipolarity of orientation and situation is removed from the frame of reference is there not a danger that the actor's subjective orientation will be pushed to the background and that the theory of action will degenerate into dreaded behaviourism? Will that not mean the definite end of the voluntaristic action theory? This would undoubtedly be the case were it not possible to include the actor's subjective orientation in the frame of reference other than as a 'point of view' or perspective. Parsons recognizes this possibility and begins to look for a new unit of analysis and, therefore, for a new frame of reference in which orientation and situation will no longer function as separate 'entrances' to the action theory but will be united in a single overall point of view.

This single overall 'point of view' is that of 'symbolic' action. The symbolic character of action can combine the two-way traffic of orientation and situation. For it comprises two aspects. First, according to Parsons, every action is symbolic in the expressive sense, i.e. every action is an *expression* of the actor's motivation or orientation. At the same time, however, the same action is also symbolic in a *cognitive* sense, i.e. the same action becomes integrated and acquires meaning for a different actor (sometimes for the same actor); the action then functions as a situational object which must be given a meaning.[32]

In other words, that single symbol, that single action is *at one and the same time* both the manifestation of an attitude i.e. actor's orientation or motivation, and a situational object, i.e. an object that is interpreted.

Thus Parsons sees action as the symbolic medium *between* the two poles of the old frame of reference, i.e. actor's orientation and situation. The most important implication of this medial character of action is that the two different perspectives are 'telescoped' together. In this way, the 'point of view' of action as a symbol transcends the awkward bipolarity which impeded the first attempt at formulating a voluntaristic action theory.

What is the significance of this accentuation of the symbolic character of action to the conceptual dilemma contained in the voluntaristic frame of reference? In what sense does this re-orientation contribute to a solution of the dilemma? In order to see this more clearly we must first see how it is in any case possible to solve a real dilemma. It will be remembered that the 'utilitarian dilemma' which Parsons constructed was solved when it was worked loose from its positivistic foundations. Apparently it was this positivistic foundation which gave rise to the utilitarian straitjacket. By removing the cause, this dilemma was averted.

The same thing applies to the conceptual dilemma; the provocation which gave rise to the dilemma is to be found in the bipolar character of the 'unit of action' and of the frame of reference based upon it. *On this basis of bipolarity* Parsons's four pretensions are in principle irreconcilable; they can only be fulfilled at the expense of each other and the result is bound to be one-sidedness or ambiguity. Therefore the only way to overcome this conceptual dilemma is to rid the frame of reference of its bipolarity.

It is precisely this relinquishment of the bipolarity of the structural-functional theory that is signified by the accentuation of the symbolic character of action. In this way Parsons makes a fresh start on his conceptualization of the action theory's premises; henceforth, the frame of reference's last unit of analysis is symbolic action. The new voluntaristic action theory is made up of different aspects of action and the relation between those aspects.

The new formulation of the unit of analysis not only provides a different conceptual translation of the first voluntaristic dimension (subjective-objective); it also has an effect on the bipolarity which Parsons used to put forward as a conceptual translation of the nominalism-realism dialectic.

Here, too, was a case of the conceptual dilemma since the bipolarity of actor and situation brought with it the conceptual bipolarity of individual and society. In that way, individual motivation and the structure of the governing institutions became more or less independent perspectives of action and this, too, failed to harmonize with Parsons's pretension to generality.

However, now that symbolic action has become the last unit of analysis, it becomes possible to transcend the opposition between the individual and society at the conceptual level as well. For actions never occur on their own but always in systems; thus the 'opposition' between the individual and society is no longer an opposition between the actor and the system – as was sometimes suggested in the structural-functional theory – but is reduced to an analytical separation into sub-systems of action. And just as the subjective orientation can be seen as an (expressive) aspect of action, so this same subjective component can also be seen as the expressive aspect of symbolic action systems. For the subjective component is now no longer a *perspective* from which to start conceptualization but an *aspect* which is involved in conceptualization. For this reason, as soon as this subjective component is translated to the symbolic plane it ceases to conflict with the significance of the concept of action systems and it becomes possible to avoid the actor-system dichotomy.

To sum up, it can be said that the double bipolarity of the voluntaristic frame of reference, as described in the two 1951 publications, is resolved in undivided symbolic action whereby the four points of view of that framework now reappear as analytical aspects of symbolic action.

The most interesting aspect of this development is that it is new only to a very limited degree. For in this accentuation of the symbolic character of action, it is not difficult to discover a return to Parsons's very first attempt at a frame of reference. In *The Structure of Social Action* (1937) is was, after all, the 'unit act' which was designated as unit of analysis and of which four analytical aspects were distinguished.[33] This return to the forgotten track of the 'unit act' proves yet again that, in Parsons's own opinion too, the structural-functional version of the action theory should be seen as a very temporary and even inadequate development of his epistemological and methodological premises. It might even be said that, from the viewpoint of Parsons's own pretensions, the structural-functional theory is no more than a detour to the formulation of a general voluntaristic action theory. The detour begins in the so-called 'unimportant' shift of the analysis unit (from 'unit act' to 'unit of action') as announced casually by Parsons in a footnote.[34]

6 The formulation of the new frame of reference: the four-function paradigm

It was never clear to Parsons himself that the developments we have been discussing mark the final end of the structural-functional version of the action theory. As we have said earlier, he continued for a long time to regard these new developments as 'recent trends in structural-functional theory'. This may be explained by the fact that Parsons never explicitly recognized the conceptual dilemma. In practice, it was the multitude of conceptual inconsistencies in the structural functional version that caused him to change his direction.

Apart from this, a confrontation with the work of Robert F. Bales led him to make a large-scale synthesis of the various classification schemata which Bales and himself had developed over the years.[35] As is usually the case, this confrontation gave Parsons new conceptual insights which he might otherwise have missed. That does not mean, however, that this new conceptual start should be regarded as completely fortuitous. For it is very possible that Parsons's desire to find a synthesis between his own work and that of others is due to the immanence of the conceptual dilemma and the instability of the structural-functional theory that resulted from it.

It is typical of Parsons's attitude that he tries to distil the fundamental structure of the new frame of reference from an arrangement of the 'old' structural-functional classification schemata. The most central of these is that of the pattern variables. This occupies a very important place in the structural-functional theory, not least because it illustrates so well the bipolarity of the voluntaristic frame of reference. For that reason it is interesting to see how Parsons reformulates this bipolar scheme of pattern variables in the light of the new unit of analysis. For, since it can now be assumed that the perspectives of orientation and situation are united in symbolic action, the question arises whether the pattern variables, distinguished according to both perspectives, cannot equally be 'telescoped' into each other. In other words, what are the intrinsic relations between the different pattern variables from the perspective of symbolic action?

Let us join Parsons in a careful examination of the different pattern variables.[36] What, for instance, is the exact meaning of 'affectivity'? 'Affectivity' means that the actor gives free rein to his inclination to satisfy his needs actively and directly. It refers to an attitude of the actor; the variable is formulated from the point of view of actor's orientation. Accentuation of the symbolic character of action has made it clear that the action resulting from this attitude can also be seen from the 'objective' or situation point of view. Well then, says Parsons, it is the variable of 'performance' which, though from a different point of view, formulates *precisely the same* as the variable of 'affectivity'. Action understood as the manifestation of an attitude, as an 'expressive' symbol (affectivity) forms from the objective observer's point of view, a 'cognitive' symbol, an event to be interpreted. Naturally, one and the same actor can use both points of view; the reflexivity of human action depends on just that.

At the overall level of symbolic action however, no differences are formulated by the two variables; they are identical. Both point to one and the same aspect of action, i.e. a direct orientation to the satisfaction of a need or the attainment of a goal.

Similar intrinsic relations can also be discovered for the other pattern variables. Affective neutrality is the opposite of affectivity; it indicates the presence of an inclination to act which, for the time being, is not transformed into direct need-satisfying action. From the objective perspective, however, this very same 'attitude' or orientation on the part of the actor is called 'quality'. The object, in this case the actor, acquires significance not through his perceptible actions but through objective qualities. However, on the level of action, when orientation and situation are united in symbolic action itself, these two qualifications are indistinguishable one from the other. Then both of them indicate one in an expressive sense, the other in a cognitive sense — a not-direct need-satisfying moment in action.

On the level of action or the action system this combination of pattern variables results in a new variable whose two poles are:
1 direct need-satisfying or goal-attaining action
(the combination of affectivity and performance)
2 indirect need-satisfying or instrumental action
(combination of neutrality and quality).

A third intrinsic relation exists between the variables of particularism and diffuseness. Particularism refers to the significance of an object e.g. an actor. It is a variable from the 'situation' set which attributes the significance of an object to the fact of its belonging to the same system of relations to which the actor belongs. Diffuseness refers to actor's orientation; here it is not the modalities of the situation but the nature of the actor's orientation or motivation that is decisive. In the case of diffuseness, the actor's orientation to the object is of a general nature. The actor's interest is aimed at the complete object and not to particular aspects of the whole. When the two qualifications are applied to action in the sense of a system of symbolic action, they both indicate the same aspect of it, i.e. the internal aspect of the complex of actions involved which Parsons sometimes calls the 'internal environment' of action.

In contrast to this there is the intrinsic relation between the variables of universalism and specificity. Here too, the relation between actor and object is defined by each from a different perspective. Specificity indicates the actor's motivational orientation to specific characteristics of the object. Universalism indicates the presence of an independent dimension of significance i.e. the significance of the object to the actor is independent of their relation one to the other. According to Parsons, when these variables are projected on to action as a system of 'unit acts' they both refer to the same aspect of it: they both go beyond the limits of the action system and signify, not the 'internal environments' but the external relation of the system to its surroundings. Here again, the combination of pattern variables on the level of action or of the action system results in a new variable.

The two poles of this new variable point respectively to the internal environment of the system or to the relation of the system to its external environment.[37]

> An important conclusion may be drawn. The pattern variable schema started with five pairs of concepts. One pair, namely the self-collectivity pair, was shown to be in the presently relevant sense of derivative significance though that fact is of very fundamental theoretical importance. Now we have shown that the other four pairs, by a relationship which crosscuts the pairing itself in *one* sense and on *one* level, reduce to only two pairs.

But of course, the expression 'pattern variables' is now no longer appropriate. For the word signifies patterns in an actor's relation to the object world and in this it fits completely into the old action-situation frame of reference. However, on the level of action or the action system these relations between actor and situation are transcended and the new variables refer particularly to the dimensions according to which action or the action system can be differentiated into different elements. Therefore, from now on, Parsons speaks of 'axes of differentiation' instead of 'pattern variables'.[38] He calls these two axes or dimensions the dimension of instrumental *versus* consummatory action and the dimension of external *versus* internal action.

Not until many *Working Papers* had been completed was Parsons able to see this combination of pattern variables as two independent dimensions. Via the conception of the four dimension poles as *phases* in the action process and a first, rather careless definition of four system problems, there develops the conceptual foundation on which the new version of the action theory is going to be formulated.

Thus the new version of the frame of reference of the action theory starts from two dimensions. Action in general – Parsons usually speaks about the general action system – can thus be divided into four analytical aspects. The most striking thing in the framework of this section is that the *same* emphasis is placed on internal and external aspects of action. The time has passed when only the internal structure of an action system was emphasized. Inasmuch as the accentuation of the internal structure can be regarded as characteristic of the structural-functional theory this is yet another proof that that version of the action theory belongs to the past once and for all.

The two axes of differentiation were looked on by Parsons as independent powers, which meant that if they were combined together, four accents of action would be distinguishable. Figure 4.3 shows the result of thus combining the two axes of differentiation.

	instrumental	consummatory
external	adaptation	goal-attainment
internal	latency	integration

FIGURE 4.3 *The differentiation of action*

This schema is the core of Parsons's 'new' conceptual and substantive work. What, then, is the meaning of these four designations?

'*Adaptation*' refers to that aspect of action which is aimed at 'manipulating' the characteristics of the external environment of the action system in question. In terms of the axes of differentiation it means that aspect of action which is both 'external' and 'instrumental'.

'*Goal-attainment*' refers to that analytical aspect of action which is aimed at satisfying needs' or 'attaining goals'. In terms of the axes of differentiation it means actions or aspects of actions which are both 'external' and 'consummatory'.

'*Integration*' refers to the analytical aspect of action which is concerned with co-ordinating the elements of the particular action system. In terms of the axes of differentiation this means those actions or aspects of action which are both 'internal' and 'consummatory'.

'Latency' refers to the analytical aspect of action which aims at or consists of maintaining the general system pattern; as such, it forms the fundamental source of tension, the 'code', which gives rise to action. In terms of the axes of differentiation it means actions or aspects of action which are both 'internal' and 'instrumental'. Parsons often refers to this last aspect of action with the more lengthy designation of 'pattern-maintenance and tension management'.

He calls this schema the *four-function paradigm*. However, the four 'functions' of adaptation, goal-attainment, integration and pattern-maintenance/tension management are no longer understood in terms of a strictly structural-functional model. The use of the word 'function' has become so stretched that one might just as well speak of 'aspects of the action system'. The concept of function, as it is used here, lacks the typical structural-functional connotations of stability and homeostasis; this implies nothing more than that action cannot exist without one of the four aspects. Thus, in a purely formal sense, the four aspects represent a 'function' of action. In his later work Parsons avoids the misunderstanding that is liable to arise from this designation and, as we shall see, he prefers to speak of the 'interchange'-paradigm.

One of the first results of the conceptualization of this four-function paradigm is that differentiation of action into sub-systems can now be based on uniform criteria. This gives to the definition of action sub-systems the clarity which it hitherto lacked. If we regard the totality of action as a general action-system, the cultural sub-system distils from it the processes of 'pattern-maintenance and tension-management'. For the first time it is now clear that this cultural system abstracts the most fundamental basis from the 'totality' of action; this is why Parsons generally uses the word 'latency' to indicate this aspect.

'Latency' refers to matters which are so common and matter-of-fact that they do not of themselves constitute subject-matter for discussion but do, in fact, make discussion *possible*. And this is what is meant, in terms of the axes of differentiation, by the instrumental character of the sub-system: in a manner of speaking, it provides the 'definition of the situation'. In Parsons's view, the cultural aspect of action, the symbol, fulfils the same function in human action as the 'gene' does in the functioning of the human organism: therefore it refers to the internal aspect of action.

Now, also, the social (sub)system can be defined with the help of the axes of differentiation and the four-function paradigm resulting from it. Henceforth the social system is an aspect of the totality of action – particularly it is that aspect that centres around the integration and co-ordination of human interaction. Thus the social system carries out the 'function' of integration for the totality of action: in other words, in the definition of the social system the integration aspect has pride of place. In terms of the axes of differentiation, integration must be understood to mean internal integration i.e. integration of elements, actions, belonging to the system and also as a directly need-satisfying aspect of action. The third system which Parsons distinguishes, the personality system, can also be fitted into this four-function paradigm. It is the personality system which differentiates the aspect of 'goal-attainment' from the totality of action. After all, says Parsons, it is the motivational orientation of individual actors that forms the motor for all action and every action system. The 'seat' of motivational orientation is within the individual actor. Therefore it is the personality system which fulfils the function of goal-attainment for the totality of action. Goal-attainment is an activity which concerns the relation between systems and environment and is therefore of an external character; at the same time this activity is consummatory and need-satisfying.

Up to now, Parsons has distinguished only three action systems, i.e. the personality, the social and the cultural system. The logic of the four-function paradigm demands the addition of a fourth subsystem. For the fourth 'function' on the action system level, the adaptation function, is still open. When Parsons picks on the 'behavioural system' for this purpose it looks as though he is making a complete *volte-face*.[39] He has always made a sharp distinction between action and behaviour in order to keep away from the behaviourism he so much fears. And now 'behaviour' is to become a very specific analytically-distinguished aspect of action. Is this contradictory? Not at all; it is an important result of a logical development in the action theory which has ceased to be hampered by the polemic attitude of the early period.

A lot of unnecessary discussion between 'behaviourists' and action theoreticians could be avoided if only both parties would recognize the analytical character of their particular activities. 'Behaviourism' in the analytical sense is a very respectable doctrine which concentrates particularly on the physiological, cerebral and motory aspect of human action. It represents an inadmissible reduction in the explanation of human behaviour only when it is reified and given an empiricist meaning. It is this combination of behaviourism and empiricism which Parsons criticizes (c.f. *The Structure of Social Action*). From this point of view it is understandable that the 'behavioural' aspect of action was ignored in the

THE INSTABILITY OF THE STRUCTURAL-FUNCTIONAL VERSION

provisional version but is now, when the behaviouristic moment is being regarded as an analytical aspect (a function) of the general action system, being given a place in the conceptual schema.

In short, Parsons distinguishes from the totality of action a fourth – adaptation – aspect which he calls the 'behavioural system'. The processes that are organized in this 'behavioural system' are of an instrumental nature and indicate the external relation between the particular action system and its environment. When projected on to the axes of differentiation schema, the analytical and functional differentiation of action into action sub-systems can be illustrated as in Figure 4.4.

	instrumental	consummatory
external	A behavioural system	G personality system
internal	L cultural system	I social system

FIGURE 4.4 *Differentiation of the action system*

Thus the four action sub-systems are organized round the four functions as distinguished above, adaptation, goal-attainment, integration and latent pattern-maintenance. This gives a considerably clear picture of action sub-systems than would have seemed possible in the structural-functional period. The social system is now no longer seen as an 'entity' but rather as an aspect or function just like all other sub-systems; this implies that the external relations between the sub-systems are going to form the nucleus of this new version of the action theory. It implies, too, that the definition of the sub-systems will be brought more into line with Parsons's epistemological option of analytical realism: concepts do not formulate concretely demonstrable things or events but abstract aspects of them. The social system formulates, not a concrete group, i.e. a concrete reality in which action occurs, but rather an aspect of action which forms an analytical part and is, in that sense, a function of action in general.

The four-function paradigm is the new frame of reference of the voluntaristic action theory. We have already remarked that this new foundation for the formulation of a voluntaristic action theory has a lot of similarity, particularly with regard to the unit of analysis, to the still largely undeveloped formulae of *The Structure of Social Action* (1937).

If we carry further the comparison between this second frame of reference and the practice runs which preceded the first (bipolar) frame of reference, we see that the similarity is very striking indeed. It is due in the first place to the fact that, in both cases, action or the action system is defined with the help of two dimensions. In *The Structure of Social Action* the dimensions were those of rationality and order; in the four-function paradigm they are the two 'new' pattern variables or axes of differentiation. The similarity, and with it the theoretical continuity between the first cautious formulation in *The Structure of Social Action* and the more definite formulation of this new phase, is most clearly seen when the two definitions are placed diagrammatically next to one another.[40]

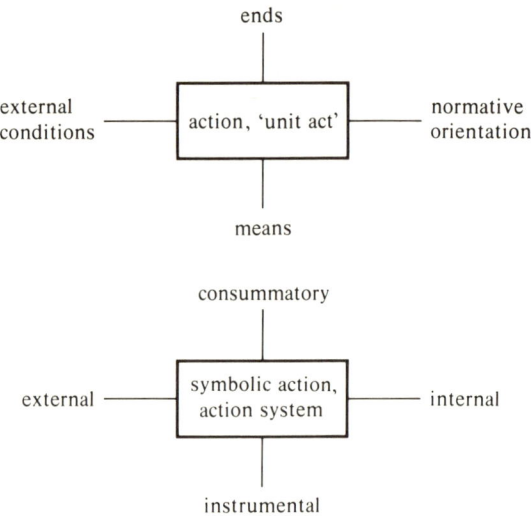

FIGURE 4.5 *Definition of action in 1937 and from c. 1953*

From Figure 4.5 it is obvious that the two dimensions of rationality and order which played such an important part in *The Structure of Social Action* also form the basis of the new action theory.

The dimension of rationality of the 'unit act' returns on the level of the action system in the 'instrumental-consummatory' axis. The 'unit act's' dimension of order returns on the system level in the 'external-internal' axis.

THE INSTABILITY OF THE STRUCTURAL-FUNCTIONAL VERSION

In a manner of speaking, the four-function paradigm could already have been formulated on the level of the 'unit act' in 1937 if Parsons had not then omitted to combine the dimensions of order and rationality with each other in the same way as he combined the axes of differentiation.

This comparison also shows the extent of the detour that Parsons made in order to arrive at a basis for a uniform general action theory. That detour is the structural-functional version of the action theory. The instability of that structural-functional theory lies in a disregard of the problems raised by a direct conceptual elaboration of the dialectic voluntaristic thought-patterns in the framework of a general theory. This leads him to formulate a frame of reference in which the thought-pattern syntheses are translated into conceptual bipolarity. The result of this is the so-called conceptual dilemma and this dilemma is evidenced by many ambiguities and inconsistencies. The fact that this instability has resolved itself, together with structural-functionalism, in the new foundation of the four-function paradigm is a proof that Parsons has continued the attempt to translate his methodological premise of voluntarism into a general and analytical theory and that he has at last succeeded in escaping from the trammels of the conceptual dilemma.

5 The new voluntaristic action theory

1 Introduction: the four-function paradigm and the levels of the action theory

In this chapter we shall show how Parsons elaborates the four-function schema, of itself a fairly simple matter, into a complex and abstract 'grand theory' in which the two central premises of voluntarism and general analytical theory are united. We shall try as far as possible to keep our exposé apart from the commentary as we did in the discussion of Parsons's provisional version of the action theory. Accordingly, this chapter will give a rough sketch of the new voluntaristic action theory and the last chapter will be devoted to an evaluation of that theory in the light of the four pretensions already mentioned.

The four-function paradigm divides action into four analytical aspects which Parsons calls the behavioural system, personality system, social system and cultural system. These four systems must be seen as conglomerations of actions each of which fulfils a particular 'function' with regard to action. That is to say: the behavioural system is a concentration of those facets of action which provide the biological-physical basis of action, the personality system a concentration of need and goal-orientation aspects, the social system one of integration or mutual co-ordination of different interaction partners and the cultural system the aspect of often implicit value-orientations and premises. Each of these four analytical sub-systems forms the subject of a particular analytical discipline (or group of disciplines) all of which are based on one and the same action theory. Parsons regards behaviouristic psychology with its related aspects of physiology, neurology and biology as the central discipline in the study of the behavioural system: functions of the brain, the way the senses work, genetical constitution are important subjects here. Psychology, as understood in the Freudian tradition to be a psychology of the structure of personality, can be defined as the discipline whose subject is the analytical notion of the personality system. The social sciences such as economics, sociology, political science and cultural anthropology are aimed particularly at the interactive aspect of action; the way in which people interact with each other and whether or not they adapt their behaviour to that of others is the central theme of these disciplines. It is more difficult to decide what disciplines are devoted to the study of the cultural system. We can only say that the subject consists of different processes of explaining the meaning of action and interaction and of the foundations on which that explanation or symbolization rests.

But, it may be argued, does not the action theory then in fact consist of four islands which can no doubt be fitted into a beautiful paradigm but whose mutual relations are examined no further? Are we then to consider the four-function paradigm and the action theory based on it to be nothing more than a classification schema?

In this respect the name 'four-function paradigm' is confusing since it does not only concern the functions fulfilled by separate parts of the action system (in other words, it is not a structural-functional schema); it has mainly to do with the way action is made up of the analytical aspects 'together' and in *relations of mutual exchange*. Thus in latter years Parsons speaks more often of the 'interchange paradigm' than of the four-function paradigm.

On the most general level, that of the action system, the action theory consists of a formulation of the exchange relations between the various sub-systems; this logically produces the six exchange relations shown in Figure 5.1.

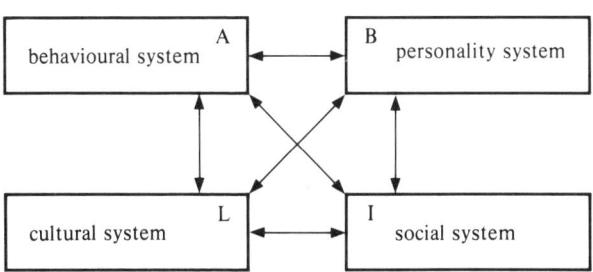

FIGURE 5.1 *The first level of the action theory*

On this level the action theory forms a basis for many disciplines. This implies that Parsons makes a sharp distinction *within the action theory* between the theory of the general action system (level

1) and, for example, the theory of social systems (i.e. one of the theories on level 2). In that way the expression action theory becomes a collective name for all theories operating on the various system levels.

With which existing theoretical interpretations can we compare the most fundamental level of the action theory? Parsons gives a clear answer of this by aligning himself with the work of W. I. Thomas. Thomas is generally looked upon as a social psychologist though he is also respected as a leading figure in sociological circles. But in Parsons's view the question as to whether Thomas is to be called a social psychologist, a sociologist or whatever else is pointless as long as the definitions of these disciplines are as variable as they are at present.[1] In Parsons's system of definition, the work of Thomas and the kind of 'social psychology' as introduced for instance by Cooley and Mead, stand model for the general level of the action theory. In this theoretical tradition, attention is given to the relations between the four primary sub-systems of action. Therefore, in his conceptual formulation of the action theory at this 'highest' level, Parsons intends to include the achievements of this theoretical tradition in the terminology of his 'interchange paradigm'.

This throws light on the significance of various so-called reductionist statements that have been made by social scientists. Parsons mentions two of them. In the first place there is the view of R. F. Bales that 'social psychology' is the most fundamental science of human action. In the second place there is G. C. Homans's view of the laws of psychology that lie at the root of 'elementary behaviour'. In both these views the word (social) psychology is used in a way which, according to Parsons, only makes sense in reference to the first level of the action theory. Bales's and Homans's statement that every theory of social systems can be finally reduced to psychological principles is then identical to Parsons's view that the theory of social systems has its foundations in the most general level of the action theory.[2]

And indeed, in working out the exchange paradigm on the level of the general action system theory, Parsons makes generous use of the concepts which Thomas used. We shall leave for the moment this elaboration of the paradigm, partly because Parsons dealt with it first and foremost on the level of the social system theory but also because it is easier to approach the theory of the action system *via* a discussion of that social system theory.

2 The new theory of social system

The fact that the development of the action theory does not really proceed until the original datum of symbolic action is once again promoted to the status of unit of analysis accords with the circumstance that in working out the four-function paradigm Parsons is greatly influenced by his original interest – the relation between economics and sociology.

In a sense this, too, is a 'return' to the pre-structural-functional period. It will be remembered that, right at the beginning of his career, Parsons seized on the discussion about orthodox and institutional economics in order to oppose their empiricist scientific views on his own analytical realism. In particular, he saw that it was possible to regard orthodox economy as a general and analytical discipline. In fact it is only surprising that Parsons did not even then try to link up with the conceptual structure of that science in a more direct kind of way. Now he is trying to make up for lost time.

In 1956, Parsons published a book with N. J. Smelser in which with the help of the four-function paradigm, they tried to clarify the relations between economic and social science. In this they aligned themselves with Max Weber's *Wirtschaft und Gesellschaft* to such an extent that they used the same title: *Economy and Society* for their own publication.[3] The half-century between the appearance of the two publications has not been favourable to the further integration of sociological and economic theory. On the contrary, according to the authors, after Weber the tendency has been backward rather than forward.[4] The main reason for this divergence of economics and sociology is the scepticism that has always existed in sociological circles with regard to the kind of general theory used in economics.

To Parsons's way of thinking it is precisely this general and analytical character of economic science that makes it a model for the other social sciences. He sees economic theory as one which is concerned with the study of one particular aspect of social systems. Thus it is part of the theory of social systems. How, then, can this social-system aspect which is the concern of economics be interpreted in the framework of a four-function paradigm? Parsons says that if we regard 'society' as the most comprehensive form of social system, we can use the aforementioned differentiation axes to differentiate this most comprehensive interactive system into social sub-systems.

Here again, the four 'functions' of adaptation, goal-attainment, integration and latency can be distinguished, as they were in the general action system. The function of adaptation (or the adaptation aspect) implies the processes of action aimed at producing the means which contribute to the achievement of general societal goals. Direct management processes themselves belong to the function of goal-attainment distinguishable in social interaction. Parsons gives the name of integrative function to the co-ordination of the different elements that play a part in social action; the cultural and motivational standards on which social action is based (e.g. values such as 'individualistic activism') belong to the function of latency.

Parsons gives very specific names to these four functions or aspects on the level of 'society'; henceforth he calls the adaptive function *'economy'* (at least on this level), he calls the goal-attainment function *'polity'*, the integrative function *'societal community'* and the latency function the *'fiduciary system'*.[5] He thinks there is sufficient reason to regard economics as the study of 'economy', i.e. of the adaptive aspect of 'society'.[6] This means that the object of economic theory becomes an analytically differentiated aspect of social action. 'Economy' does not refer to a concrete reality but to analytical aspects of such a concrete reality. In other words, 'economy' is not identical to the conglomerate of businesses, banks, consumers, etc.; if that were so, 'economy' would be a particular *sector* of social action. Not so, says Parsons; 'economy' embraces that aspect of social action which fulfils the adaptation-function for the social system in question ('society'). Thus economic theory, in the analytical sense, concerns the abstract reality aspect which Parsons calls 'economy'. The four-function paradigm makes it clear that 'economy' cannot be studied to any purpose unless relations with the other sub-systems of social action are also examined. Therefore Parsons tries to fit the theory of economics into the theory of social systems by modelling the other sub-disciplines such as sociology on the example of economics. This means that all these social science disciplines are forced up to a higher degree of abstraction than ever before in the history of social science.

This incorporation of economics into a theory of social systems naturally begins with fitting the theory of economics into the four-function paradigm. The result is the conception of three so-called inter-system relations as shown in Figure 5.2.

The obvious question now is how to fill in these three relations. According to both authors, the external relations of the 'economy' are generally conceptualized in the science of economics in terms of inputs and outputs. The imputs in the economy are the so-called production factors. The development of economic theory has led to the differentiation of four of these, *land, labour, capital and organization*. In the 'economy' these production factors, or inputs, are combined together into products, the outputs of the 'economy'.

The question is whether these production factors and outputs of economy can be related to the differentiation of social systems which ensues from the four-function paradigm. For instance, can production factors be regarded as inputs from the three other sub-systems? If this is indeed the case, Parsons has found the key to an adequate elaboration of the action theory at the level of social systems.

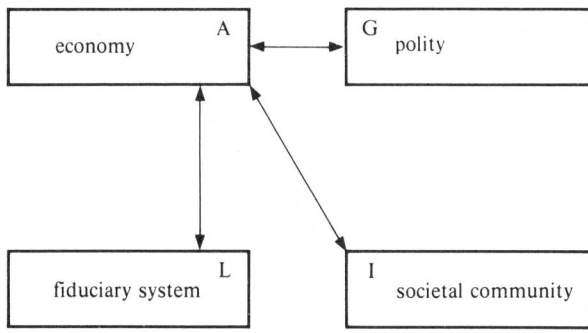

FIGURE 5.2 *The inter-system relations of the economy*

Very briefly, he argues as follows: what, he asks, is the contribution or input that can be made to the economy from the three other sub-systems bearing in mind their analytical definition?[7] From the fiduciary system it must consist of some kind of motivational and cultural involvement. In a way, this L-sub-system is the producer of 'commitments'; it regulates and controls the value-commitment of the interaction partners. When orientated to economy this involvement can be interpreted into the fundamental willingness of actors to offer their labour. The offering of this 'labour factor' expresses the actors' immediate involvement in the goals at which the economy is aiming. Therefore Parsons regards the labour factor as originating in the L-sub-system of society. A large proportion of the processes that occur in this L-sub-system can be placed in the concrete phenomenon of 'family'. It is the family especially, which, *via* the process of socialization and all kinds of control mechanisms, pushes people's individual motivation in particular directions. This does not mean that the 'analytical' L-sub-system is synonymous with the 'concrete' family but that the family occupies an important place in this L-function.

The next question is what contribution could be made to the economy from the sub-system of polity. Polity is the analytically differentiated aspect of interaction processes which is directed to, or is concerned with, the achievement of collective goals. It aims at the 'production' of effectiveness. From this point of view it goes without saying that its contribution to the economy will be in the framework of increasing the latter's effectiveness. Therefore, according to Parsons, it is quite possible to regard the factor of capital as an input from polity. This factor gives the economy the opportunity, as it were, to increase its own effectiveness. Here, too, it is clear that polity and 'government' must not be considered identical. It is true that government has an important place in the processes of polity but it does not exhaust those processes; money-lending institutions such as banks also play their part in this input into the economy of the effectiveness or capital factor.

The integrative social sub-system (the societal community) specializes in a product to which Parsons gives the name of 'solidarity'. In a wide sense this means that the crux of this sub-system consists of processes of mutual adaptation and co-ordination. With regard to the contribution it makes to the economy, this function of co-ordination is translated into the standards with the help of which the economy is able to combine the other factors of production with each other. In economic theory this has been called by the special name of 'organization'.

This way of putting the case presents a problem. In the theory of economics there were four production factors, yet logically there is room in the four-function paradigm for only three inputs. Is this where the theory of economics ceases to run parallel to the four-function paradigm? Parsons does not think so. For the fourth production factor (land) occupies a very special position in the theory of economics. In contrast to the three previously mentioned production factors, the factor of land is not in a direct sense included in the economic schema of supply and demand; it can rather be said to symbolize a set of given circumstances within which the economic process takes place. Those 'givens' need not consist simply of physical matters such as raw materials but also, especially, of cultural value-patterns within which the economic process is framed.[8] Parsons extends the meaning of 'land' as a production factor to include all factors which are not in a direct sense dependent on the economic process and on exchange relations at the level of social sub-systems. The factor of 'land' provides, as it were, the most elementary structure of the economy. Parsons likens it to the programme of a computer; A computer's operations are carried out in the framework of a programme and have no direct influence on that programme. The three factors that fall in the category of 'land'[9]

> are committed to economic production on bases other than the operation of short-term economic sanctions. They are 'fed into' the economic machine prior to current operations; consequently they must be treated as a given determinant of subsequent processes.

Up to now we observe a parallelism between the four-function paradigm on the one hand and the economic theory of production factors on the other. But the parallelism between the four-function paradigm goes further than that. For in economics these inputs or production factors are combined together into 'goods and services'. Thus the production of goods and services is the output of the economy. Can this output be differentiated into social subsystems in the same way as the inputs? Parsons is convinced that it can and his conviction is strengthened by the fact that in economic theory, too, the four production factors are matched by four so-called 'shares of income', i.e. wages (against labour), interest (against capital), profit (against organization) and rent (against raw materials or 'land'). It is true that we are here concerned with a division of economy-output into four monetary, rather than real, elements but that does not alter the fact that the envisaged differentiation of the economy-output appears, in principle, to be possible.[10] What, then, is the aspect of production output that compensates, as it were, for the labour input? In other words, what is the output of the economy to the fiduciary system? Here economic theory points to the supply of goods as the primary output. The fiduciary system, in which as we have seen, the private household plays an important part, receives goods in exchange for the labour it has offered. From the point of view of the four-function paradigm, polity also receives a share of the products or outputs of the economy. The important aspect here is the definition of both economy and polity. For does not the economy produce the means by which the aims of the interaction system can be fulfilled? Thus the 'economy' is of service to the polity and in this light it is understandable that Parsons regards the 'services' which the economy produces as being particularly important in this interchange relationship.[11]

Finally, what share does the societal community receive from the economy's productivity output?[12]

> The answer is based on the fact that the outputs of the economic process . . . have a variety of symbolic meanings throughout the society. Distribution of wealth, for instance, raises many integrative problems. Furthermore, appropriate combinations of goods and services are necessary to symbolize a style of life adequately. In these two respects and many others the economy has integrative significance for the society. The primary output of the economy to the integrative sub-system consist therefore of those *new product combinations* which have symbolic significance in non-economic contexts.

The inter-system relations of the economy are given in Figure 5.3.

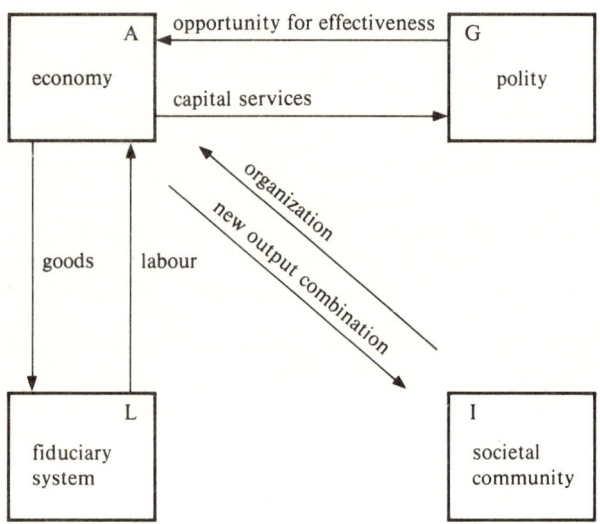

FIGURE 5.3 *The primary interchange relations between the social systems*

But even now, the matrix of societal exchange relations is not complete; for it would be too much of a simplification to suggest that the exchange between, for example, the sub-systems A and L comprises only the categories of goods and labour. In fact, there is no question of a direct exchange of labour for goods and vice versa. In modern society, characterized as it is by a progressive division of labour, the worker in a shoe factory does not receive shoes for wages nor does he pay for his food in kind. In order to simplify exchange relations, modern society uses the 'intermediary mechanism' of money. Goods are bought for money and labour is paid for with money. Thus the exchange relation between A and L appears in Figure 5.4.

Thus the two middle categories point to an intermediary exchange relation which is inserted, as it were, between the primary exchange of goods and labour. Moreover, these two middle categories, spending and wages, point to the symbolic medium of money which regulates the total of exchange relations, the market.

In modern society with its high degree of differentiation, the idea of a market and the freedom of exchange that it implies are not restricted to the A-L relation. They can also be applied to the interchange relation between the sub-systems A and G (economy and polity). Here, too, it is not a question of a simple or 'barter-like' exchange but of a double one in which the exchange of 'oppor-

THE NEW VOLUNTARISTIC ACTION THEORY

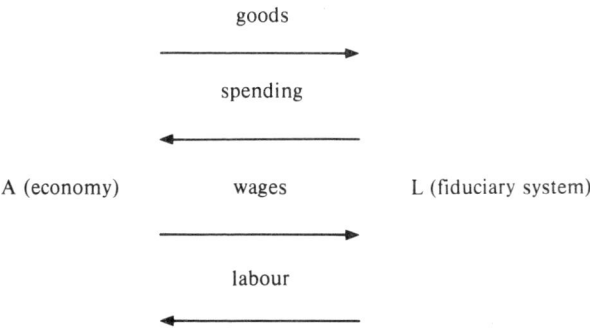

FIGURE 5.4 *The primary and intermediary interchange between A and L*[13]

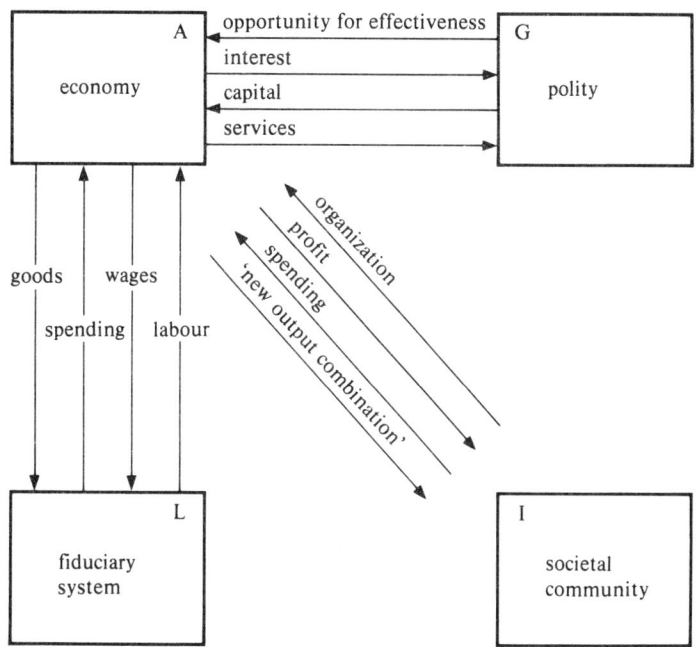

FIGURE 5.5 *The interchange between the economy and the other sub-systems*
(The outer arrows symbolize the primary exchange relations; the inner arrows symbolize the intermediary exchange relations in which money, in one form or another, plays a part.)[14]

tunity for effectiveness' for services is mediated by that of capital for interest. So here again, money is an intermediary mechanism.

The same can be said about the relation between the sub-systems A and L. In a modern, differentiated society it is the medium of money which mediates the primary interchange of movement between the input of organization and the output of new product combinations. The monetary reward for 'organization' is profit whereas the supply of new product combinations is matched by consumer demand (i.e. readiness to spend) for such outputs of the economy. This means that the interchange relations between the economy on the one hand and the three other social sub-systems on the other hand can, in the analytical sense, be divided between three markets each of which consists of a double exchange relation.

Meanwhile it is now becoming clearer why Parsons sees the economy as *part* of the theory of social systems. The theory of economics is principally concerned with only three of the six logically possible markets or interchange-systems. The theory of social systems must be applicable to *all* of those markets.

This means that, disregarding possible overlappings, three such systems of exchange or 'markets' can be studied from the point of view of polity, the societal community and also from the fiduciary system. Apart from the three exchange systems that have to do with the economy and are discussed in *Economy and Society,* Parsons also deals fairly thoroughly with the markets in which the polity plays a crucial part. He considers these three markets to be the principle object of the study of political science. A theoretical sketch of this is given in part IV of Parsons's collection of articles *Politics and Social Structure* (1969)[15] in the same way as it is done for economics in *Economy and Society.*

It took a long time before the exchange systems which centred on the societal community and the fiduciary system were theoretically elaborated and even today, the elaboration is still of a fairly summary nature. Up to now, Parsons's views on this point have been confined to a number of articles.[16]

It would be uneconomical to discuss in the context of this section all these exchange relations and their complicated and abstract terminology. Suffice it for the time being to stipulate that the method used in the theory of economics is the model for elaborating these exchange relations.

3 The social system's symbolic media of interchange: money, power, influence and value-commitment

Because Parsons tries to find the key to a general formula for the theory of social systems in the confrontation between economic theory and the four-function paradigm, it is natural that he should start to wonder whether the so-called intermediary mechanism of 'money' which plays such an important part in the economy's exchange relations, does not have a parallel in the exchange relations of the other social sub-systems. He wonders whether money belongs to a special class of exchange media. The logic of the four-function paradigm clearly encourages this attitude and this inspires Parsons to elaborate[17] on the idea:[18]

> For me the primary model was money . . . but another which has been conspicuous in recent years . . . is language. There has, however, been a tendency to treat each of these phenomena as unique in itself and not related to other phenomena in the action system. This postulate of the uniqueness of money on the one side, language on the other, is one of the traditions which some of us have been challenging. Our attempt has been to treat each of them as members of a much more extensive family of media.

The classical economists, says Parsons, distinguished three functions of the phenomenon of money. In the first place it is a medium of exchange which has *no intrinsic value* but only *value in use*. Compared to the situation of direct, primary exchange between labour and goods, for example, the use of money gives the user more freedom of choice of the goods he desires. Next, money is a *measure* of the value of goods and services which are thus mutually comparable. Finally, money makes it very easy for value to be *stored*.

How can these characteristics of the phenomenon of money be summed up in one common denominator? *The most fundamental characteristic of money as a medium of exchange is its symbolic nature.* The symbolic nature is evidenced by the fact that money has (or need have) no intrinsic value. The value of money is tied to a set of rules and agreements; without those rules and agreements it is worthless even as a medium of exchange. In this symbolic character, a medium such as money may be likened to 'linguistic symbols, [e.g.] the word "dog", though signifying a species of mammalian quadruped, can neither bark nor bite, though the concrete dog can do both.'[19] The relation between the word 'dog' and the animal that it signifies is the same as the relation between money and the value which it symbolizes.

This symbolic nature of the medium overlies four other characteristics. From the above we have already seen that a medium, a symbol, acquires meaning only when it is embedded in a wider *institutional order,* in a set of rules and agreements. For the ordinary man, the institutional order in which the phenomenon of money is embedded is such an objective matter of course that the complicated system of explicit and implicit agreements from which it derives significance often eludes him completely. That institutional order consists mainly of the following three institutions: property, occupation and contract.[20]

In the same way as words acquire communicative meaning by being embedded in a grammatical and syntactic code, so does money acquire meaning as a medium of exchange from a code or institutional context. Thus money becomes equally a medium of communication.

This brings us directly to a second characteristic of this kind of symbolic medium: it acquires significance only in the framework of an institutional code, it has no meaning outside that code. In other words, a medium is characterized by a certain degree of *specificity*.

Thus money is a medium of interchange which has communicative value in some particular interchange relations but has none in a great many others. Diplomas cannot be bought, a doctor's degee cannot be bought and neither can love. In that kind of relation, money as a medium does not 'work' because the institutional code it belongs to does not 'cover' such relations.

The third characteristic of a medium of exchange mentioned by Parsons is that it can be *circulated*. Money in the sense of a set of property rights can be passed from one owner to another and this should be equally true of the other media which play a part on the level of social systems. Control of a certain quantity of the medium can pass from one actor to another. We shall see later how Parsons projects this characteristic on to the other media.

Last, Parsons mentions a fourth characteristic which is obviously derived from the exchange medium of money but which he considers to be valid for other symbolic media as well. He refers to the *absence of the 'zero-sum' quality in the medium*. By this he means that the medium is not tied to a particular unchanging quantity but can increase or decrease in amount. The fact that it can be circulated need not mean that one party loses exactly the same amount of the medium as the other party gains so that on balance, the total quantity remains the same. This characteristic of the money medium is fairly well recognized. Money entrusted to banks by private individuals is lent out again by the banks to institutions or (other) individuals. The 'savers' retain their property rights while the 'investors' are allowed to make use of those property rights. In that way a dual function is fulfilled: in a sense, money is created, the medium of exchange increases.

On the level of the social systems Parsons distinguishes four symbolic media of exchange, each of them an integral part of one of the four sub-systems. The medium that belongs to the economy is, of course, money. That is to say that, in the exchange relations between the economy and the other sub-systems, money plays a dual role. On the one hand, it 'controls' the 'inputs' of the economy; on the other hand, it is a medium in which the 'outputs' of the economy can be expressed. Parsons extends this idea to the other three sub-systems and the other media. Thus, the medium of power, which we shall discuss in the following section, belongs to the sub-system of polity of which it 'controls' the 'inputs' or effectiveness factors while being at the same time a medium by which the polity's outputs are expressed. In the same sort of way, the medium of *influence* is connected to the societal community and that of *value-commitment* to the fiduciary system.

This representation of the situation calls for some further explanation. After all it is most unusual to relate and compare power, influence and value-commitment to the phenomenon of money in this way. There are no examples of it in the tradition of social science; moreover, the strictly analytical character of a theory built around such symbolic media of exchange is a departure from the over-riding tendency in social science to keep as close as possible to 'concrete reality' when it comes to forming concepts.

The considerations which led Parsons to conceive three more symbolic media of exchange on the level of social systems analogous to that of money can, of course, be deduced mainly from the logic of the four-function paradigm: if money is understood to be a 'generalized capacity' in the acquisition of goods, then it is natural to suppose that other such 'generalized capacities' will operate in the realization of effectiveness (polity), the realization of solidarity (societal community) and the implementation of general patterns of value (fiduciary system). As Parsons says, all these analytically distinguishable 'capacities' have up to now nearly always been brought under the common denominator of *power*. In that way, power became a rather diffuse category which was defined as '*any* capacity for an acting unit in a social system to "get what it wants", as Weber said, with or without opposition, in a nexus of social relationships'.[21]

Thus the medium of money has also come to be regarded as a form of power and it has almost become impossible to differentiate between power and influence. *Parsons's definition of power breaks away from this 'diffused' concept;* on the one hand he regards power as a general symbolic medium, i.e. a medium of exchange that is not tied to any special concrete 'particulars'; on the other hand this general symbolic medium is also a very specific 'capacity':[22]

> Power then, is generalized capacity to secure the performance of binding obligations by units in a system of collective

organization, when the obligations are legitimized with reference to their bearing on collective goals and where in a case of recalcitrance there is a presumption of enforcement by negative situational sanctions, whatever the action agency of that enforcement.

What strikes the reader immediately in this definition is that Parsons's concept of power is bound up with the fulfilment of obligations in the framework of *collectivity* and that the exercise of power takes place in a context of *legitimacy*. Both of these facets imply a different attitude to the concept of power from the one generally adopted; Parsons's concept diverges strongly from normal sociological and political usage particularly in its emphasis on the characteristic of legitimacy.

To Parsons, however, this is a logical outcome of his view of power as a separate symbolic medium of exchange: in the same way that money acquires exchange value from its position in an institutional context (property), so does the medium of power acquire meaning and exchange value from its legitimization in the institution of authority. Authority is the code which makes power a significant means of communication.

Thus the relation between Parsons's concepts of power and authority is very different from the 'normal' view of authority as a legitimized form of power. In this latter view, power and authority form the two extremes of the dimension of legitimacy. It sees a crisis of authority as a situation in which the normal subordinative relationship is increasingly considered illegitimate; when the legitimacy of authority is contested in this way there remains only a subordinate relationship based on power i.e. the right of the strongest. Parsons's definitions imply a completely different relation between power and authority. Here, authority is not the legitimized form of power, nor is power the same thing as authority without legitimacy; authority is the code within which power operates and acquires meaning as a medium of exchange. Just as the institution of 'property' forms the framework within which the medium of money becomes significant, so it is the institution of authority which gives meaning to the use of power.[23]

Does all this mean that Parsons is closing his eyes to the non-legitimized forms of power and creating once again the impression that he prefers to regard society as a peaceful Utopia? It would be a mistake to draw such a conclusion. Parsons feels very strongly that his definition of power as a general symbolic medium of exchange helps to resolve the argument as to whether power is based on consensus or on coercion. Completely in accordance with the voluntaristic synthesis, Parsons tries to connect the two aspects – institutional legitimization and coercion. He sees coercion as the 'intrinsic basis' of the medium of power, i.e. when there is resort to coercion in its purest, and therefore physical, form in the process of creating effectiveness, power can no longer be regarded as a 'symbolic' medium of exchange. Indeed, Parsons sees coercion as a 'limiting case' of the medium of power. Power can only be regarded as a *symbolic* medium when its intrinsic basis is wrapped up, as it were, in a complicated set of institutional (or symbolic) rules and agreements.

The parallel with the medium of money will help to explain. The 'intrinsic basis' or value of money lies in the value of the metal from which it is made or which serves to 'back it up'. If ever it were necessary to fall back on the intrinsic value of money it could no longer be regarded as a symbolic medium. The exchange would not be symbolic because *intrinsically valuable things* would be changing hands instead of cultural *expectations* concerning the general exchangeability of the medium. In a modern differentiated society it is normal for the symbolic exchange value of the medium of money to exceed its intrinsic value; this means that money is wrapped up in a complex of institutional expectations of which the most important is that of property. Unless people were confident that the expectations offered in an exchange transaction could indeed be realized (i.e. converted into goods), not many of them would be prepared to buy or sell goods for money.

Confidence in the exchangeability of money has a parallel in the legitimacy of power. Unless the use of power is in one way or another embedded in a set of rules and agreements, the medium loses its surplus-meaning (i.e. the meaning that transcends the intrinsic basis) and also its symbolic character. As we see in our immediate surroundings, power has very often retained its surplus-meaning: effectiveness is not always realized by means of physical coercion; a slight hint is often sufficient to make people act in a certain way.

However, the legitimacy or the degree of institutionalization of power must not be regarded as a constant but only as a variable – and this is the essential element in Parsons's view of power. In the same way as confidence in the symbolic value of money can increase or decline, so can the legitimacy of the wielding of power fluctuate as well. This means that the degree of legitimacy of the institutional code which lends the medium its communicative value is subject to change and also that the exchange value of the medium of power is variable. This leads Parsons to project the analogy of economic theory into the problem of 'zero-sum' – a debatable subject in political science.

Before embarking on this problem we must explain precisely the *exchange character* of the relations involving the medium of power. The comparison between exchanging money for goods and power for subordination, appears to have one obvious fault. When goods are bought for money, that money is transferred to the possession of the seller. Can it then also be said that when binding obligations are imposed by means of power, there is an exchange in the true sense of the word? Does the person who becomes subordinate receive something in exchange? If he does, is it the exchange medium of power which he receives, in analogy with the exchange of money for goods? Is then the exchange medium of power a circulating medium, like money, which can be transferred from one person to another? Curious though it may seem, this is indeed the case. Let us follow Parsons's argument in detail.

In Parsons's opinion, the most significant aspect of the exchange of money for goods and vice versa is its symbolic or communicative character. This means that whereas 'ego' (the buyer) acquires concrete goods, valuable in themselves, 'alter' (the seller) is left with nothing but money which is intrinsically worthless. To put it in a more positive way, 'alter' is offered a set of (symbolic) expectations in exchange for his goods – expectations that this intrinsically worthless money can be reconverted into goods. The same applies to the exchange that involves the medium of power. 'Ego' (the person who wields the power) ensures that certain actions will be performed which are intrinsically valuable to the effectiveness of the system. In exchange, 'alter' receives nothing but an intrinsically worthless medium of exchange, power.

In Parsons's words, this exchange[24]

> leaves the recipient, the performer of the obligation, with 'nothing of value'. This is to say that he has 'nothing' but a set of expectations, namely that in other contexts and on other occasions, he can invoke certain obligations of the part of other units.

On the strength of this parallel Parsons dares to speak of a symbolic exchange, i.e. an exchange of meanings, even in reference to the exercise of power. It might have been less confusing if he had used the expression 'communication' instead of 'exchange'. For to Parsons, the spending of money and the exercise of power are both ways of communicating which take place on the basis of a code. Here the parallel with language is so pronounced that we are not surprised by Parsons's statement, as follows: 'Hence for my purposes, I would like to say not merely that money [and the other media] resembles language, but that it *is* a very specialized language, i.e. a generalized medium of communication through the use of symbols given meaning within a code.'[25]

Thus, the exchange value or communicative meaning of the medium of power is dependent on the degree of institutionalization of the code of authority. Parsons takes the parallel with the medium of money still further and develops a most unusual view on the increase and decrease of the amount of power-medium in circulation. This discussion of the so-called 'zero-sum' problem with regard to power proceeds from the assumption that the total amount of power in the polity can increase or decrease in the same way as money does in the economy. The factors which are responsible for the variability in the amount of power and what names should be given to the processes involved in that variation can only be discussed to any purpose if we use the familiar example of the creation of money and the processes of inflation and deflation connected with them.

The primary economic process can be described as a circular flow of producing and consuming units. Within the framework of a complicated system of constant factors or parameters, the circular flow continues undisturbed; there is an equilibrium in the exchange between input and output of the economy and this means that there is no change, either, in the total amount of money by which this exchange is represented. Nevertheless, it is possible for this equilibrium in the primary 'economic' circular flow between the A and L sub-systems to be 'disturbed'. This disturbance of the normal circular flow between the A and L sub-systems is called the process of investment. This means the provision of financial possibilities to increase production. The banks play an important part in this process by seeing to it that money deposited by individuals does not remain unproductive but is used in the form of capital input to provide opportunities for higher productivity.

Actually, this offering of opportunities is a form of power; it is the phenomenon of power, *in the sense of a symbolic medium of exchange,* which disturbs the equilibrium of the cycle and its monetary aspect. This input of power causes the amount of money in circulation to increase. Thus the exchange medium of power has a controlling or steering function with regard to the economy's productivity; it provides the economy with extra means for increasing productivity. This disturbance of the regular circular flow between the A and L sub-systems is accompanied by two other phenomena, inflation and deflation.

In principle, the concept of a flexible amount of money makes the relation between the exchange value of money and the goods that can be bought with it also a variable one. If the process of creating money is not accompanied by a proportionate increase in production, we have inflation, i.e. a process in which the value of the symbolic medium declines in relation to the goods to be bought.

Money loses its purchasing power. Deflation signifies the opposite situation: a decrease in the total amount of money (e.g. through redemption of credit) causes the value of the medium to rise in relation to the goods to be bought.

To sum up the 'zero-sum' question concerning money we can say that the circular flow between the sub-systems A and L is broken by the input of power; that this starts a process of investment which, in turn, is dependent on the provision of credit, i.e. a growth in the amount of money; that discrepancies between the amount of money and productivity are to be called inflation and deflation.

In this framework we can now turn to a useful discussion of the 'zero-sum' question about power as a symbolic medium.[26] According to Parsons, most political scientists regard power as a phenomenon the quantity of which remains constant; an increase in the power of Mr A is accompanied by a decrease in the power of Mr B so that the sum total of power remains the same. This picture of the situation is based on implicit acceptance of the idea of the circular flow. The political system's circular flow[27]

> is conceived as the locus of the 'routine' mobilization of performance expectations either through invoking obligations under old contractual (. . .) relations, or through a stable rate of assumption of new contractual obligations, which is balanced by the liquidation typically through fulfillment, of old ones.

However, the logic of the four-function paradigm shows that this circular flow, too, can be broken in such a way that − in analogy to the function of banks − power can be 'created' without a decrease in power elsewhere in the system. Parsons situates this 'power bank' in the institution of 'political leadership'. For instance, the political support given to leaders by means of elections results in a kind of process of investment: the chosen leader is placed in a position that can be compared with that of a banker; like the latter, he is able to promote a growth in the quantity of the medium. Instead of simply having to fulfil the demands of his supporters, he also has the opportunity to initiate 'new' projects and to impose binding decisions on his supporters, even though they may not have asked for such decisions to be taken. In this way the total quantity of power is increased and the original circular flow is broken.[28]

In principle, the variability of the total quantity of power contained in a system makes it possible to project the idea of inflation and deflation on to this medium. In the same way that inflation and deflation of money occurs when a discrepancy arises between the growth of money and the growth of productivity, where the medium of power is concerned, a discrepancy can arise between the increase of power and the increase of political effectiveness in a system. In a situation where the creation of power cannot be converted into new, binding obligations, power loses some of its communication or exchange value and inflation occurs. When 'demands' are made on the existing quantity of power-credit, the process of power-deflation occurs.

Power-deflation is a process in which the 'credit' that has been given to political leaders is drawn upon or withdrawn. In this kind of situation, political leaders are held on a very tight rein with regard to their policies and are allowed little freedom of decision. In Dutch politics this process has been very noticeable since the early 1970s; the spiral of power-deflation began with complaints about the so-called political ambiguity. Leaders have been less and less able to prevent their supporters from adding very specific demands to the party programmes; they are expected to choose coalition partners before elections take place and, as leaders, to be what is euphemistically called 'open' to a programme put together by the party members which may vary from really political programmes to various interpretations of the gospel. In short, political leaders are allowed less power-credit, less free rein. There may be a close connection between inflation and deflation of power. No doubt the present deflationary trend has a lot to do with a situation in which (often considerable) power-credit has failed to produce the desired result. One way of reacting is to protest about decisions that have been taken; such decisions are less and less regarded as binding (power-inflation). Another way is to withdraw credit (power-deflation).

So far, two of the four symbolic media have been discussed, money and power. Discussion of the other two follows the same principle.

The third medium to play a part in the interaction process is that of *influence*. Just like the other media already discussed, this medium, too, controls various aspects of the total interaction or social system. The exercise of influence can, in the same way as the use of money and power, be regarded as 'a way of getting results':[29] the spending of money results in control of goods, the exercise of power binds people to decisions; the exercise of influence can persuade people to behave in a particular way not because they are obliged to do so but because they become convinced of the rightness of such behaviour. Thus, influence is equally to be regarded as a medium of communication or exchange.[30]

> Influence is a means of *persuasion*. It is bringing about a
> decision on alter's part to act in a certain way because it is felt

to be a 'good thing' *for him,* on the one hand independently of contingent or otherwise imposed changes in his situation, on the other hand for positive reasons, not because of the obligations he would violate through non-compliance.

What, then, is the consequence of regarding influence as another 'generalized symbolic medium of interchange'? In the first place, of course, it means that a direct form of persuasion linked to one specific situation cannot be regarded as influence. In order for it to be generalized, influence as a medium of exchange must be able to circulate freely without being restricted to strictly defined exchange relations. In other words, a number of degrees of freedom must be incorporated in the concept of influence to ensure that this medium of exchange can be applied in many different directions. This general character of the medium of influence is expressed most clearly in the concept of 'reputation': people are more readily convinced by someone with a great reputation for expert knowledge, reliability, etc., than by another who lacks such a reputation.[31]

Then there is the symbolic character of the medium of influence. Just as in the case of the other media, influence has outgrown its intrinsic basis in a strongly differentiated society. The intrinsic basis of this medium, Parsons suggests, can be found in a 'common belongingness in a *Gemeinschaft* type of solidarity [that] is the primary "basis" of mutual influence, and is for influence systems the equivalent of gold for monetary and force for power systems.'[32] For Parsons, it is the primary relations of solidarity like those within the family which form the basis for the medium of influence. However, if influence and the processes of mutual conviction are enacted only on the fringe of the *Gemeinschaft* relation, their symbolic significance is limited. In modern society the medium of influence reaches far beyond the primary relations of solidarity. In the course of its development it has acquired a degree of freedom with regard to its strict *Gemeinschaft* basis. In other words it begins to operate in a market. By this means, influence can play an active part in wider systems of communication as well. Of course, the increased freedom (and with it the symbolic meaning of the medium) still goes hand in hand with the development of a set of institutional regulations. Without an institutional code, influence as a medium of exchange is worth as much as 'suspect' currency or unlegitimized power: it then reverts to its intrinsic basis. For Parsons, the institutional code that gives influence its symbolic meaning consists mainly of a set of attitudes which regulate the ways in which people ought to, or are able to, associate with one another.

In this case, Parsons sees the right of free association as an institution parallel with those of property and contract where money is concerned and with authority with regard to power.[33]

It is just because of this freedom of association, which lends importance to other than primary *Gemeinschaft* relations, that relations of influence, or rather of persuasion, begin to develop far beyond the original primary goods.

However, this does not invalidate the principle that influence and persuasion remain tied to a certain degree of mutual attachment; new 'in-groups' are constantly being formed through all different kinds of association. It is only by creating this sort of collective attachment that interaction partners acquire the 'right to persuade' each other.

The total quantity of the medium of influence, like that of the other media, is also variable. Here too, the circular flow of the 'power' of persuasion that is 'normal' to the system can be disturbed and influence can be created or destroyed.

In his article 'The Matthew Effect in Science', Merton gave what Parsons considered to be one of the better examples of the process of influence creation:[34]

> In this paper Merton analyzes the 'reputations' of Nobel Prize winners as evidenced by references to their work in the scientific literature. His finding is that these reputations have been on the average substantially enhanced following the receipt of the award. Clearly this cannot be accounted for by actual improvement in the quality of their scientific contributions – Merton carefully considers this possibility – but must derive from their membership in the very select company of Nobel laureats. We interpret this finding to mean that the Nobel awards serve to create influence which is placed in the hands of the actual scientists, and through them enhances the prestige of the type of scientific contributions which their work exemplifies. This should then be a net addition to the volume of influence circulation in the scientific world.

Because the medium of influence is variable, processes of inflation and deflation can occur. Influence deflation means that the quantity of the generalized medium has decreased. In other words, the criteria by which a person can reach an 'influential' position and make a reputation for himself have become more narrowly defined. The number of group loyalties has decreased; large sections of what used to be the 'in-group' now belong to the 'out-group'.

This kind of influence-deflating process can be observed in various social organizations. In the Churches, the universities and the different political parties 'reputations' are destroyed by the hundred. Members of such organizations tend to be extremely particular in the matter of loyalty and it is often a case of 'He who is not for me is against me.' In other words, the basis for association is restricted and becomes more like a *Gemeinschaft* solidarity. There is no place for persuasion and influence except along very narrowly defined party-lines. The exercise of influence on more universalistic grounds, such as the power of argument, becomes relatively unimportant. As an example, Parsons often refers to McCarthyism in the United States – a political movement which set out to diminish relations of loyalty and solidarity, to reduce the credit of influence.[35]

If influence deflation indicates a process in which the generalized persuasive power of reputations is reduced, influence inflation is a situation in which the creation of new influence fails to coincide with an expansion of the power to convince which holds good for the system.

We have already shown that the medium of influence, like the other media, can, in principle, vary in quantity. When this happens, there is a break in the balanced circular flow formed by an unvarying quantity of influence. The question as to why this break occurs still remains to be answered. It is natural that Parsons should look for some institution which operates as a kind of 'influence bank'. The analogy with banking as a monetary institution leads him to the conclusion that 'voluntary association' fulfils the same function in respect of the medium of influence. He compares the members of such an association with investors in a bank. They each place their own particular amount of influence in the hands of the association, and of its leaders in particular.

This makes it possible for the top men of the association or society to use whatever amount of influence is deposited with them to induce others to act in a certain way and to persuade them of the rightness of their action without consulting their members. In this way fresh influence is added to the amount that already exists.[36]

The last of the media to be discussed on the level of social systems is that of value-commitment. The context in which this concept becomes significant is rather complicated and requires some explanation. In the same way as the other three media are rooted in the social sub-systems of economy, polity and the societal community respectively, so is the medium of value-commitment rooted in the fiduciary system. This immediately raises the acute question as to how far we can distinguish between the general social patterns of value which are at the heart of this sub-system and value-commitment as a medium.[37]

A general pattern of value has no operational significance until it is translated into specific situations. Part of this specification has already been discounted in the value-orientations that form the basis of the other three social sub-systems, i.e. productivity, effectivity and solidarity. In fact, these three principles give an indication as to how the general value-pattern is 'filled in'. For instance, one of the general value-patterns of this modern era is 'individualistic activism' which plays an important part in Parsons's views on the development of modern society. This value-pattern acquires concrete meaning only in its implementations; even the specification of the general pattern into productivity, effectiveness and solidarity remains very formal and gives no clear idea of the concrete institutional lines along which action moves.

It is especially on this dimension of generalization *versus* specification that the concept of value-commitment as a medium of exchange becomes meaningful; it is 'a generalized capacity to effect the implementation of values'.[38]

Value-commitment as a symbolic medium of exchange or communication can be seen as the medium which controls the way in which values become concrete in interactions. The general character of this exchange medium ensures that the actor in the collectivity has a degree of freedom to make up his, or its, own general value-pattern. There are hardly any societies or other concrete social systems with so little differentiation that they decree *exactly* the way in which values have to be implemented or specified. The strongly differentiated character of modern society requires the functioning of such a medium of exchange: for the process of specification of general values by the participants in an interactive system is wrapped up with a complicated totality of unforeseeable 'exigencies' which necessitate continuous adaptation.

Value-commitment is a symbolic as well as a generalized medium. Just like the other media, it too has grown out of its intrinsic basis – a basis which, for this medium, consists of fundamentalism or value-absolutism, i.e. the complete absence of freedom in the implementation of value-patterns.

Thus value-commitment is 'used' by the participants in the social system to implement values. The fact that the medium can be circulated means that some persons or institutions have more value-commitment than other persons or institutions. Therefore these are the people or institutions which are able to come forward as society's moral leaders; they are the ones best able to decide what are legitimate forms of value-implementation. But such institutions have yet another function – that of influencing the quantity of the medium in circulation.[39]

I should like to suggest that institutions possessing marked 'moral authority' in societies, may on the one hand function as relatively 'custodial' guardians of unit commitments, but that on occasion they may engage in the innovative extension of commitments with the consequence of reorganizing the value-institutionalization system.

Parsons regards Weber's view of charismatic leadership as one of the most significant sociological formulations of the process of creating value-commitment.

He, Parsons, emphasizes that the charismatic breakthrough did not, as is so often suggested, imply a complete change in the general value-pattern. If that were the case, the charismatic leader would not last long; there would be a 'run' on the charisma's commitment bank which, like every other bank in similar circumstances, would very soon become insolvent.[40] According to Parsons, these charismatic movements only add to the existing system of implementation possibilities. In that sense, the amount of value-commitment is increased.

This brings us to the processes of inflation and deflation. The creation of value-commitment as a medium of exchange can coincide with an increase or decrease in the extent to which value-commitment might result in moral obligations. Inflation, then, refers to an increase in 'commitments' which remain unfulfilled. In the case of charismatic movements, inflation can be measured by the extent to which new pretensions are, or are not, embedded in a set of institutional procedures: there is no question of inflation when the new ways of implementation have, in Weber's terminology, become 'routinized'.[41]

Deflation in the medium of value-commitment means, just as it does in the other media, a reduction of degrees of freedom. In the particular case of value-commitment it means that the possibilities for implementation are limited. This kind of deflationary process may be the result of an inflationary increase in the total amount of value-commitment; when promises are not fulfilled and are not routinized in an institutional framework, traditionalistic or fundamental counter-movements may develop which will impose very rigid restrictions on the different ways of implementation so that individual behaviour is squeezed into a narrow straitjacket of norms.[42]

This completes our introduction of the four symbolic media of exchange present in the social system. Parsons's original idea that the exchange medium of money is not a unique phenomenon but rather part of a larger group of media led eventually, and by way of an often complicated conceptual operation, to the symbolic media being fitted into the four-function paradigm.

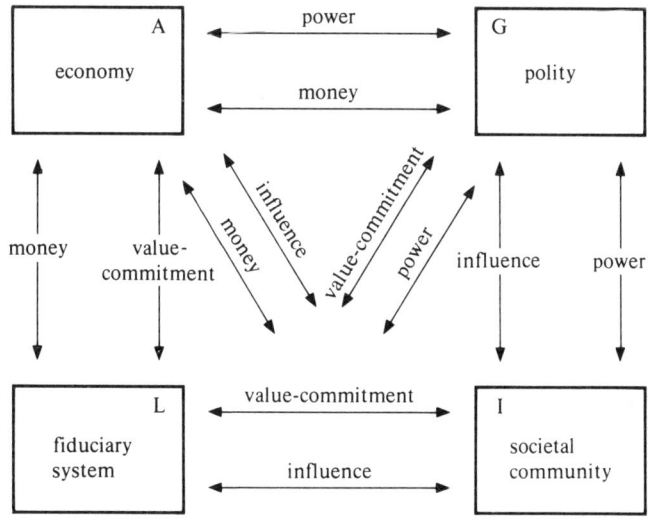

FIGURE 5.6 *The interchange paradigm with respect to media*

There is one aspect of this which should be noted in particular. The symbolic media are regarded as means of exchange through which certain 'things can be done'; money 'controls' the acquisition of goods, labour, etc.; power, influence and value-commitment also control a number of concrete ways of interacting. But, apart from this, the relations of exchange between the four primary social sub-systems can also be effected directly via the media. Figure 5.6 illustrates this double exchange on the level of the symbolic media.

4 Hierarchical relations between sub-systems and media

In a number of formulations, particularly those concerning the expansion of the amount of medium, there is implicit acceptance of an aspect of the cybernetic arrangement that exists between the sub-systems. The idea of a circular flow with regard to the circulation of money was only partially valid in the framework of the four-function paradigm; the circular flow was interrupted by the input of a phenomenon controlled by the medium of power, 'opportunity for effectiveness'. The same thing applied to other imaginable circular flows or systems of equilibrium. They were all interrupted by the input of a so-called 'medium of a higher order'. What does Parsons mean by this hierarchy?

The hierarchy of media stems from the general hierarchical element which Parsons ascribes to the four-function paradigm itself. The differentiations A, G, I and L stand in a particular hierarchical relation to each other *regardless of the level* which they concern. In order to eliminate any deterministic view of the inter-system relations Parsons here refers to a *cybernetic hierarchy*. This cybernetic hierarchy shows the sequence in which the sub-systems *control* each other. The highest place in this hierarchy of control is occupied by the L-system or sub-system. Continuing for a while our reference to the social system, we observe that the highest controlling or cybernetical function in the process of human interaction is carried out by the value-patterns of a society. Value-commitment in the sense of a general capacity to implement values is thus the medium which, cybernetically, fulfils the most important steering function in comparison with the other media. It is followed in the cybernetic hierarchy of control by the integrative sub-system and the medium of influence, then by the polity and the medium of power and, last, by the economy and the medium of money.

The character of this cybernetic arrangement of the four functions of the paradigm should be well understood. In particular, the high score of the L-function sometimes gives the impression that Parsons's theory of social systems should be regarded as a so-called value theory. This is an unjustifiable criticism of the new version of the action theory; although values *control* and direct the process of interaction, they do not *determine* it. The values of a society act as a code within which concrete interactions take place. But the concrete shape of society is no more determined by its values than is the content of a message determined by the grammatical code. The non-deterministic character of the cybernetic hierarchy of control implies the existence of another hierarchy, that of *conditioning factors*. In Parsons's opinion, control and conditioning are opposing, complementary processes. The implementation of values takes place within a set of 'objective' conditions affecting action. Here too, the scale of conditions can be arranged in a kind of hierarchical order. Projected on to the four functions of the interchange paradigm, this hierarchy is opposite to the hierarchy of control. At the top of the hierarchy we now have the A-function (and with it the A-sub-systems on their respective levels), followed by the G-, I- and L-functions.

With regard to the level of social systems, the highest conditioning factor in society is the economy which occupies a subordinate position (i.e. a more or less operative one) in the hierarchy of control. In contrast, the most important type of control is formed by the fiduciary system which contains, as it were, the very nature of society. Nevertheless, within the frame of the social system, this sub-system has no conditioning or determining influence.

The standard example of this kind of relation is the thermostat which is programmed in a particular way in order to 'control' the temperature of a central heating boiler and keep it within certain limits. In terms of a cybernetic relation the thermostat is therefore 'above' the boiler. Nevertheless, the process of control takes place within a set of objective conditions; for instance, no thermostat can release the air from a heating system or reignite the pilot light. It is for the boiler to supply 'energy' and for the thermostat to 'inform' the boiler just when to do so.

5 The general theory of action

Most attention so far has been given to the way the four-function paradigm was worked out on the level of the theory of social systems. This theory is only one of the specialisms in the wide range of Parsons's action theory — specialisms which can themselves be differentiated. Figure 5.7 illustrates the limitations of the social-system theory; it shows the various disciplines according to the lines of the four-function paradigm.

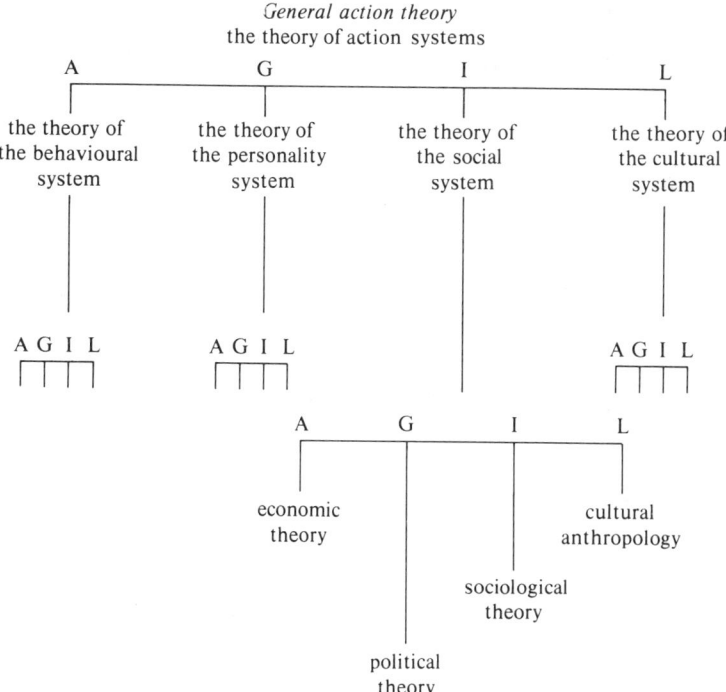

FIGURE 5.7 *The action theory and its differentiations*

This figure shows too, how Parsons's theoretical activity has left gaps in the theory of the social system itself. Thus, it is true that he has designed a schema of exchange relations for the processes *between* the primary sub-systems of society as the most widespread social system, together with the respective paradigm of symbolic exchange media, but his subsequent elaboration towards the lower level of the differentiations themselves is quite summary.

In the case of the other three primary theoretical systems in the framework of the action theory, there are far more blank spaces. The fact that Parsons has indeed ventured into some of these fields is more significant as an illustration of the possibilities offered by the four-function paradigm than as a well-considered theoretical contribution. It represents a kind of invitation to students of the various disciplines in the field of action to delve deeper into the possibilities of the paradigm and to contribute in that way to the integration and unity of science.

We are left now with the most general level of the action theory, the theory of action systems. As we remarked at the beginning of this chapter, the development of this level of the action theory is linked to the tradition of social behaviourism as expounded by Cooley, Mead and Thomas. The theory of the action system gives a formulation of the fundamental relations between the various analytical aspects of action. The relations between the four 'functions' or aspects of the action system constitute the most important theme of this theory. Between the four functions, the behavioural system, the personality system, the social system and the cultural system, it is possible to differentiate six exchange systems which are regarded as 'markets' in pursuance of the theory of social systems.

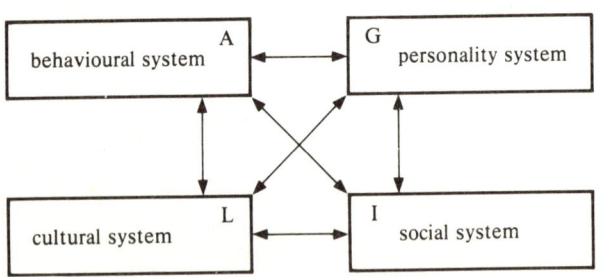

FIGURE 5.8 *The general action system*

The use of the idea of market on the level of the action system has a number of implications. In the first place it means that it is, in principle, possible to construct a scheme of concrete interchange relations in the same way as for the social system. Second, the idea of a market suggests degrees of freedom in respect of exchange relations and also the possibility of conceiving four symbolic exchange media on this level.

Just as in the case of the social system, it would be too much to discuss in this section all these exchange relations separately. Suffice it to say that the logical structure of this exchange schema is identical with that of the social system.

We shall now examine in greater detail the second implication, the conception of four symbolic media. In an analogous way to the procedure he adopted with regard to the social system and its symbolic exchange media, Parsons also tries to fill out the four-function paradigm on the level of the general action system with a schema of four symbolic exchange media each of which is anchored in one of the differentiated sub-systems.

Again, the symbolic media are regarded as circulating media with very little, if any, intrinsic value but which are important because of the fact that they can be translated into many very specific 'particulars'.

Where does Parsons 'happen' to find these media? It is especially on this point that the work of W. I. Thomas has eased the way to conceptualization of the action system theory.

Before confronting the reader with Thomas's work we would point out that the media to be newly constructed have the same characteristics as the media on the level of the social system; they are general rather than specific, they are of a symbolic nature and have therefore no intrinsic value, they circulate in the action system and function with other media in exchange traffic, as media they can fluctuate in 'quantity' and can therefore be involved in inflationary and deflationary processes.

It would serve little purpose to discuss all these characteristics of symbolic media for every medium separately; this chapter is long enough without repetitions. For this reason we shall discuss only the first medium in detail so that the others can be dealt with in a more summary manner.

In his famous work, *The Unadjusted Girl*,[43] W. I. Thomas mentions four fundamental desires or orientations which inspire and direct human action: the desire for response, for recognition, for new experiences and for security. Thomas formulated this schema of 'wishes' with the particular purpose of stressing that the behaviouristic tendency to explain action by 'instincts' gives insufficient recognition to the subjective motivational orientation which is inherent in action. He discussed the specific manifestations of these four wishes with the help of a large number of examples. Parsons is greatly impressed by Thomas's social behaviourism and feels that his (Thomas's) classification of general human 'needs' has such depth of validity that it cannot be ignored in an elaboration of the action theory. This means that Parsons has to find out whether, and to what extent, this schema of the 'four wishes' can be related to the four-function paradigm and, more especially, to the idea of general symbolic exchange media.[44]

Let us first consider the wish for new experiences on the one hand and the wish for security on the other hand. Parsons sees both these wishes as different aspects of one and the same fundamental human problem, the question of how a person will react to his external, or natural, environment: will he venture on a rational manipulation of that environment and thus break out of his present situation, or will he prefer not to take such risks but to accept as far as possible the security of his familiar surroundings? Both possibilities refer to the same fundamental aspect of action, namely the adaptation aspect (in terms of the four-function paradigm). Parsons identifies the behavioural system as the adaptation aspect of action; by this he means those processes which precede the realization of goals and which even constitute conditions for the realization of those goals. On the level of action these functions generally have a physical-neurological context. They are sensory processes which originate in the nervous system. In other words, the adaptation function on the level of action is concerned with a conglomeration of processes around awareness of one's external environment, discrimination of objects in that environment and the solution of general cognitive problems. Parsons formulates this 'function' as 'the capacity of an acting unit, usually the individual, effectively to mobilize the resources requisite to the solution of cognitive problems.'[45] He uses the term 'intelligence' to describe this capacity. At the same time he regards intelligence as a symbolic medium. For the only alteration effected in the above description of the adaptation function on the level of action by the conception of intelligence as a symbolic medium is the addition of the word 'generalized'. A symbolic medium is invariably a 'generalized capacity'; i.e. a medium which, in principle, controls a large number of 'particulars' whereby it can be 'used' in various different ways as means of exchange or communication.

Thus intelligence as a symbolic medium embraces the two wishes for new experiences and for security which are included in Thomas's schema of the 'four wishes'. Like every other medium, it links a material or organic facet of action to a cultural or symbolic superstructure. In the case of the medium of intelligence, that material basis consists of the objective conditions or possibilities in the human nerve system (brain capacity). The cultural superstructure of the medium consists of an institutional code which makes it possible to 'spend' intelligence on knowledge in general 'independent of any particulars of knowledge'.[46]

The fact that Parsons puts intelligence in the behavioural system and not in the personality system does not mean that the intelligence which a person possesses must be regarded as invariable. Just like every other medium intelligence, too, can fluctuate in quantity. As we have already seen in respect of the social system, any idea of equilibrium or regular circular flow must be treated with the greatest of caution. On the level of action it is possible for the total quantity of intelligence in one unit to increase or decrease by means of the exchange relations which constitute action.

In analogy with banking in the economic sense, Parsons distinguishes the institution of intelligence bank. This intelligence bank is able to cause an increase in the total quantity of intelligence circulating in the action system (individual or collectivity). This means that the 'generalized capacity' to solve cognitive problems becomes greater. One of the institutions which carries out this function of banking is the university, 'the operations of which under favourable conditions, result in net increases in the amount of intelligence circulating in the system.'[47]

Thus the answer to the 'zero-sum' question is the same in the case of the intelligence medium as in that of the other media we have discussed. This medium is equally subject to the processes of inflation and deflation. An example given by Parsons of intelligence inflation is that of the recent expansion of higher education:[48]

> In the face of rapid expansion of higher education intelligence inflation was created. The resources necessary for the increase in the volume of knowledge and in its diversification were not, and probably could not be, increased rapidly enough to meet the demand; the effect was an upward price spiral for knowledge, that is, an increasing amount of intelligence was required for advancing and disseminating the same output of knowledge. The consequence was a depreciation of the unit of value of intelligence.

There is no doubt that intelligence deflation may be one of the reactions to such a depreciation in the medium. Are not deflationary processes generally the result of declining confidence in the symbolic significance of the medium? A concomitant of this is often a relative increase in the symbolic significance of other media. Once again Parsons gives the example of the university where, after the period of rapid expansion and the accompanying intelligence inflation, confidence in the significance of cognitive problem-solving has declined considerably in favour of non-cognitive, and particularly 'affective', activities.

The use of the four-function paradigm necessitates the formulation of three more exchange media analogous to that of intelligence. Parsons relates these three media as well to Thomas's categories. Thus, for example, Thomas sees the manifestation of the 'wish for recognition' in 'the general struggle of men for position in their social group, in devices for securing a recognized enviable, and advantageous social status'.[49]

Parsons is chiefly concerned with the origins which give rise to this kind of social action. These origins are generally to be found in an urge to achieve i.e. in a motivation to attain goals and to 'achieve' in that very general sense. In the four-function paradigm this orientation to the satisfaction of needs lies in the G-function and thus, on the level of the action system, in the personality system. The urge to achieve is the same thing as the 'capacity' to satisfy needs or to achieve goals, as the case may be. When the urge to achieve is no longer restricted to *particular* achievements but becomes more general – 'capacity' becomes 'generalized capacity' – then we can say that a symbolic medium exists; Parsons speaks in this respect of 'performance capacity'.[50]

The character of performance capacity as a medium is expressed in Weber's publication of the Protestant ethic. The activism so characteristic of both the Calvinistic mentality and capitalism is in fact a generalized urge to achieve; it is not restricted to fully specified activities but can be fulfilled in innumerable ways. This exchange medium, too, can increase in quantity and is therefore subject to the processes of inflation and deflation.

Of Thomas's schema of 'four wishes' there remains only the desire for response. According to Thomas, this desire 'is primarily related to the instinct of love, and shows itself in the tendency to seek and to give signs of appreciation in connection with other individuals.'[51] It indicates the reciprocity of affective relations, the 'need' to be absorbed into a unified society. In the terms of Parsons's four-function paradigm, this desire runs parallel to the integrative function or the social system dimension. The integrative aspect of action consists of the 'capacity' to achieve interactive relationships and to attune the different elements of the action system one to the other. What Thomas calls a desire or a wish is formulated by Parsons as a function or capacity.

This integrative capacity too can be generalized to a general symbolic medium which is of course characterized by a certain freedom of use; it is not restricted to any specific 'particulars' but can be concretely evinced in a number of ways of acting. Parsons uses the word 'affect' to describe this medium, which is anchored in the social system: it is the 'generalized capacity' of interaction partners to integrate.

Thomas suggests that the material basis of this fundamental desire lies in the erotic complex. Parsons agrees with him. On that intrinsic basis a complex of symbolic meanings has evolved which has given affect an importance as a freely circulating medium in many forms of association besides the strictly erotic. The effect of this medium in the process of co-ordination is variable. As a circulating medium its absolute quantity can be increased by the process of affect creation. The possible discrepancy which may then arise between the increase of the generalized medium and the extent to which it fulfils its co-ordinative function is the process of affect-inflation. In contrast, the deflationary process robs affect of some degrees of freedom and brings it closer to its intrinsic basis.

The four-function paradigm suggests a fourth symbolic medium. Thomas's schema of the 'four wishes' appears not to offer any connecting link here; the four wishes have already been translated into the terms of the four-function paradigm and Thomas's schema is thereby exhausted. However, if we look at the nature of the sub-system in which this fourth medium must be anchored (the cultural system), we can at least give a definition of the capacity or function of this system. For we are concerned with the 'latent' cultural basis, the most general forms of symbolization which lie at the root of action. In a manner of speaking, this system contains the symbolic code which is specified in the codes of the other sub-systems.

In the same way as value-commitment as a medium of the social system, so too must the symbolic medium with which we are here concerned be placed on the dimension of the specification of the general latency pattern. Thus the medium might be described as the 'generalized capacity' to specify the symbolic code of the action system (comparable to the DNA-molecule or the biological gene) to more concrete situations. With this definition, Thomas's schema of categories suddenly seems to offer an adequate connecting link in this respect when he coins the notion of 'definition of the situation'. To Thomas, this definition of the situation is equally a sort of code which precedes the designation of the four fundamental desires.[52] This completes the parallel between his scheme of categories on the one hand and Parsons's four-function paradigm on the other; on the level of the action system the 'definition of the situation' fulfils the latency function. As a 'generalized capacity' this definition of the situation can be seen as a symbolic medium. It is a medium of exchange which contributes to the specification of the symbolic nature of action in the exchange with other media.

These four symbolic media control the exchange relations that take place between the four action sub-systems. The identification of the six logically possible exchange systems and their elaboration to the level of direct exchange relations represent the most important direction for the action theory to take at this moment.

This, then, is the extent of our exposé of the new version of the action theory. In many respects this new version is still incomplete. However, as we shall show in the following chapter, this action-theoretical version, in spite of its incompleteness, still represents a more adequate fulfilment of Parsons's pretensions than did the structural-functional one.

6 Testing the theory against its premises

1 Introduction

In the previous chapter, the new action theory was introduced by means of four of its central themes: the four-function paradigm, the differentiation of various levels of the action theory, the conception of symbolic exchange media and the double hierarchy incorporated in the four-function paradigm. All of this represents only a rough outline of the new version. There were two reasons why the presentation was of necessity incomplete. In the first place, Parsons's action theory has not yet been conceptualized on all levels and differentiations. Second, we were unable in the space of one chapter to do justice to all the nuances characteristic of the theory formulated thus far. Yet these limitations need not prevent us from answering the crucial question of this final chapter, which is this: *does the new version of the action theory represent a better conceptual translation of the epistemological and methodological premises than did the structural-functional version?*

So far we have only ascertained that the development of this new version was made possible by the transcendence of the conceptual dilemma contained in the first elaborated voluntaristic frame of reference. As long as the formulation of the action theory was entangled in this conceptual dilemma, Parsons's epistemological and methodological premises could not be upheld simultaneously. Since the dilemma has been solved it is now possible, at least in principle, to fulfil the premises simultaneously and in combination with each other. This does not, however, answer the question as to whether Parsons does, in fact, make use of the possibility. In order to answer that question the new theory – and in particular the four central themes of the theory mentioned above – must be tested against its premises.

TESTING THE THEORY AGAINST ITS PREMISES

This testing will be the main subject of the following section. In section 3 we shall see how our interpretation compares with a number of the best-known and most widely read criticisms of Parsons's action theory. Our plan of interpretation and the conceptual dilemma both play an important part in this comparison.

2 The premises and the new theory

The premises which Parsons formulated at the beginning of his career are of two kinds, the epistemological and the methodological. From an epistemological point of view Parsons thinks that the action theory should be of a general and analytical nature; from the methodological point of view it must do justice to both the voluntaristic patterns of thought. So it follows as a matter of course that in this paragraph we shall discuss the four different premises in turn and see whether we can rediscover them in the four themes – the four-function paradigm, the conception of different levels, the idea of symbolic media and the notion of a double hierarchy.

The general character of the new version

We pointed out in the first chapter that Parsons's pretension to generality concerns not only each separate concept but also the complex of inter-related concepts called *theory* or discipline.[1]

His pretension to generality in respect of the separate concept becomes apparent in his discussion of Weber's ideal types. In that discussion he shows that Weber introduces the ideal types in order to resist the individualizing tendency in conceptualization to be found in the idealistic or historicist tradition. Throughout Parsons's development, including the structural-functional version, it was never a problem for him to realize this facet of the pretension to generality. His concepts were always the 'universals' which embraced a multitude of concrete 'particulars'; this applies to the first elaborated frame of reference, to the concepts in the structural paradigm (the pattern variables) and to the dynamic-functional categories in the motivational paradigm.

In the new action-theoretical version this situation remains unchanged; it may even be that the general character of the concepts stands out more clearly. Thus the four-function paradigm consists of four functions which can be projected on to any concrete action system and thereby acquire a specific content of their own, depending on the particular action system concerned. The idea of levels within the action theory also emphasizes the general character of the four-function concepts: for the empirical referent of the function varies with the level of action. The general character of the concepts used is very clearly expressed in the idea of symbolic media; definition of the media includes the information that they are 'universals', 'generalized capacities' which are able to control a number of concrete actions. Finally, the conception of the cybernetic hierarchy, far from being restricted to concrete and special action, concerns a general formula which can be applied on all levels and differentiations.

However, when the pretension to generality is projected on to the theory or discipline in the sense of a coherent totality of concepts, it is apparent that Parsons found it difficult to fulfil that pretension. In the structural-functional period the pretension to generality became entangled with the conceptual dilemma and this led to a conflict with the conceptual translation of the two voluntaristic patterns of thought. The results of this could take three different directions and lead respectively to obscurity, one-sidedness or 'complementarity' of the action theory. Parsons regularly refers to his structural-functional theory as a general theory of action; this means that, at this period he has not yet noticed the constrained situation in which he is placed on the level of conceptual theory. It also means that in the structural-function version of the action theory, aspects of all three abovementioned offshoots of the conceptual dilemma are beginning to show. The most important offshoot with regard to the generality premise is that of the so-called complementarity of the structural-functional version. This complementarity can be seen in a number of perspectives or points of view which compete with each other in the framework of the structural-functional theory. Therefore we have decided that the structural-functional theory of action should really be seen as a sort of federative system of various different theories. There is actually no question of one general theory; multi-perspectivism is irreconcilable with the pretension to generality.

In the new voluntaristic frame of reference – the four-function paradigm – this perspectivism has disappeared. The four-function paradigm sees action only from the overall point of view of 'symbolic' action; orientation and situation, formerly two rival perspectives whose mutual relation was obscure, are united in the symbolic nature of action. Now the idea of different system levels takes the place of the perspectivism of orientation and situation. What used to be a conflict of perspective in the structural-functional period – for example, the subjective or 'social behaviouristic' point of view as opposed to the standpoint of an objective system structure – is replaced in the new version by the differentiation of one and the same theory into the level of the general action system and the level of the social system respectively.

Differentiation of system levels means that Parsons's claim to generality reaches beyond the boundaries of the various human sciences. The essence of this far-reaching claim to generality lies in the view that the four-function paradigm and the dimensions on which it is based are so general that they are applicable to all variances of the 'action system' category at least and probably also to the wider category of 'living systems'.[2]

In this way, the four-function paradigm is gradually turning into a general statute which heralds the coming of a new kind of 'unity of science'. It can be said with justification that such a programme of unity is the logical finishing point of all pretensions to generality. But the idea of a uni-science – a 'unified theory' – is stigmatized; as a rule it is thought to be inseparable from a strictly objectivistic methodological position. This kind of attitude is understandable in the light of the historical circumstance that claims for such a unified programme have nearly always come from a background of natural or physical science. As we shall see (in section 3) this physical connotation of the idea of unity of science is often seized upon as proof that Parsons has forgotten his Weberian heritage. However, when he tries to make good the pretension of generality in a construction of the action theory built up round the subjective or symbolic moment, this charge of physicalism proves to be without foundation. Parsons does not reduce human cultural and symbolic reality to *Natur* (as Rickert would say) but uses his general theory of action to break through the all-too-readily accepted connection between pretension to generality and physicalism. In this respect Weber was his predecessor.

To conclude this discussion, which aims to show that Parsons's pretension to generality is made good in the new version of the action theory, it is necessary to forestall a possible misunderstanding. It would be wrong to regard the claim to generality as a claim to a kind of exclusiveness. There is no suggestion that, because of its general character, the theory is the only 'right' one. To Parsons, however general the theory may be, it remains a construction of the human mind and is, in that sense, of an analytical nature. The idea of exclusiveness cannot fit in with the analytical view and can only be put forward in an empiricist scientific attitude. The first chapter of this book showed how far Parsons was removed from such an attitude. Of course, he does not think either that his action theory is simply a shot in the dark. Apart from its fruitfulness with regard to orderly construction of empirical reality, it is especially its close connection with the classical tradition that inspires Parsons with confidence in its possibilities.

The analytical character of the new version

As in the case of the general character of Parsons's concept of theory, we can divide our discussion of the analytical premise into two parts: on the one hand it is possible to project the analytical view on to the individual *concept;* on the other hand we can project that analytical view into *theory* or discipline, conceived as a system of concepts.[3]

We have already explained the analytical character of Parsons's concepts by means of a discussion of his so-called analytical-realistic position in the first chapter. We emphasized that this epistemological view must be regarded as a variant of Weber's ideas concerning the relation of concept to reality. In the same way as did Weber's ideal types, Parsons's concepts also select from concrete reality; but they do so in a different way. These are not 'types' that refer to hypothetically concrete constructions but 'analytical elements' that refer to abstract aspects of concrete reality. The prototypes of these analytical elements are the pattern variables. Each variable represents only one aspect of a concrete phenomenon and in that way types are differentiated into their component variables.

However, we have also seen that the structural-functional version of the action theory sometimes resulted in formulations which cast doubt on the analytical character of some concepts. In particular, the definition of the concept of system and the ambiguity with regard to the criteria by which sub-systems in the action system were differentiated gave rise to misunderstandings. The bipolarity of the voluntaristic frame of reference was certainly one of the reasons why the contradiction of individual and society and, with it, the dichotomy of actor-system were to play a part in the structural-functional version.

In the new version of the action theory the concept of system is given a clearly analytical meaning. Thus systems like the personality system, the social system and the cultural system refer to abstract aspects of action. This means that the accent is more than ever on the system's external rather than internal relations. For instance, the emphasis is no longer placed exclusively on the system's internal structure which was the most important theme of *The Social System*. It also means that the questions about the reducibility of sociological to psychological regularities are placed in quite a different light: personality system, social system, cultural system and behavioural system appear in mutual relations of exchange and it is in those interchange relations that concrete action is manifested; none of these systems is reducible to the three others; together, with their mutual relations, they form the substance of the action theory.

In the sense that Parsons intended, the categories of the four-function paradigm itself are also of an analytical nature; they do not refer to concrete processes of action but to abstract aspects of such processes. Therefore, as suggested above, the adaptation function on the level of social systems (the economy) should not be identified with the concrete concept of 'business'; therefore too, polity is not identical to 'government' nor the fiduciary system to the concrete family. In principle this analytical way of dividing social action cuts across the concrete division of society into groups, collectivities and sectors.

There is no doubt whatever as to the analytical character of the symbolic media. Money, power, influence, value-commitment, as well as the media on the fundamental level of action refer not to tangible things but to abstract 'capacities'. The cybernetic hierarchy is also incorporated in the analytical character of the four-function paradigm; it is a hierarchy of functions or abstract aspects.

This brings us to the second facet of the analytical premise, namely the analytical nature of theory or scientific discipline. Within the framework of the four-function paradigm, Parsons defines the various human sciences as analytical disciplines. In order to clarify the character of this kind of analytical definition and its analytical-realistic background, suffice it to give Parsons's definition of 'political theory':[4]

> First, 'political theory', as here interpreted, which is not simply to be identified with the meaning given the term by many political scientists, is thought of as an abstract analytical scheme in the same sense in which economic theory is abstract and analytical. . . . Political theory thus conceived is a conceptual scheme which deals with a restricted set of primary variables and their interrelations that are to be found operating in all concrete parts of social systems. . . . Secondly, following on this, I assume that the empirical system to which political theory in this sense applies is an analytically defined, a 'functional subsystem' of a society, not, for example, a concrete type of collectivity. The conception of the economy of a society is relatively well defined. I should propose the conception of the *polity* as the empirical system of direct relevance to political theory as here advanced. The polity of a given society is composed of the ways in which the relevant components of the total system are organized with reference to one of its fundamental functions, namely effective collective action in the attainment of the goals of collectivities.

The complex of concepts which constitutes 'political theory' thus refers to an abstract aspect of social action. This abstract aspect, the polity, forms the empirical referent of political science at least according to Parsons.

The same thing naturally applies to all disciplines which Parsons differentiates on the various system levels. Thus economics is the study of the economy, sociology the study of the societal community and cultural anthropology or the theory of culture is the study of the fiduciary system. The empirical referents of these various sciences concern the abstract rather than the concrete. Therefore the relation between theory and referent is an analytical-realistic one.

For Parsons, one of the consequences of this analytical view of the nature of scientific disciplines is that the social scientist should become, first and foremost, proficient in the theory of social systems before going on to specialize in the study of the four abovementioned aspects of it. In the study of a concrete phenomenon, the different aspects of it should be combined in a more general theory of social systems and if necessary the higher level of the action system should be included – this is in fact a Parsonian plea for interdisciplinary integration. However, it is more than a plea: for, with the four-function – or interchange – paradigm, Parsons provides the general statute within which the analytical disciplines can be linked together. This general statute is interesting because most modern pleas for a multi- or interdiscipline spring from the empiricist desire for a clearer picture and better control of reality; thus the origin of such a plea lies in the subject itself. Parsons's multidiscipline, however, is a direct result of the analytical character of the four-function paradigm; in fact, the action theory is, of itself, a multidiscipline.

Every research that is guided by the conceptual structure of the action theory situates the phenomenon to be studied on different system levels and in the exchange relations belonging to them. A good example of this is to be found in Parsons's and Platts's book on *The American University* (1973).[5] Here the concrete phenomenon of university is subjected to an action-theoretical analysis on two levels; i.e. the level of the social system and the level of the general action system. To conclude, it is our opinion that in the new version of the action theory, Parsons's analytical-realistic premise is fulfilled to a greater extent than ever before.

The first voluntaristic thought pattern and the new version

The so-called conceptual dilemma is at the centre of our interpretation of the way Parsons's action theory developed. As we have seen, that dilemma was to a large extent caused by the dialectic nature of the voluntaristic patterns of thought. At first sight it was almost inevitable that these methodological premises should be polarized on their translation to the conceptual level. But because, in this way, a conflict arises between the methodological and the epistemological premises – generality relapses into complementarity – the conceptualization of those premises presents a dilemma. Only when the two voluntaristic patterns of thought are no longer conceptualized as opposite poles but as aspects of the same (symbolic) course of action, is it in principle possible to solve this conceptual dilemma.

The question in this section is whether the voluntaristic option on the methodological dimension between a subjective and an objective approach to human action has in fact been built into the new general theory. In other words, is there any difference with regard to this particular point between the new version of the action theory and the structural-functional version? In a previous section (2) we have already ascertained that the new action theory may indeed be considered 'general'; Parsons will come a good deal closer to realizing his pretensions if it can also be shown that the particular voluntaristic thought-pattern can be found in the central sections of the new theory.

If we examine the four central themes of the new version of the action theory we can have no possible doubts that it is voluntaristic in Parsons's sense of the word. The *four-function paradigm* is based most directly on this translation of voluntarism. Parsons deduced the two axes of differentiation on which this paradigm is based from the 'old' scheme of pattern variables by 'telescoping' the two points of view of that scheme into each other. For Parsons, the two differentiation axes acquire such general significance, comparable with dimensions in natural science like time and space, that he proclaims the resulting four-function paradigm as the frame of reference *par excellence* for human sciences. He sees this new framework as a 'real' paradigm, i.e. a schema that will guide research into the human sciences for a long time to come. This general paradigm can justifiably be called voluntaristic. The supposition is strengthened by the fact that Parsons's very first typification of the 'unit act', which was made at a time when even his sharpest critics had no doubts about the voluntaristic nature of his views, shows a remarkable similarity to the new four-function paradigm and is based on the same dimensions of order and rationality.

The *differentiation into various levels* of the action theory and its object helped Parsons thenceforth to avoid attributing the two types of factors included in the definition of voluntarism to separate disciplines. We have seen that in the structural-functional version of the action theory there was a tendency to put the subjective component into the theory of the personality system, as far as possible, and the objective component more especially in the social system theory. In the new version this is certainly no longer the case and every discipline based on the action theory and following its tenets may now be called voluntaristic.

The most significant translation of this voluntaristic thought-pattern is undoubtedly into the symbolic media. According to Parsons, a common factor of all the media is that they link together the objective and subjective moment. He distinguishes in the media an intrinsic and a symbolic meaning which, in a manner of speaking, form the extremes of one dimension. The intrinsic basis of such a medium lies in its objective (i.e. material or organic) parameters: money has its intrinsic or objective basis in precious metal, power in physical force, affect in the so-called erotic complex and intelligence in objective brain capacity.[6] It is characteristic of the action theory that it is not satisfied with this objectivism and that it stresses the subjective or symbolic aspects of action. It assumes that the objective parameters in modern differentiated society will be overwhelmed by complicated complexes of symbolic significance i.e. institutions. In those institutions the subjective, orientational or motivational aspect of typical human action comes into play. That is why the symbolic character of Parsons's media points with such clarity to the institutional context or code which gives the medium its significance as a means of exchange. It is interesting to note, too, that Parsons uses exactly this dimension of intrinsic *versus* symbolic meaning in order to dynamize his action theory. In contrast to the 'normal' course of action processes (the idea of a circular flow or equilibrium), the creation or destruction of a quantity of medium indicates a change of structure in the system concerned. This structural change always consists of the revaluation of one exchange medium in relation to the other media on the same level of system. Parsons describes in this way the shift of our culture, based as it is on cognitive rationality, to one which gives more space to affective orientations.[7]

The double hierarchy that is built into the four-function paradigm shows for the first time the relationship between the two types of factors that play a part in the voluntaristic pattern of thought. Up to now, Parsons's conception of voluntarism has actually done little else than to place the subjective and objective factors *next to one another*. From the moment the structural-functional version of the action theory is replaced by a version which substitutes the unity of symbolic action for the bipolarity of the frame of reference, the *relation* between the objective and the subjective aspect has to be sketched in more clearly. The conception of a cybernetic hierarchy answers this purpose. The development of cybernetics and the theory of information makes it possible for Parsons to describe the relation between the four functions and thus also the relation between the underlying subjective-objective dimension in terms of control, steering or information on the one hand and conditioning, determination or energy on the other. It goes without saying that the two functions which lie on the subjective (or internal) side of the axis of differentiation, the L- and I-functions, play a strong steering or controlling role. They score 'high' in informative strength but 'low' in conditioning or determining strength. For instance, the fiduciary system gives *direction* to the interactive processes in society; it forms the institutional code from which symbolic social action derives its meaning. But, there is nothing definite in the code about the specific and concrete form which action should take. The general value-patterns of the fiduciary system in no way constitute specific dictates for action any more than grammar or syntax specify what is to be said or written. Conversely, the conditioning force is greatest in those functions which are very directly connected to the external or objective conditions of the action system in question such as the A- and G-functions in the four-function paradigm. The steering or controlling power of these 'functions', however, is very limited.

In this way Parsons connects the four functions of the paradigm in two opposing hierarchies, i.e. one of conditioning factors and another of controlling factors. This means that the subjective and objective aspects are no longer separate from each other but are mingled together in various ways.

The introduction into the action theory of a terminology which originated in the theory of cybernetics is not as new and surprising as it may appear. In the structural-functional version, Parsons had already tried to build the controlling or steering aspect of action into a functionalistic teleology. In fact, concepts such as mechanism, and homeostasis are nothing but manifestations of Parsons's need to give conceptual form to the subjective or steering aspect of action. It is just because this subjective-teleological aspect could not be connected up to the objective conditioning aspect of action and could therefore be regarded only as the homeostatic counterpart of objective disturbing factors that the functionalistic form of analysis is marred by a certain one-sidedness. This one-sidedness can also be seen as the result of the rigid separation of subject from object, characteristic of the first voluntaristic frame of reference.

One of the more interesting examples of a cybernetic analysis in its preliminary stages is Weber's study of the relationship between Protestantism and capitalism. As soon as Weber attempts a causal imputation of the *Wahlverwandtschaft* of Protestantism and capitalism, two types of factors present themselves − the objective and the subjective. *Via* his own typical logic of the 'objectively possible' − which, as we have already remarked, shows a striking resemblance to Parsons's structural analysis − Weber isolates the influence of subjective factors from that of objective factors in an almost experimental way. With his conclusion that objective material conditions for the development of capitalism were no more favourable in the West than in various other parts of the world, Weber is able to demonstrate the 'cybernetic' or steering power of a subjective factor like the ethic of Protestantism. Just as Weber's analysis implies that capitalism does not become established unless objective conditions are in its favour, so too does it imply that capitalism cannot develop without the necessary steering mentality. This means that neither the subjective nor the objective factor provides, of itself, a sufficient condition for capitalism to develop; it was only their mutual reciprocity which led to modern capitalism.

Meanwhile, it is sufficiently clear that this first voluntaristic pattern of thought was incorporated into the new theory in a way which was reconcilable with Parsons's pretensions to generality.

The second voluntaristic pattern of thought and the new version

Right at the beginning of his scientific career Parsons expressed the hope that, in his attempt to formulate a general theory of action, he would be able to overcome not only the dichotomy of positivistic and idealistic explanations but also the dilemma of individualistic and collectivistic ones.

In chapter 2 we showed how Parsons transcended this dilemma on the level of methodological thought-patterns. It was especially his comparison of the work of Weber and Durkheim which put him on the track of the 'dialectic' voluntaristic thought-pattern. But we have also seen that this thought-pattern still had to be translated to a conceptual system and that this led to the so-called conceptual dilemma. We have seen that the structural-functional version of the action theory deteriorated into a bipolarity of viewpoints. His emphasis on the symbolic character of action meant that Parsons broke away from this structural-functional version because the new conceptual translation of the voluntaristic thought-pattern resulted in one overall point of view. We have established more than once that this new translation of voluntarism into the 'symbolic' means that from now on the individualistic-subjective aspect that forms part of the voluntaristic thought-pattern is incorporated in the conceptual schema not as 'the actor's point of view' but as an aspect of action.

This breakaway also has its effect on the second voluntaristic thought-pattern, i.e. individualistic *versus* collectivistic explanations. For, as soon as action becomes the basis of the frame of reference and it is certain that the typically subjectivistic aspect of voluntarism will not thereby be eliminated, it is possible to speak with impunity of action *systems*. By 'impunity' we mean without fear that in this way the subjective aspect of action will once more be ignored. As we have seen, Durkheim interprets the methodological opposition between individualistic and collectivistic explanations in terms of the 'anthropocentric postulate', i.e. the methodological individualists could not conceive of social scientific explanation without man as its centre. This criticism of Durkheim's should not be seen as a plea for collectivistic objectivism; as we have seen, this is not the direction that Durkheim takes. In the framework of the development of Parsons's action theory his criticism of the 'anthropocentric postulate' takes on a more graduated meaning which may be interpreted as follows: *try in the conceptual theory to preserve the subjective and steering aspect that is inherent in action, but do not build that theory up from the viewpoint of the individual actor.*

This new conceptual translation of the 'first' voluntaristic thought-pattern makes it possible for the dialectic character of the second voluntaristic thought-pattern also to be translated to the conceptual level of theory without it disintegrating into complementarity or perspectivism. The redundancies and ambiguities of the structural-functional conceptualization can, in principle, be avoided. The actions of individual actors, the interaction of a number of actors or the whole of society as an overall totality – all these can be equally regarded as action systems. In Parsons's action theory, the so-called antithesis between individual actor and overall system is not regarded as such but as a differentiation of levels. In Parsons's view every action, whether of an individual or a collectivity, constitutes a system.

The different levels of systems and their specific differentiations are systematically linked together in the action theory. In other words, Parsons's theory of the system of action can justly claim to translate the voluntaristic thought-pattern on the dilemma of individualism *versus* collectivism to the level of conceptual theory unambiguously – and thus in a way which is reconcilable with the pretension to generality – without at the same time making one of the poles the conceptual starting-point. Instead of two complementary theoretical points of view – which Martindale calls social behaviourism and macro-functionalism – there is now one general action theory which must be differentiated into levels rather than points of view.

Thus the four-function paradigm and the differentiation of system levels are very directly related to this second voluntaristic thought-pattern. The same can be said of two other important components of the action theory in its new version – the symbolic media and the cybernetic hierarchy. For, just as the concept of system is now completely independent of the dimension of individual-collectivity, so, in principle, are the symbolic media also independent of that dimension.

Intelligence, affect, influence, power, etc., are all characteristics of action systems; they are tied to networks of actions and not to individuals or collectivities. These characteristics can be related to the individual or to collectivities according to whatever concrete system of action is being studied. The same is true also for the cybernetic hierarchy; this too is quite independent of the dimension of individual-collectivity. It does not formulate the relation between 'actor and system' but rather that between the objective and subjective factors that play a part in every concrete action system (whether of individual or collectivity) and on each of the analytically differentiated levels of those systems.

Thus we are able to conclude that the new version of the action theory fulfils the pretension expressed by Parsons in *The Structure of Social Action* of overcoming the dilemma of individualism-collectivism not only on the level of methodological thought-patterns but also on that of conceptual systemization. He is now able to incorporate this voluntaristic aspect, too, into the general theory.

All in all, it is now apparent that the four epistemological and methodological premises which formed the original basis of Parsons's theoretical work have gradually become conceptualized in the new version of the action theory. This means that the new version is a decided improvement on the 'old' structural-functional version. In our opinion it also means that it would be a rewarding exercise to continue further along the course which Parsons has embarked upon, however roundabout his approach may have been. For it should be clearly understood that the new version of the action theory is anything but a cut-and-dried construction; in many places it is, and will always remain, a 'tentative' formulation. The important thing, however, is that the theory of action has, in spite of everything, been satisfactorily raised to the conceptual level. It is only on that level that the action theory can give systematic guidance to the formulation of an empirically based substantive theory. And let it be quite clear that he sees the level of conceptual theory not as an end in itself but simply as an instrument which is necessary for the achievement of the ultimate scientific goal – the construction of so-called 'dynamic knowledge'.

In the last section we tried to see if the new version of the action theory fulfilled its own premises. That this proved to be indeed the case means that, to say the least, Parsons offers an interesting perspective to all those who share in these epistemological and methodological premises. It is a perspective with many gaps remaining to be filled and it still needs the important contributions which would stem from a codification of social-scientific theory; but it offers the prospect of systemization of the present chaotic state of social scientific theory with all its schools, movements and perspectives and their utterly vague relations one to the other.

3 Average criticism and the conceptual dilemma

To end this publication it is interesting to confront the views here recorded of the development of Parsons's work and our favourable judgment of the possibilities offered by his action theory with the views of others. In general, these other views are in a more negative vein. Meanwhile, negative criticism has become so overwhelmingly predominant that so-called 'sympathetic reviews' are sometimes no longer taken seriously. In his necrology of Parsonianism, Gouldner underlines what he regards to be the obvious truth of his opinions as follows:[8]

> Yet it must not be supposed that the obscurity of Parsons's style had only the effect of impeding the understanding and diffusion of his ideas. For, the sheer difficulty in understanding Parsons can be overcome, if at all, only by considerable effort, which constitutes an appreciable personal investment in his work and engenders what is, in effect, a vested interest in it.

This 'reflexive sociology' is, of course, always in the right: negative criticism of Parsons's work as being completely inadequate is based on scientific criteria; positive approbation of it is intellectual weakness in the critic. Naturally, this kind of sophism is not generally typical of Parsons-criticism. Even Gouldner pays some attention to the subject-matter of Parsons's work. Yet there is no doubt at all that in the 1950s and 1960s there was widespread agreement about the negative qualities of Parsons's theory and that this negative criticism has gradually become established as a 'taken-for-granted-opinion'.

In this section we hope to draw some conclusions from our method of interpretation. This means that we shall try to examine the criticism to which Parsons's work is subjected.

It is characteristic of the best-known critical literature on Parsons's work that it concentrates almost exclusively on what is supposed to be his *magnum opus, The Social System.* This is natural enough in some cases which were written very soon after the publication of that work. But no such excuse can be put forward for the criticisms we are most concerned with in this discussion. Martindale,[9] Dahrendorf[10] and Mills[11] all committed their remarks to paper at a time when the structural-functional schema in the strictest sense of the word had already been superseded and the interchange paradigm had made its undeniable appearances. Thus their one-sided concentration on *The Social System* can only mean that they attach little importance to the conceptual changes which Parsons introduced into his schema after 1953. This constitutes the very obvious difference between their view and the one we have propounded here and we shall now confront these two opposing views.

Given the concentration on *The Social System,* what is the theme of the average Parsons criticism? If our plan of interpretation and our theory of the conceptual dilemma are of any value at all in explaining the development of Parsons's action theory, they must also give some insight into the trend followed by most criticism of his work. We concluded in chapter 4 that the structural-functional version is entramelled in the conceptual dilemma of the voluntaristic frame of reference which makes it impossible to harmonize the epistemological and the methodological premises in one conceptual schema. We saw that, logically, this conceptual dilemma might reveal itself in three different ways: first, through ever-increasing ambiguity; second, through emphasis on voluntarism at the expense of the pretension to generality; third, through emphasis on the pretension to generality at the expense of the voluntaristic premise. In our opinion Parsons made particular use of the first of these three logically-possible 'escape-routes' when writing *The Social System*; unaware of the dilemma in which he had become entangled, he tried to reconcile the irreconcilable.

It is obvious that authors who concentrate their attention mainly on *The Social System* and thereby lose sight of the fact that it deals with the conceptualization of earlier premises, will not interpret the ambiguity resulting from Parsons's escape attempt as such but will become absorbed in the *deduction* or imputation of epistemological and methodological – sometimes even metaphysical[12] – premises on which Parsons founded his theory of the social system at that period. Thus these authors build an image of the theory of the social system which completely matches up with the third escape-route mentioned above. In other words, average criticism of *The Social System* sees Parsons's structural-functional theory of social systems as one which fails to live up to its promise of voluntarism and, in spite of this, regards itself as a general theory.

In order to take a closer look at this type of criticism we can best turn to Don Martindale's article, 'Talcott Parsons' theoretical metamorphosis from social behaviorism to macrofunctionalism' (1959).[13] This article is primarily a criticism of *The Social System* but one which is at the same time incorporated into a view on the development of Parsons's work. It was particularly this article which, for a long time, determined the content of the average Parsons-criticism.

Martindale constructs an opposition between social behaviourists on the one hand and functionalists on the other. He counts himself among the first category and sees *The Social System* as a prototypical product of a functionalistic author. In order to characterize the opposition between the two positions, Martindale makes use of the social realism-social nominalism dimensions. Social behaviourists regard individual action as 'the only thing that really ever exists'[14] and refuse to see the world of more comprehensive institutional structures as a reality of its own; they simply consider it to be nothing but 'a manner of speaking'. On the other hand the functionalists, according to Martindale, take as their starting-point the 'causal primacy of the whole over the part'.[15] He says that these two currents of thought are becoming more pronounced but also more strongly opposed to each other in sociological theory. According to Martindale this opposition did not fail to have its effect on Parsons's work as well.[16]

> The extent to which Talcott Parsons stands astride the main theoretical trends of his time is revealed by the fact that he has undergone the development from one position to the other and from the worm of Social Behaviorism has metamorphosed into the butterfly of Macrofunctionalism. One may assume that so fundamental a change must have been accompanied by considerable inner drama. Perhaps some day Parsons will explain his reasons for the shift. Meanwhile, one can only account for the dramatic sense of excitement that clings to some phases of his work as a byproduct of the radical nature of the theoretical change they contain.

Meanwhile, Parsons still has not responded to Martindale's expectations and explained why he deserted social behaviourism for macro-functionalism, social nominalism for social realism or, according to Martindale, Weber for Durkheim. This seems strange since Parsons is not the kind of man to be unaware of such important shifts of position in his own work. We shall show that Martindale's hope *could* not be fulfilled since there was never any question in *The Social System* of a shift in the sense that Martindale intended; the metamorphosis he speaks of was certainly at variance with Parsons's intentions.

How does Martindale arrive at the idea of a theoretical metamorphosis? The procedure is very simple; it is based on the misrepresentation of both the start (*The Structure of Social Action*) and the finish (*The Social System*) of the shift. Misrepresentation of *The Structure of Social Action* is most obvious in Martindale's opinion that: 'conclusions in Parsons's *Structure of Social Action* are most noteworthy for their thoroughgoing nominalism. At this time Parsons was a Social Behaviorist of the Weber type.'[17]

It is surprising, to say the very least, that Martindale's estimation of *The Structure of Social Action* is based on the (social) nominalism which he imputes to it. For Parsons has always tried his utmost to escape from this one-sided nominalism and it is partly on this account that he arrived at the conception of voluntarism, in which social nominalism and social realism were combined in a dialectical pattern of thought. No wonder that Martindale has subsequent difficulty with some of the passages in *The Structure of Social Action* since it refers to a number of matters which are difficult to reconcile with the qualification of 'thorough-going nominalism': 'The only indication of a potential break from this nominalistic orientation is the suggestion that systems of social actions may have "emergent" properties not analyzable into unit acts.'[18]

From Martindale's preconceived and erroneous standpoint that Parsons's starting position should be qualified as nominalistic, everything that is intended to represent the dialectical aspect of voluntarism is thus taken as a sign of a possible metamorphosis.

The second surprising facet of Martindale's characterization of *The Structure of Social Action* is that he identifies Parsons's views with those of Weber. We, too, have strongly emphasized Parsons's affinity to Weber's work; however, the difference between Martindale's article and the view presented here is that we have sought to show on which levels of theory that affinity exists. As we have seen, it was particularly from an epistemological point of view that Weber was Parsons's example and point of reference. But because Martindale makes no distinction between the epistemological and the methodological levels of theory, he has not realized that Parsons's affinity with Weber is especially on the first level; on the second level he regards Weber's contribution on the voluntaristic theory of action as being on a par with that of Durkheim. The inability to differentiate between these two levels of theory leads Martindale to put forward some very dubious evidence to prove his theory: his familiarity with Parsons's critique on Weber's *Wissenschaftslehre* in chapter 16 of *The Structure of Social Action* (pp. 579–639) does not prevent him from considering passages from a later work in which Parsons only *repeats* that *epistemological criticism* as proof of his theory of a *methodological* metamorphosis.

For instance, in chapter 1 we read that Parsons wanted to go further with the generality of an action theory than Weber did. He regarded Weber's ideal types as an epistemological 'half-way point' which would never lead to a really general theory but would become bogged down in a kind of 'mosaic theory'.[19] When, ten years later in his structural-functional period, Parsons makes the same epistemological criticism of Weber's work, Martindale sees this as a proof of a theoretical (or methodological) metamorphosis from nominalism to realism, from Weber to Durkheim:[20]

> In this context, Parsons launches against Weber the characteristic functionalistic complaint against the Social Behaviorist. Weber's whole methodology, Parsons maintains, tends to degenerate into a kind of 'type atomism'. Without the slightest ambiguity, Parsons makes it clear that in his opinion adequate analysis proceeds from the whole, not from the part.

Thus it might be said that by first eliminating an aspect of Parsons's definition of voluntarism, Martindale makes up a one-sided picture of that voluntarism, then decides that after all the aspect thus eliminated does indeed play a part in Parsons's theory and, finally, instead of revising his idea of voluntarism, concludes that a theoretical metamorphosis has taken place.

In Martindale's view, Parsons's *Social System* represents the prototype of a social-realistic pattern of thought. Individual human action is entirely determined by institutions and every motivational orientation on the part of the actor is eliminated. In fact, Martindale accuses the structural-functional theory of the kind of 'sociologistic positivism' which Parsons detected in a particular phase of Durkheim's work. Once again, Martindale 'proves' the social-realistic character of Parsons's thought-pattern by confusing the epistemological with the methodological level of theory; he uses an epistemological fact, the fission of ideal types into so-called analytical elements (pattern variables), as a proof of a social-realistic – and therefore methodological – position.[21]

However that may be, the social-realistic character imputed to *The Social System* has gradually acquired the status of unassailable reality. The supposition of a theoretical metamorphosis is based on the completely fallacious interpretation of *The Structure of Social Action* on the one hand and the distorted interpretation of the indisputably ambiguous *The Social System* on the other; in other words, it is based on quicksand.

Of greater importance, however, is the fact that this

'given' – the social-realistic character of Parsons's theory of social systems – is being emphasized at about the same time in various publications by Ralf Dahrendorf, C. Wright Mills, David Lockwood, Alvin Gouldner and Dennis Wrong.[22] All of these writers take a stand against what they call the over-accentuation of the aspect of 'common-values'. Just like Martindale, they regard Parsons's model of social systems as a normative-deterministic whole which allows the individual no alternative than to adapt himself. They paint a picture of Parsons's model in which order and regularity, harmony and consensus constitute the 'normal' elements, conflict and change the abnormal. To lend support to this interpretation, quotations are produced from *The Social System* asserting that the social system in a state of equilibrium has a tendency to self-maintenance and defining equilibrium in terms of absolute complementarity. In this connection Parsons himself speaks of a 'theoretical' assumption and it probably never occurred to him that this theoretical assumption would be taken to be an indicator for such widely differing things as an empirical statement and a metaphysical supposition. When Parsons says that 'the complementarity of role expectations, once established, is not problematical . . .',[23] he is saying neither more nor less than that his theory is not concerned with the purely academic question as to the ins and outs of a system in a state of equilibrium. To Parsons, this kind of system is just as fictitious as the famous frictionless machine. Yet Gouldner appears to be convinced that this Parsonian assumption hides 'a variety of tacit *empirical* assumptions',[24] he does seem to be interested in the question whether an absolutely stable state of the social system does not already contain a nucleus of human conflicts; so he takes the same attitude as the mechanic whose chief worry is why his frictionless machine keeps stopping . . .

The result of this kind of assertion is that Parsons's theory of social systems is considered unsuitable for explaining human action in general or conflict and change in particular. We do not claim that the structural-functional theory of social systems is suitable for these purposes; indeed its pluri-perspectivism makes it inadequate as a general theory. We do, however, claim that the positive assertion that conflict and change are outside the scope of Parsons's systems model can only be based on a one-sided, streamlined, social-realistic interpretation of that model.

In Dahrendorf's conflict-sociological essays, including the famous 'Out of Utopia', it is assumed that Parsons's theoretical assumption of equilibrium is based on a 'Utopian' view of society which makes no allowance for change and conflict.[25] If we compare this assumption of equilibrium with Newton's law of inertia – a comparison which, disrespectful as it may be, is made by Parsons himself – it is immediately apparent that few natural scientists have made history by claiming that Newton's law obscured the view on movement and change of movement. For, like that of Parsons, this first law of Newton's is no substantive, empirically verifiable thesis on natural reality, but a theoretical assumption which belongs in the conceptual frame of reference of classical mechanics. Just as Newton's law would be unaffected by the conclusion that not everything remains at rest or in a constant rhythmical movement so too is Parsons's assumption of equilibrium unaffected by the conclusion that concrete social systems are not generally in this state of equilibrium. One might go so far as to say that, just like Newton's law, Parsons's assumption made it possible to get a grip on the movement and change of action. In spite of its shortcomings, there is no doubt at all that *The Social System* and the scheme of concepts which it formulates emphasize the instability of concrete societies: it is true that the structural analyses of *The Social System* take a dominant value as starting-point, but the analysis aims to show why it is that this value is never fully realized in practical reality. The constructions of the functional requirements and the compatability imperatives played an important part here.[26] These constructions are Parsons's explicit expression of the view already expounded in *The Structure of Social Action* that concepts which refer to individual or collective consciousness can never of themselves apart from their interplay with objectively conditioning factors, determine the face of society.

Dahrendorf was not able completely to disregard this conflict orientation of Parsons's structural-functionalism. In a footnote he says that there is, indeed, a great deal of disagreement on the question as to whether structural-functionalists assert the stability of every concrete society and that 'assertions to the contrary are found in the works of Parsons, Merton and others'.[27] But, he reasons further, from a consistently structural-functional point of view, these assertions can be nothing more than 'mere declarations' since 'the concept of equilibrium and the concept of a system would have little sense if they did not make the assumption of the stability of societies.'[28] In other words, Dahrendorf's view of structural-functionalism – which only throws light on half of Parsons's structural-functionalism – is in no way affected by 'assertions to the contrary'; on the contrary, his view is so self-evident that no counter-evidence is possible.

Dahrendorf introduces a new element into the discussion with his assertion that when conflict and change are introduced into *The Social System* by hook or by crook, Parsons is unable to explain them sociologically but has to resort to psychological variables.

This means that Dahrendorf does not include motivational factors, which indeed play an important part in Parsons's structural-functionalism (the motivational paradigm), in sociology. Apparently, Dahrendorf's theory of social systems accepts only those explanatory factors which are connected with 'the structure of social positions'. Thus Dahrendorf's idea of the task of sociology is quite different from that of Parsons; he considers that sociology ought to be a 'factor' theory, i.e. one which explains human action from a particular factor, in this case that of social positions. But Parsons's sociological theory must not be regarded as a factor theory such as this: for in Parsons's view, sociology is distinguished from other action disciplines not according to the kind of explanatory factor it uses but by the aspect of action with which it is concerned.

For Parsons, the fact that sociology is an aspect science does not mean that from the totality of possible *explanatory factors* it chooses only one (e.g. sociology is the study of human behaviour inasmuch as it is determined by common value-systems), but that from the totality of action it selects one aspect that must be explained by a number of factors which fit into the frame of reference of the action theory (e.g. sociology is 'that aspect of the theory of social systems which is concerned with the phenomena of the institutionalization of patterns of value-orientation in the social system').[29]

Yet it is because of this idea that Parsons's sociology is a factor theory in the above sense of regarding the structure of the social system as an overall determining factor, that Dahrendorf's conflict sociology developed. Did not W. I. Thomas say 'a situation which is defined as real, is real in its consequences'? Dahrendorf's structural conflict-sociology is an example of this.

The assertion that the Parsonian sociology can explain conflict, deviation and change only by relinquishing sociological, i.e. 'structuralistic' tenets is for Dahrendorf a reason to conceive a new model which will be able to explain conflict and change without having to resort to motivational or social-psychological phenomena. This reaction of Dahrendorf's is the complete opposite of that of Homans, who, in his essay 'Bringing men back in',[30] also asserts that whenever structural-functionalists like Parsons start to explain social phenomena, including change and conflict, they are unable to dispense with individual and motivational factors. But for Homans this is a happy thought and another proof of the inevitability of a 'psychological' reduction. Homans has not been slow to observe that motivational factors play an important part in Parsons's theory of social system. Against this background, Dahrendorf's magnanimous and final conclusion that in his 'structural' sociology there is a place for both models can only be regarded as inconsistent. This brings us finally to the second aspect of the average criticism of *The Social Systems:* i.e. criticism of Parsons's pretension to generality.

It goes without saying that the predominating social-realistic interpretation of Parsons's theory of social systems results in a forthright rejection of his claim to generality. It is C. Wright Mills in particular who points his criticism of Parsons at the generality of *The Social System*. His *Sociological Imagination*[31] is an attack on the abstract-theoretical schemas which ensue from the claim to generality.

Mills appears to subordinate the construction of a conceptual paradigm for the study of human action to a direct study of concrete social problems. The fact that in so doing he prefers to ignore the boundaries between the different social scientific disciplines and to opt for a 'unified social science'[32] does not quite mean that he shares Parsons's pretensions to generality. On the contrary, Mills opposes every form of conceptualization which is not directly concerned with concrete reality. In that respect he really resembles Veblen who, sixty years earlier, had made a plea for institutional economics which expanded the science of economics into one of human action.[33] Mills's programme for the unity of science is arranged round the unity of social problems, not round the formulation of a single, general paradigm that forms the basis of action sciences. For Mills, this kind of paradigm is nothing more than a glorified theory which, of necessity, ignores some of society's essential structural characteristics.

Not all of Parsons's critics agree with Mills's complete rejection of general theory; but they do support his rejection of Parsons's claim to generality. After all, according to them that claim was founded on a (social-realistic) half-truth. It would be of little use to turn the spotlight on still more criticisms of Parsons by like-minded authors. On most of the essential points they subscribe to the interpretation of Martindale and Dahrendorf. If there is one thing that is obvious from the average criticism, it is that in the 1950s and 1960s many authors at least tried to form an unambiguous and consistent picture of the structural-functional theory. It is also clear that they all concentrate on the 1951 publications and try to get an insight into Parsons's total work from that point. It is particularly this one-sided concentration on the structural-functional theory of *The Social System* that is to blame for the average criticism and also for the fallacies in that criticism. Because of this one-sided concentration, *The Social System* has come to be regarded as a separate, individual monograph rather than a conceptual elaboration of the premises which were formulated in *The Structure of*

Social Action. The result of this is that the average criticism of *The Social System* is not concerned with the question whether or not the structural-functional theory represents an adequate translation of those previously-formulated premises but itself goes in search of the premises which may be presumed to lie somewhere behind the conceptual chaos of *The Social System*. When this procedure results in a clear picture — and certainly when the intersubjectivity of the forum of critic-colleagues confirms the validity of that picture — then is the time to launch the idea of a theoretical metamorphosis; to create the impression that the premises on which *The Social System* is so intersubjectively based are not the same as the explicit pretensions made by Parsons ten years earlier.

In this discussion of the average criticism we have shown that the arguments which form the basis of the line of interpretation are often founded on the *confusion between various principally distinguishable levels of theory*. It is not important how those different aspects are distinguished from each other nor what names they are given. The important thing is that epistemological arguments should not be used as proof of methodological theories. This brings us to a very obvious shortcoming in the average criticism. Almost without exception, the authors ignore Parsons's epistemological confrontation with Weber's *Wissenschaftslehre*. This means that they are not in a position to judge the typical conceptual manifestation of analytical realism according to its worth. If he had been aware of this confrontation, it would not have been possible for Dahrendorf to take Parsons's analytical conception of the sociological discipline to be a factor-theory rather than one which, from an analytical and general frame of reference, concentrates on one aspect of a particular field of study included in that framework. Nor has Parsons's claim to generality ever been directly related to Weber's *Wissenschaftslehre*. The average criticism even suggests that the break with Weber is here most evident. Some authors go so far as to accept as a fact that this pretension to generality is evidence of physicalistic presuppositions of the Lundberg type and consider the modernistic terminology of cybernetics and informations as proof of this.[34]

The average criticism is absolutely clear about Parsons's methodological premises: it places the nostalgia of 'social-behaviouristic' voluntarism from *The Structure of Social Action* against the accusation of sociologistical positivism levelled at *The Social System*. But Parsons's voluntarism does not correspond with that construction. Therefore, in many respects, the contrast between *The Social System* and *The Structure of Social Action* is only so in appearance.

Finally, the fruitfulness of our differentiation into four levels of theory is illustrated by the fact that the average critic has not always known how to deal with the difference between substantive statements on the one hand and the conceptual constructions on which analysis of action must be based on the other. The confusion of a number of fundamentally different levels of theory has given rise to an interpretation of Parsons in which the social-realistic 'common values' aspect is the all-decisive factor.

In this, too, the average criticism is at variance with our interpretation. It is not that we disagree with it entirely, but the conceptual dilemma has taught us that every unambiguous interpretation of *The Social System* has failed to recognize a number of 'facts'. The fundamental ambiguity and lack of precision in *The Social System*, which translates voluntarism into a double bipolarity, makes the structural-functional theory a hotch-potch from which to pick and choose according to one's book. If only for this reason, the great synthesis, the king-pin of Parsons's convergence theory can be said to have failed in the structural-functional version and a fresh attempt will have to be made.

But the average criticism has squeezed *The Social System* into a straitjacket and is therefore unaware of any such attempt. It tends to fit all new publications into the social-realistic picture;[35] it is unable to see the connection between the accentuation of the symbolic, the subjective, the concurrence with Weber's definition of action, etc. and the search for a general theory. Thus, according to the average criticism, it is impossible for the subjective-symbolic pole of Parsons's action theory to transcend the level of 'mere declarations'.

The big difference between the average criticism and our line of interpretation lies in the way we assess the continuity of Parsons's development. The critics make a distinction between the 'young' Parsons and the 'old'. They see an almost complete break between the two phases of Parsons's work and assume, therefore, that its development was discontinuous. In our interpretation, the question of continuity is inseparable from the various levels that we have distinguished in Parsons's action theory. We have laid particular emphasis on the continuity in its epistemological and methodological premises which, for half a century, have formed the constant element in Parsons's work on the action theory. Certainly, there is discontinuity on the conceptual level but it should be interpreted in the light of the premises and not as a thing apart. The conceptual dilemma plays its important role here.

Thus, the two interpretations are diametrically opposed to each other; the average criticism supposes that development was discontinuous on the epistemological and methodological level, while regarding the various attempts at conceptualization as identical and continuous rather than separate and distinct from each other. We, on the other hand, see the continuity in Parsons's work mainly on the level of epistemological and methodological premises; because of the conceptual dilemma it becomes clearly discontinuous on the conceptual level. That is why we feel that our interpretation throws fresh light on the voluntaristic action theory and may lead to serious reconsideration of its new developments. Then, perhaps, Parsons will be given the criticism he deserves instead of the 'average' criticism to which he has thus far been subjected.

Notes

Explanatory introduction

1 Cf. A. C. Zijderveld, 'Twee dilemma's, vier denkvormen' (Two dilemmas, four patterns of thought), *Sociale Wetenschappen,* 17, 1, 1974, pp. 49-66 and A. C. Zijderveld, *Institutionalisering,* Hilversum, 1966, Meppel, 1974. The subtitle reads as follows: 'a study of the methodological dilemma of the social sciences'.

1 The general and analytical character of theory: Parsons's epistemological premise

1 T. Kuhn, *The Structure of Scientific Revolutions,* Chicago, 1970 (1962).
2 G. Allport, 'The open system in personality theory', *Sociometry,* 24, 2, 1961, p. 301.
3 K. Boulding, 'General systems theory − the skeleton of science', in W. Buckley, ed., *Modern Systems Research for the Behavioral Scientist,* Chicago, 1968, p. 4.
4 T. Parsons, 'The present position and prospects of systematic theory in Sociology', 1945, in Talcott Parsons, *Essays in Sociological Theory,* rev.ed., New York, 1954 (1949), p. 214.
5 T. Parsons, *The Structure of Social Action,* Glencoe, Ill., 1949 (1937), p. 29.
6 Cf. T. Parsons and E. Shils, eds, *Toward a General Theory of Action,* Cambridge, Mass., 1951, New York, 1962, pp. 3-4; 50-1.
7 Parsons dedicates *The Social System* in the following words: 'To Helen, whose healthy and practical empiricism has long been an indispensable balance-wheel for an "incurable theorist".'
8 Cf. A. C. Zijderveld, *Institutionalisering,* Hilversum, 1966, Meppel, 1974.
9 Cf. H. Rickert, *Kulturwissenschaft und Naturwissenschaft,* Tübingen, 1926 (1899). pp. 15, 55-6.
10 Cf. M. Weber, *Gesammelte Aufsätze zur Wissenschaftslehre,* Tübingen, 1922 (1968). Weber uses the word 'nomological' on more than

one occasion. By consistently placing it between inverted commas he is pointing out that it refers to so-called *'generelle Erfahrungsregeln'* (general rules of experience) rather than to immutable 'objective' laws. See the quotation in Parsons, *The Structure of Social Action,* p. 585.
11 Cf. Weber, op. cit., pp. 175-9 and Parsons, *The Structure of Social Action,* p. 592.
12 T. Parsons, Introduction to: Max Weber, *The Theory of Social and Economic Organization,* New York, 1947, pp. 10-11.
13 Ibid., p. 11.
14 Cf. Parsons, *The Structure of Social Action,* pp. 603-10.
15 The expression 'hypothetically concrete construction' should not be confused with a 'hypothetical construction'. The ideal type does not formulate an expected course of action but an imaginable one.
16 Cf. Parsons, *The Structure of Social Action,* p. 621.
17 Parsons, Introduction to: Max Weber, *The Theory of Social and Economic Organization,* p. 13, my italics.
18 Parsons, *The Structure of Social Action,* p. 730.
19 R. Merton, *Social Theory and Social Structure,* New York, 1957 (1949), pp. 9-10. This discussion between Parsons and Merton was carried out mainly in the *American Sociological Review,* 13, 1948, pp. 156-68. Parsons wrote an article, 'The position of sociological theory', to which Merton replied with one called 'On the position of sociological theory'.
20 Merton, 'On the position of sociological theory', pp. 164-5.
21 R. Merton, 'Puritanism, pietism and science', in *Social Theory and Social Structure* pp. 574-606.
22 Parsons, *The Structure of Social Action,* p. v.
23 It should be noted that a distinction is made here between the words 'empiristic' and 'empiricistic'. The first refers to the one-sided emphasis on the more or less quantitatively oriented empirical or substantive theory, without attention to all other theory-levels. The second word, however, reflects a view which is significant on the so-called epistemological level.
24 Cf. M. Weber, 'Die "Objektivität" sozialwissenschaftlicher und sozialpolitischer Erkenntnis', in *Gesammelte Aufsätze zur Wissenschaftslehre,* pp. 190-3 or, in the translation of Shils and Finch, *The Methodology of the Social Sciences,* New York, 1949, pp. 90-2.
25 Cr. A. Schutz, 'Common sense and scientific interpretation of human action', in *Collected Papers* I, The Hague, 1962, pp. 3-47; A. C. Zijderveld, 'The problem of adequacy', *European Journal of Sociology,* 13, 1972, pp. 176-90.
26 Schutz, op. cit., p. 44.
27 Cf. A. C. Zijderveld, *De theorie van het symbolisch interactionisme,* Meppel, 1973, pp. 214-19.
28 Cf. Rickert, op. cit., p. 30.
29 Parsons, *The Structure of Social Action,* p. 730.
30 Ibid., my italics
31 T. Parsons, 'Sociological elements in economic thought', I and II, *Quarterly Journal of Economics,* 1934-5, pp. 414-53, 646-67.
32 T. Parsons, ' "Capitalism" in Recent German Literature: Sombart and

Weber', I, *Journal of Political Economy,* 36, 6, 1928, pp. 641-61, and II, *Journal of Political Economy,* 37, 1929, pp. 31-51.
33 Cf. A. N. Whitehead, *Science and the Modern World,* New York, 1925, p. 75.
34 Parsons, *The Structure of Social Action,* p. 476.
35 Parsons, 'Sociological elements in economic thought', I, p. 439.
36 Parsons, *The Social System,* New York, 1951, p. 548.
37 Ibid., p. 552, Parsons's italics.

2 The voluntaristic pretension; Parsons's methodological premise

1 T. Parsons, 'On building social system theory: a personal history', *Daedalus,* 99, 1970, 4, p. 830
2 T. Parsons, *The Structure of Social Action,* Glencoe, Ill., 1949 (1937), p. 74.
3 It is characteristic of Durkheim's work, especially of *Les Règles* (1895), that he is trying to find an objective and scientific yardstick for deciding what should be regarded as normal and what as pathological; no doubt an important factor here was the positivistic tendency of wanting to interfere in an objective and rational way in social development.
4 Parsons, op. cit., pp. 61-2
5 Ibid., pp. 87-470
6 Ibid., pp. 87-125, and T. Parsons, 'Utilitarianism', *International Encyclopedia of the Social Sciences,* vol. 16, New York, 1968, pp. 229-31.
7 J. O. Urmson, 'Utilitarianism', *International Encyclopedia of the Social Sciences,* vol. 16, New York, 1968, pp. 224-5.
8 Quoted in Parsons, *The Structure of Social Action,* p. 65.
9 Cf. ibid., pp. 89-94 (Hobbes and the Problem of Order).
10 Cf. Parsons, *The Structure of Social Action,* pp. 95-102 (Locke and the Classical Economics).
11 Ibid., p. 102.
12 Cf. ibid., pp. 60-9 (The Positivistic Theory of Action).
13 Ibid., p. 64.
14 Ibid., pp. 129-77; 452-4.
15 Ibid., pp. 178-300; 454-60.
16 Quoted in Parsons, *The Structure of Social Action,* p. 198.
17 Ibid., p. 206.
18 Ibid., pp. 301-450; 460-70.
19 Ibid., p. 323.
20 Cf. ibid., p. 383.
21 Ibid., p. 379.
22 Ibid., p. 82.
23 M. Weber, 'Die Protestantische Ethik und der Geist des Kapitalismus' (1905), in *Gesammelte Aufsätze zur Religionssoziologie,* vol. I, Tübingen, 1920. For Parsons's way of interpreting Weber's substantive theory of this methodological dimension, see Parsons, *The Structure of Social Action,* pp. 500-78.
24 Cf. A. C. Zijderveld, *Institutionalisering,* Hilversum, 1966, Meppel, 1974.
25 Ibid., p. 207.

26 Parsons, *The Structure of Social Action*, p. 238.
27 Cf. ibid., pp. 150-1
28 Cf., ibid., pp. 219-41
29 E. Durkheim, *Les Règles de la methode sociologique*, Paris, 1967 (1895). Preface to the second edition.
30 Parsons, *The Structure of Social Action*, pp. 311, 319.
31 E. Durkheim, *De la Division du travail social*, Paris, 1967 (1893). For Parsons's interpretation of Durkheim, see Parsons, *The Structure of Social Action*, pp. 301-450.

3 The structural-functional version of the action theory; the first attempt at conceptualization

1 T. Parsons, *The Structure of Social Action*, Glencoe, Ill., 1949 (1937), p. 43.
2 Cf. ibid., p. 44.
3 Ibid., p. 43.
4 Ibid., p. 77.
5 Ibid., pp. 739-40.
6 Ibid., pp. 743-4.
7 Cf. ibid., p. 745.
8 T. Parsons and E. A. Shils, eds, *Toward a General Theory of Action*, New York, 1962 (1951); Parsons, *The Social System*, New York, 1951.
9 Cf. Parsons, *The Social System*, p. 9.
10 Cf. Parsons and A. Shils., eds, op. cit., pp. 58-60. Although this publication was supervised by the two authors, both of whom may claim responsibility for the main contribution, 'Values, Motives and Systems of Action', we shall mention only Parsons's name in our references to it rather than repeatedly referring to Parsons and Shils.
11 The original Greek meaning of the concept 'cathexis' was 'to grasp'. Parsons uses it in the specific sense of 'emotional attachment in respect of need-satisfaction'.
12 Cf. Parsons and Shils, op. cit., p. 71.
13 Ibid., p. 59.
14 Ibid., pp. 57-8.
15 Cf. ibid., p. 67.
16 In the history of American sociology the period that included the Second World War was the one in which first attempts were made to systematize a functionalistic method of analysis. Cf. T. Parsons, 'The present position and prospects of systematic theory in sociology', 1945, included in T. Parsons, *Essays in Sociological Theory*, New York, 1964 (1954, 1949), as well as a number of more substantively orientated articles such as 'Democracy and social structure in pre-Nazi Germany' (1942), 'An analytical approach to the theory of social stratification' (1940) and 'The professions and social structure' (1939), all of which were included in the abovementioned *Essays in Sociological Theory*.
17 Parsons, 'The present position and prospects of systematic theory in sociology', p. 216.
18 Cf. ibid., p. 217.
19 Cf. ibid., p. 216.

20 Ibid., p. 217.
21 Cf. Parsons and Shils, op. cit., p. 77.
22 Cf. ibid., pp. 76-88
23 Here we see something of the result of the indistinct differentiation between subject and object in the frame of reference; specificity *versus* generality is described as an orientation-modus whereas, in the frame of reference, it was seen as an object-modality, i.e. the scope of significance dimension.
24 This pattern variable, too, reflects ambiguity as a result of the conceptual scheme's indistinct differentiation of individual and society on the one hand and subject and object on the other. See chapter 4.
25 Included in Parsons, *Essays in Sociological Theory,* pp. 34-49.
26 At first, Parsons adopts R. Linton's terminology and calls this pattern variable 'ascription vs. achievement'. Later on, he generally uses the more general terms 'quality vs. performance'.
27 Cf. E. Devereux, 'Parsons's sociological theory', in M. Black, ed., *The Social Theories of Talcott Parsons,* Englewood Cliffs, N.J., 1961, p. 42.
28 Parsons, 'The present position and prospects of systematic theory in sociology', p. 218.
29 Cf. Parsons, *The Social System,* pp. 204-5, and T. Parsons, 'An outline of the social system', in T. Parsons *et al.*, eds, *Theories of Society,* New York, 1961, pp. 37-8.
30 Cf. W. B. Cannon, *The Wisdom of the Body,* New York, 1932.
31 Cf. Parsons and Shils, op. cit., p. 108
32 Parsons, *The Social System,* p. 480. Parsons's italics.
33 As in other phases of his work, Parsons does not now confine his attention to the conceptualization of the social system. Especially since his penetrating study of the work of Freud, he is also interested in the theory of the personality system. In his preface to the second edition of *The Structure of Social Action* he points to the necessity of including Freud in the list of classical authors discussed in that book: 'So much is this the case that a full-dress analysis of Freud's theoretical development seen in the context of "the theory of social action" – and adaptation of the rest of the book to the results of such an analysis – would seem indispensable', op. cit., p. B-C.
34 Cf. Parsons and Shils, op. cit., p. 75.
35 Ibid., p. 76.
36 Cf. Chapter 4.
37 Parsons, *The Social System,* p. 3.
38 Ibid., p. 29.
39 Ibid., p. 34.
40 Parsons and Shils, op. cit., p. 23.
41 Parsons, *The Social System,* p. 114.
42 It should be observed that in Parsons's later work the concept of power acquires a totally different meaning. Cf. chapter 5.
43 Cf. Parsons, *The Social System,* p. 71.
44 Cf. ibid., p. 137.
45 Cf. ibid., 152.

46 Cf. ibid., pp. 153-67.
47 Ibid., p. 167.
48 Cf. ibid., p. 178. This idea of compatibility is also mentioned in R. Merton, 'Manifest and latent functions', albeit under the epithets 'structural context' and 'structural constraint'. Cf. R. Merton, *Social Theory and Social Structure,* New York, 1957, pp. 52-3.
49 T. Parsons, *The Social System,* pp. 168-9.
50 In this respect, too, there is obvious similarity between the work of Parsons and that of Weber. Weber's method of causal imputation makes use of a mental experiment to relate the so-called 'ontological' knowledge to the 'nomological' and thus introduces a causal logic of the 'objectively possible'. Parsons's structural analysis seems to have a similar 'probabilistic' basis. In *The Structure of Social Action* (pp. 610-24) Parsons himself dealt so thoroughly with Weber's views on causal imputation that he must undoubtedly have incorporated that knowledge into his model of structural analysis. He himself gives evidence of this in *Essays in Sociological Theory,* p. 227, and in his Introduction to Max Weber's *Theory of Social and Economic Organization,* New York, 1947.
51 No doubt under the influence of the psychologists with whom he co-operated in the project that resulted in the publication *Toward a General Theory of Action,* Parsons increasingly substitutes the term 'motivation' for 'orientation'. This means, however, that the concept of motivational orientation is going to represent one pole of the frame of reference, leaving unanswered the question as to whether the other pole should consist of value-orientation or of situation. The ambiguity in the relation orientation-situation (or subject-object) is having its effects here.
52 Parsons, *The Social System,* pp. 204-5.
53 'It is certainly contrary to much of the common sense of the social sciences, but it will nevertheless be assumed that the maintenance of the complementarity of role-expectations, once established, is *not problematical,* in other words that the 'tendency' to maintain the interaction process is the *first law of social process.* This is clearly an assumption, but there is, of course, no theoretical objection to such assumptions if they serve to organize and generalize our knowledge.' Ibid., p. 205, Parsons's italics.
54 See Alvin Gouldner, *The Coming Crisis of Western Sociology,* London, 1971 (1970), p. 232. Gouldner seems unable to differentiate between theoretical and empirical assumptions; he understands the theoretical assumption cited here to be a 'tacit empirical assumption'; consequently he subjects it to empirical tests and comes to the conclusion that it lacks validity on various counts. He has failed to realize that the purpose of this theoretical assumption is to reveal whatever is contradictory to it.
55 Parsons, *The Social System,* p. 42, footnote.
56 Cf. ibid., pp. 201-48.
57 Cf. ibid., pp. 249-325.
58 Ibid., p. 321.
59 Ibid., pp. 300-1.

4 The instability of the structural-functional version of the action theory

1 Max Black, ed., *The Social Theories of Talcott Parsons*, Englewood Cliffs, N.J., 1961. In particular, Black's own contribution completely ignores the developments that can be seen in the formulation of Parsons's voluntaristic action theory after 1951.
2 Alvin Gouldner, *The Coming Crisis of Western Sociology*, London, 1971 (1970); for that matter, the criticism of Parsons to which roughly 200 pages of this so-called 'most important book in this field since C. Wright Mills' (according to *The New York Times*) are devoted is of very dubious quality.
3 Walter Buckley, *Sociology and Modern Systems Theory*, Englewood Cliffs, N.J., 1967, pp. 23-31
4 This is the English version of the original, T. Parsons, 'Die jüngste Entwicklungen in der strukturell-funktionalen Theorie', *Kölner Zeitschrift für Soziologie and Sozialpsychologie*, 16, I, 1964, pp. 30-49.
5 See chapter 3.
6 See especially chapter 3, note 25.
7 Cf. Talcott Parsons, *The Social System*, Glencoe, Ill., 1951, p. 502, and T. Parsons and E. Shils, eds, *Toward a General Theory of Action*, New York, 1962 (1951), pp. 96-8 and fig. 5, p. 253.
8 Ibid.
9 See chapter 3, p. 73.
10 See chapter 3, pp. 75-6.
11 See chapter 3, p. 71.
12 See chapter 3, p. 75.
13 The best known publications in this field are *(inter alia)*: C. G. Hempel, 'The logic of functional analysis', in L. Gross, ed., *Symposium on Sociological Theory*, New York, 1959; W. W. Isajiw, *Causation and Functionalism in Sociology*, London, 1968; E. Nagel, 'Teleological explanation and teleological systems', in H. Feigl and M. Brodbeck, eds, *Readings in the Philosophy of Science*, New York, 1953, pp. 537-58; H. C. Bredemeier, 'The methodology of functionalism', *American Sociological Review*, 21, 1956, pp. 129-35; A. L. Stinchcombe, *Constructing Social Theories*, New York, 1968, especially pp. 80-116.
14 A. C. Zijderveld, *Institutionalisering*, Hilversum, 1966, Meppel, 1974.
15 Ibid., pp. 207-8. Zijderveld's italics.
16 See chapter 2, pp. 29-41.
17 See Don Martindale's remarks in his article 'Talcott Parsons' theoretical metamorphosis from social behaviorism to macrofunctionalism', in *Alpha Kappa Delta*, winter 1959, pp. 38-46.
18 Cf. Parsons and Shils, op. cit., p. 53, footnote: 'The present position of the theory of action represents in one major respect a revision and extension of the position stated in Parsons' *The Structure of Social Action* ... particularly in the light of psychoanalytic theory, of developments in behavior psychology, and of developments in the anthropological analysis of culture. It has become possible to incorporate these elements effectively, largely because of the conception of a

system of action in both the social and psychological spheres and their integration with systems of cultural patterns has been considerably extended and refined in the intervening years.'
19 Cf. T. Parsons, *The Structure of Social Action*, p. 46.
20 Cf. Parsons and Shils, op. cit., pp. 57-8 and fig. 2, p. 248.
21 Cf. ibid., fig. 2, p. 248 and fig. 5, p. 253.
22 G. C. Homans, 'Bringing men back in', *American Sociological Review*, 29, 1964, pp. 809-18.
23 See note 17.
24 In this connection the following statement by Parsons is typical: 'The unit of all social systems is the human individual as actor . . .', cf. 'The present position and prospects of systematic theory in sociology', *Essays in Sociological Theory*, rev. ed., New York, 1954, p. 228.
25 Cf. Parsons, *The Social System*, p. 207: 'The allocation of personnel between roles in the social system and the socialization processes of the individual are clearly *the same processes viewed in different perspectives.* Allocation is the process seen in the perspective of functional significance to the social system as a system. Socialization on the other hand is the process seen in terms of the motivation of the individual actor.' (Parsons's italics.)
26 See note 24.
27 Martindale, op. cit., p. 41.
28 D. Wrong, 'The oversocialized conception of man in modern sociology', *American Sociological Review*, 26, 1961, pp. 183-93.
29 R. Dahrendorf, 'Out of Utopia: toward a reorientation of sociological analysis', *American Journal of Sociology*, 64, 1958, pp. 115-27.
30 J. Berting, 'Ruiltheorie', *Intermediair*, 12, 22, 1976, p. 51.
31 T. Parsons, R. Bales and E. Shils, eds, *Working Papers in the Theory of Action*, Glencoe, Ill., 1953.
32 Cf. T. Parsons, 'The theory of symbolism in relation to action', in *Working Papers in the Theory of Action*, pp. 31-62.
33 See chapter 3, section 2.
34 See chapter 3, section 3.
35 Cf. T. Parsons and R. Bales, 'The dimensions of action-space' in *Working Papers in the Theory of Action*, pp. 63-110, and T. Parsons, R. Bales and E. Shils, 'Phase movement in relation to motivation, symbol formation and role structure', pp. 163-269.
36 Cf. T. Parsons, 'The theory of symbolism in relation to action', especially the appendix. Also, T. Parsons, 'Pattern variables revisited: a response to Robert Dubin', *American Sociological Review*, 25, 4, 1960, included also in T. Parsons, *Sociological Theory and Modern Society*, New York, 1967, pp. 192-220; and T. Parsons, 'The point of view of the author', in Black, ed., op. cit., pp.311-63.
37 T. Parsons, 'The theory of symbolism in relation to action', pp. 61-2. Parsons's italics.
38 T. Parsons, 'Some problems of general theory', in J. McKinney and E. Tiryakian, eds, *Theoretical Sociology*, New York, 1970, p. 31.
39 Parsons speaks originally of 'behavioral organism'; perhaps because he realized that the name did not sufficiently express the analytical

character of this sub-system, he refers later mainly to 'behavioral system'.
40 A similar comparison is also to be found in D. Gerstein, 'A note on the continuity of Parsonian action theory', *Sociological Inquiry*, 45, 4, 1975, pp. 11-15.

5 The new voluntaristic action theory

1 Cf. T. Parsons, 'Some problems of general theory', in J. McKinney and E. Tiryakian, eds, *Theoretical Sociology*, New York, 1970, p. 46.
2 Cf. ibid., p. 49. In this way Parsons rejects the division between social behaviourism or symbolic interactionism on the one hand and social-system theory on the other. Exclusion of the first tradition from sociological education on the ground that its place is in the study of psychology deprives sociology of its action theoretical basis. If this is the meaning of Homans's 'psychological reductionism' then, according to Parsons, the epithet may not be the right one but the idea is correct.
3 T. Parsons and N. J. Smelser, *Economy and Society*, London, 1956. N. Smelser, like R. Bales, is an important figure in the development of the four-function paradigm. Just as the first exercises with this paradigm were developed on the micro-level of interaction through the co-operation with Bales (cf. *Working Papers in the Theory of Action* (1953) and *Family, Socialization and Interaction Process* (1955), so, too, did co-operation with Smelser lead to the first elaborated study on the macro-level of society, understood as the most comprehensive social system.

Without in any way wishing to minimize Smelser's contribution to the development of the action theory on this level, we shall not henceforth continue to repeat the names of both authors.
4 Cf. ibid., p. xvii.
5 The last two names in particular are of fairly recent date. The concept 'societal community' was used explicitly for the first time in T. Parsons, *Societies, Evolutionary and Comparative Perspectives*, Englewood Cliffs, N.J., 1966, p. 17. It is, in fact, Parsons's equivalent of Tönnies's concept of *Gemeinschaft* though the former concept should be seen as an analytical element and the latter as an ideal type. The expression 'fiduciary system' dates from T. Parsons and G. Platt, *The American University*, Cambridge, Mass., 1973, p. 89, footnote.
6 Parsons and Smelser, op. cit., pp. 20-1 and p. 39.
7 Cf. ibid., pp. 51-70.
8 Cf. ibid., pp. 25-6.
9 Ibid., p. 70.
10 Cf. ibid., pp. 51-70.
11 In later work Parsons differentiates between goods and services in the sense that services represent more especially output to the polity. This is a departure from normal economic theory. Cf. T. Parsons, 'On the concept of political power', in T. Parsons, *Politics and Social Structure*, New York, 1969, pp. 357-8 and 400-1.
12 Parsons and Smelser, op. cit., p. 66.

13 Cf. ibid., p. 71
14 This schema is distilled from *Economy and Society,* in particular the section 'Double interchanges at the boundaries', pp. 70-85. Some adaptations were made in view of some of Parsons's later work including the aforementioned 'On the concept of political power'.
15 Parsons, *Politics and Social Structure,* pp. 311-522.
16 Cf., *inter alia,* Parsons, 'On the concept of influence' and 'On the concept of value-commitments', which are also included in the volume *Politics and Social Structure,* pp. 405-29 and pp. 439-72.
17 This elaboration was carried out in the two essays mentioned in note 16. A fairly recent exposé is T. Parsons, 'Social structure and the symbolic media of interchange', in P. Blau, ed., *Approaches to the Study of Social Structure,* New York, 1975, pp. 94-120; this forms the basis of our exposé.
18 Ibid., p. 94.
19 Ibid., p. 96.
20 Ibid., pp. 97-8.
21 Ibid., p. 99.
22 Parsons, 'On the concept of political power', p. 361.
23 Cf. ibid., pp. 371-2.
24 Ibid., p. 362.
25 Parsons, 'On the concept of influence' p. 407.
26 Parsons, 'On the concept of political power', pp. 383-95.
27 Ibid., p. 388.
28 Cf. ibid., p. 390.
29 Parsons, 'On the concept of influence', p. 410.
30 Cf. ibid., pp. 415. Parsons's italics.
31 Cf. ibid., p. 418.
32 Cf. ibid., pp. 416-17. Parsons's italics.
33 Cf. ibid., p. 417.
34 Parsons and Platt, op. cit., p. 322.
35 Cf. Parsons, 'On the concept of political power', pp. 392-4.
36 Cf. Parsons, 'On the concept of influence', p. 428.
37 This discussion is based on Parsons, 'On the concept of value-commitments', in Parsons, *Politics and Social Structure,* pp. 439-72.
38 Ibid., p. 456.
39 Ibid., p. 467.
40 Ibid., p. 468.
41 Ibid., p. 469.
42 Ibid., p. 469.
43 W. I. Thomas, *The Unadjusted Girl,* New York, 1967 (1923).
44 Parsons, 'Some problems of general theory', p. 46.
45 Parsons, 'Social structure and the symbolic media of interchange', pp. 105-6.
46 Parsons and Platt, op. cit., p. 71.
47 Ibid., p. 77.
48 Ibid., p. 318.
49 Thomas, op. cit., p. 13.
50 Parsons and Platt, op. cit., p. 78. Their italics.

51 Thomas, op. cit, p. 17.
52 Ibid., p. 42.

6 Testing the theory against its premises

1 See chapter 1, pp. 14-19.
2 T. Parsons, 'Some problems of general theory', in J. McKinney and E. Tiryakian, eds, *Theoretical Sociology*, New York, 1970, p. 29.
3 See chapter 1, pp. 20-7.
4 T. Parsons, 'On the concept of political power', in T. Parsons, *Politics and Social Structure*, New York, 1969, p. 355.
5 T. Parsons and G. Platt, *The American University*, Cambridge, Mass., 1973.
6 See chapter 5, sections 3 and 5.
7 Cf. Parsons and Platt, op. cit., pp. 305-8, 316-20.
8 A. Gouldner, *The Coming Crisis of Western Sociology*, London, 1971 (1970), pp. 202-3.
9 Cf. D. Martindale, 'Talcott Parsons' theoretical metamorphosis from social behaviorism to macrofunctionalism', *Alpha Kappa Delta*, winter 1959, pp. 38-46.
10 Cf. R. Dahrendorf, 'Toward a theory of social conflict', *Journal of Conflict Resolution*, 2, 1958, pp. 1958, pp. 170-83, also included in W. Wallace, *Sociological Theory*, London, 1969; and 'Out of Utopia: toward a reorientation of sociological analysis', *American Journal of Sociology*, 64, 1958, pp. 115-27, also included in L. A. Coser and B. Rosenberg, eds, *Sociological Theory*, New York, 1976 (1964).
11 Cf. C. Wright Mills, *The Sociological Imagination*, New York, 1959.
12 Cf. Gouldner, op. cit., p. 199: 'Undergirding the phantasmagorical conceptual superstructure that Parsons has raised there is an unshakable metaphysical conviction: that the world is one, and must be made safe in its oneness. Its oneness, Parsons believes, is the world's most vital character'.
13 See note 9.
14 Martindale, op. cit., p. 39.
15 Ibid., p. 39.
16 Ibid., p. 40.
17 Ibid., p. 41.
18 Ibid., p. 41.
19 See chapter 1, p. 17.
20 Martindale, op cit., p. 42.
21 Cf. Ibid., p. 43-4
22 D. Wrong, 'The oversocialized conception of man in modern sociology', *American Sociological Review*, 26, 1961, pp. 183-93; D. Lockwood, 'Some remarks on the social system', *British Journal of Sociology*, 7, 1956, pp. 134-46.
23 T. Parsons, *The Social System*, Glencoe, Ill, 1951, p. 205.
24 Gouldner, op. cit., p. 232.
25 Cf. R. Dahrendorf, 'Out of Utopia'.
26 See chapter 3, pp. 81-2.

27 R. Dahrendorf, 'Toward a theory of social conflict', quoted from Wallace, op. cit., p. 225, footnote 9.
28 Ibid., p. 255, footnote 9.
29 Parsons, *The Social System,* p. 552.
30 G. C. Homans, 'Bringing men back in', *American Sociological Review,* 29, 1964, pp. 809-18.
31 Wright Mills, op. cit; quotations are from the 1970 edition.
32 Ibid., pp. 154-8.
33 Cf. Mills's introduction to Thorstein Veblen, *The Theory of the Leisure Class,* New York, 1953 (1899).
34 Cf. M. J. Wibier, *C. Wright Mills als socioloog en wetenschapstheoreticus,* Deventer, 1976, pp. 10-16.
35 Cf. Gouldner, op. cit., pp. 199-245.

Bibliography

ADORNO, T. W., ed., *Der Positivismusstreit in der deutschen Soziologie,* Neuwied and Berlin, 1969.
ADORNO, T. W., ed., 'Zur Logik der Sozialwissenschaften', in T. W. Adorno, ed., *Der Positivismusstreit in der deutschen Soziologie,* Neuwied and Berlin, 1969, pp. 125-43.
ADRIAANSENS, H. P. M., 'Parsons' eerste fase', *Sociale Wetenschappen,* 15, 1, 1972, pp. 1-25.
ADRIAANSENS, H. P. M., 'Parsons' tweede fase', *Sociale Wetenschappen,* 15, 4, 1972, pp. 241-62.
ADRIAANSENS, H. P. M., 'Sociologie, een humanity', *Sociale Wetenschappen,* 16, 4, 1973, pp. 227-35.
ALLPORT, G., 'The open system in personality theory', *Sociometry,* 24, 2, 1961, pp. 301-10, and in W. Buckley, *Modern Systems Research for the Behavioral Scientist,* Chicago, 1968, pp. 343-50.
ATKINSON, D., *Orthodox Consensus and Radical Alternative: a study in sociological theory,* London, 1971.
BALES, R. F., *Interaction Process Analysis: a method for the study of small groups,* Reading, Mass., 1950.
BALES, R. F., PARSONS, T. and SHILS, E., eds, *Working Papers in the Theory of Action,* New York, 1953.
BERGER, P. and LUCKMANN, T., *The Social Construction of Reality,* New York, 1966.
BERSHADY, H. J., *Ideology and Social Knowledge,* Oxford, 1973.
BIERSTEDT, R., 'Nominal and real definitions', in L. Gross, ed., *Symposium on Sociological Theory,* New York, 1959, pp. 121-44.
BIERSTEDT, R., ed., *Florian Znaniecki, On Humanistic Sociology,* Chicago, 1969.
BLACK, M., ed., *The Social Theories of Talcott Parsons,* Englewood Cliffs, N.J., 1961.
BLAIN, R., 'A critique of Parsons' four-function paradigm', *Sociological Quarterly,* 11, 1970, pp. 157-68.
BLAIN, R., 'An alternative to Parsons' four-function paradigm as a basis

for developing general sociological theory', *American Sociological Review,* 36, 1971, pp. 678-92.

BLAU, P., ed., *Approaches to the Study of Social Structure,* New York, 1975.

BLUMER, H., *Symbolic Interactionism,* Englewood Cliffs, N.J., 1969.

BOULDING, K., 'General systems theory, the skeleton of science', in W. Buckley, ed., *Modern Systems Research for the Behavioral Scientist,* Chicago, 1968, pp. 3-10.

BOULDING, K., *A Primer on Social Dynamics; history as dialectics and development,* New York, 1970.

BOURRICAUD, F., *Introduction à Talcott Parsons; éléments pour une sociologie de l'action,* Paris, 1955.

BRANDENBURG, A. G., *Systemzwang und Autonomie; Gesellschaft und Persönlichkeit bei Talcott Parsons,* Düsseldorf, 1971.

BREDEMEIER, H. C., 'The methodology of functionalism', *American Sociological Review,* 21, 1956, pp. 129-35.

BREDEMEIER, H. C. and STEPHENSON, R. M., *The Analysis of Social Systems,* New York, 1962.

BRODBECK, M., ed., *Readings in the Philosophy of the Social Sciences,* New York, 1968.

BRODBECK, M. and FEIGL, H., eds, *Readings in the Philosophy of Science,* New York, 1953.

BUCKLEY, W., *Sociology and Modern Systems Theory,* Englewood Cliffs, N.J., 1967.

BUCKLEY, W., ed., *Modern Systems Research for the Behavioral Scientist; a sourcebook,* Chicago, 1968.

CANCIAN, F., 'Functional analysis of change', *American Sociological Review,* 25, 1960, pp. 818-27.

CANNON, W. B., *The Wisdom of the Body,* New York, 1932.

CHAZEL, F., *La Théorie analytique de la société dans l'oeuvre de Talcott Parsons,* Paris, 1974.

COHEN, J., HAZELRIGG, L. E. and POPE, W., 'De-Parsonizing Weber; a critique of Parsons' interpretation of Weber's sociology', *American Sociological Review,* 40, 1975, pp. 229-41.

COHEN, P. S., *Modern Social Theories,* London, 1968.

COOLEY, C. H., *Social Organization; a study of the larger mind,* Glencoe, Ill., 1956, (1909).

COSER, L. A., *The Functions of Social Conflict,* Glencoe, Ill., 1956.

COSER, L. A. and ROSENBERG, B., eds, *Sociological Theory,* London, 1976, (1957).

DAHRENDORF, R., 'Struktur und Funktion; Talcott Parsons und die Entwicklung der soziologischen Theorie', *Kölner Zeitschrift für Soziologie und Sozialpsychologie,* 7, 4, 1955, pp. 491-519.

DAHRENDORF, R., *Sozialen Klassen und Klassenkonflikt in der Industriellen Gesellschaft,* Stuttgart, 1957.

DAHRENDORF, R., 'Out of Utopia; toward a reorientation of sociological analysis', *American Journal of Sociology,* 64, 1958, pp. 115-27.

DAHRENDORF, R., *Homo Sociologicus; ein Versuch zur Geschichte, Bedeutung und Kritik der Kategorie des sozialen Rolle,* Cologne, 1959.

BIBLIOGRAPHY

DAHRENDORF, R., *Gesellschaft und Freiheit: Zur soziologischen Analyse der Gegenwart,* Munich, 1961.

DAHRENDORF, R., 'Toward a theory of social conflict', in W. Wallace, ed., *Sociological Theory,* London, 1969, pp. 213-26. Also in *Journal of Conflict Resolution,* 1958, 2, pp. 176-83.

DEMERATH, N. J. and PETERSON, R. A., eds, *System, Change and Conflict,* New York, 1967.

DEUTSCH, K. W., 'Mechanism, teleology, and mind', *Philosophy and Phenomenological Research,* 12, 1951, pp. 185-223.

DEUTSCH, K. W., 'Mechanism, organism and society; some models in natural and societal science', *Philosophy of Science,* 18, 1951, pp. 230-52.

DEUTSCH, K. W., *The Nerves of Government,* New York, 1963.

DEVEREUX, E. C., 'Parsons' sociological theory', in: M. Black, ed., *The Social Theories of Talcott Parsons,* Englewood Cliffs, N.J., 1961, pp. 1-63.

DOMHOFF, G. W. and BALLARD, H. B., eds, *C. Wright Mills and the Power Elite,* Boston, 1968.

DUBIN, R., 'Parsons' actor; continuities in social theory', *American Sociological Review,* 25, 1960, pp. 457-66.

DURKHEIM, E., *Le Suicide: Etude de sociologie,* Paris, 1960 (1897).

DURKHEIM, E., *De la Division du travail social: Étude sur l'organisation des sociétés supérieures,* Paris, 1967 (1893).

DURKHEIM, E., *Les Règles de la méthode sociologique,* Paris, 1967 (1895).

DURKHEIM, E., *Les formes élémentaires de la vie religieuse; le système totemique en Australie,* Paris, 1968 (1912).

EASTON, D., *A Framework for Political Analysis,* Englewood Cliffs, N.J., 1965.

EMERSON, A. E., 'Dynamic homeostasis; a unifying principle in organic, social and ethical evolution', *Scientific Monthly,* 78, 1954, pp. 67-85.

EMMET, D., and MACINTYRE. A., eds, *Sociological Theory and Philosophical Analysis,* London, 1970.

ETZIONI, A., *The Active Society,* New York, 1968.

FALDING, H., 'Toward a reconciliation of Mills with Parsons', *American Sociological Review,* 26, 1961, pp. 778-80.

FEIGL, H. and BRODBECK, M., eds, *Readings in the Philosophy of Science,* New York, 1953.

GERSTEIN, D. R., 'A note on the continuity of Parsonian action theory', *Sociological Inquiry,* 45, 4, 1975, pp. 11-15.

GIDDENS, A., *Capitalism and Modern Social Theory; an analysis of the writings of Marx, Durkheim and Max Weber,* Cambridge, 1971.

GIDDENS, A., ed., *Emile Durkheim; selected writings,* with introduction, London, 1972.

GIDDENS, A., ed,. *Positivism and Sociology,* London, 1974.

GODDIJN, H. P. M., *Het functionalisme in de sociologie,* Assen, 1963.

GODDIJN, H. P. M., *De sociologie van Emile Durkheim,* Amsterdam, 1969.

GODDIJN, H. P. M., et al., *Geschiedenis van de sociologie; achtergronden, hoofdpersonen en richtingen,* Meppel, 1971.

BIBLIOGRAPHY

GOULDNER, A., 'Reciprocity and autonomy in functional theory', in L. Gross, ed., *Symposium on Sociological Theory,* pp. 240-70.

GOULDNER, A., *The Coming Crisis of Western Sociology,* London, 1971, New York, 1970.

GRINKER, R., ed., *Toward a Unified Theory of Human Behavior,* New York, 1956.

GROSS, L., ed., *Symposium on Sociological Theory,* New York, 1959.

GURVITCH, G. and MOORE, W. E., eds, *Twentieth Century Sociology,* New York, 1945.

HABERMAS, J., 'Analytische Wissenschaftstheorie und Dialektik', in T. W. Adorno, ed., *Der Positivismusstreit in der deutschen Soziologie,* Neuwied and Berlin, 1969, pp. 155-91.

HAFERKAMP, H., *Soziologie als Handlungstheorie,* Düsseldorf, 1972.

HEMPEL, C., 'The logic of functional analysis', in L. Gross, ed., *Symposium on Sociological Theory,* New York, 1959, pp. 271-307.

HOMANS, G. C., *Social Behaviour: its elementary forms,* London, 1961.

HOMANS, G. C., 'Bringing men back in', *American Sociological Review,* 29, 1964, pp. 809-18.

ISAJIW, W. W., *Causation and Functionalism in Sociology,* London, 1968.

JOHNSON, H. M., *Sociology, a Systematic Introduction,* London, 1961.

KUHN, T., *The Structure of Scientific Revolutions,* Chicago, 1970 (1962).

LEVY, M., *The Structure of Society,* Princeton, N.J., 1952.

LOCKWOOD, D., 'Some remarks on the social system', *British Journal of Sociology,* 7, 2, 1956, pp. 134-46.

LOCKWOOD, D., 'Social integration and system integration', in E. K. Zollschan and W. Hirsch, eds, *Explorations in Social Change,* Boston, 1964, pp. 244-57.

LOOMIS, C. P., *Social Systems, essays on their persistence and change,* Princeton, N.J., 1960.

LOOMIS, C. P. and LOOMIS, Z., *Modern Social Theories; Selected American Writers,* Princeton, N.J., 1961.

MCKINNEY. J. and TIRYAKIAN, E. A., eds, *Theoretical Sociology: perspectives and developments,* New York, 1970.

MARTINDALE, D., 'Talcott Parsons' theoretical metamorphosis from social behaviorism to macrofunctionalism', *Alpha Kappa Delta,* winter 1959, pp. 38-46.

MARTINDALE, D., *The Nature and Types of Sociological Theory,* Boston, 1960, London, 1961.

MARTINDALE, D., *Community, Character and Civilization,* New York, 1963.

MEAD, G. H., *Mind, Self and Society; from the standpoint of a social behaviorist,* Chicago, 1967 (1934).

MERTON, R. K., 'On the position of sociological theory', *American Sociological Review,* 13, April 1948, pp. 164-8.

MERTON, R. K., *Social Theory and Social Structure,* New York, 1957, rev. ed., 1949.

MERTON, R. K., 'Structural analysis in sociology', in P. Blau, ed., *Approaches to the Study of Social Structure,* New York, 1975, pp. 21-52.

MERTON, R. K., BROOM, L, and COTTRELL, L. S., eds, *Sociology Today,* New York, 1958.
MILLS, C. WRIGHT, *The Power Elite,* New York, 1956.
MILLS, C. WRIGHT, *The Sociological Imagination,* New York, 1959.
MILLS, C. WRIGHT, *Power, Politics and People: the collected essays of C. Wright Mills,* New York, 1963.
MITCHELL, W., *Sociological Analysis and Politics; the theories of Talcott Parsons,* Englewood Cliffs, N.J., 1967.
MOOR, R. A. de, *De Verklaring van het Conflict,* Assen, 1961.
NIJHOFF, P., 'Talcott Parsons', in L. Rademakers and E. Petersma, eds, *Hoofdfiguren uit de sociologie,* Utrecht/Antwerp, 1974, vol. 2, pp. 23-38.
PARETO, V., *The Mind and Society, Treatise on General Sociology,* New York, 1935.
PARETO, V., *Sociological Writings,* ed., S. E. Finer, London, 1966.
PARSONS, T., ' "Capitalism" in recent German literature: Sombart and Weber', I, *Journal of Political Economy,* 36, 1928, pp. 641-61.
PARSONS, T., ' "Capitalism" in recent German literature: Sombart and Weber', II, *Journal of Political Economy,* 37, 1929, pp. 31-51.
PARSONS, T., 'Sociological elements in economic thought', I, *Quarterly Journal of Economics,* 49, 1934/35, pp. 414-53.
PARSONS, T., 'Sociological elements in economic thought', II, *Quarterly Journal of Economics,* 49, 1934/35, pp. 645-67.
PARSONS, T., 'The place of ultimate values in sociological theory', *International Journal of Ethics,* 45, 1935, pp. 282-316.
PARSONS, T., *The Structure of Social Action,* Glencoe, Ill., 1949 (1937).
PARSONS, T., 'The role of theory in social research', *American Sociological Review,* 3, 1938, pp. 13-20.
PARSONS, T., 'The role of ideas in social action', *American Sociological Review,* 3, 1938, pp. 653-64 (also in: *Essays in Sociological Theory,* rev. ed., pp. 19-33).
PARSONS, T., 'The professions and social structure', *Social Forces,* 17, 1939, pp. 457-67 (also in: *Essays in Sociological Theory,* rev. ed., pp. 34-9).
PARSONS, T., 'Democracy and social structure in pre-Nazi Germany', *Journal of Legal and Political Sociology,* I, 1942, pp. 96-114 (also in *Essays in Sociological Theory,* rev. ed., pp. 104-23).
PARSONS, T., 'The present position and prospects of systematic theory in sociology', in G. Gurvitch and W. E. Moore, eds, *Twentieth Century Sociology* (also in *Essays in Sociological Theory,* rev. ed., pp. 212-37).
PARSONS, T., ed., *Max Weber: The Theory of Social and Economic Organization,* with introduction, New York, 1947.
PARSONS, T., 'The position of sociological theory', *American Sociological Review,* 13, 1948, pp. 156-64.
PARSONS, T., *Essays in Sociological Theory Pure and Applied,* New York, 1949. From 1954 known as *Essays in Sociological Theory,* New York, 1954.
PARSONS, T., 'The prospect of sociological theory', *American Sociological Review,* 15, 1950, pp. 13-16 (also in *Essays in Sociological Theory,* rev. ed., pp. 348-69).

PARSONS, T., *The Social System,* New York, 1951.

PARSONS, T., 'Some comments on the state of the general theory of action', *American Sociological Review,* 18, 1953, pp. 618-31.

PARSONS, T., 'A sociological approach to the theory of organization', *Administative Science Quarterly,* I, 1956, pp. 63-85, II, pp. 225-39 (also in: *Structure and Process in Modern Society,* pp. 16-58).

PARSONS, T., 'The distribution of power in American society', *World Politics,* 10, October 1957, pp. 123-43 (also in: *Structure and Process in Modern Society,* pp. 199-225).

PARSONS, T., 'General theory in sociology', in R. K. Mertin, L. Broom and L. S. Cottrell, eds, *Sociology Today,* New York, 1958, pp. 3-38.

PARSONS, T., 'An approach to psychological theory in terms of theory of action', in S. Koch, ed., *Psychology: A Study of a Science,* vol. 3, New York, 1959, pp. 612-711.

PARSONS, T., 'Voting and the equilibrium of the American political system', in E. Burdick and A. Brodbeck, eds, *American Voting Behavior,* New York, 1959, pp. 80-120 (also in: *Sociological Theory and Modern Society,* pp. 223-63, and in: *Politics and Social Structure,* pp. 204-40).

PARSONS, T., 'Durkheim's contribution to the theory of integration of social systems', in K. H. Wolff, ed., *Emile Durkheim, 1858-1917: A Collection of Essays,* Columbus, Ohio, 1959, pp. 118-53 (also in: *Sociological Theory and Modern Society,* pp. 3-34).

PARSONS, T., *Structure and Process in Modern Societies,* New York, 1960.

PARSONS, T., 'Pattern variables revisited; a response to Robert Dubin' *American Sociological Review,* 25, 1960, 4, pp. 467-83 (also in: *Sociological Theory and Modern Society,* pp. 192-219).

PARSONS, T., 'The point of view of the author', in M. Black, ed., *The Social Theories of Talcott Parsons,* Englewood Cliffs, N.J., 1961, pp. 311-63.

PARSONS, T., 'Some considerations on the theory of social change', *Rural Sociology,* 26, 3, 1961, pp. 219-39.

PARSONS, T., 'Introduction' to Max Weber, *The Sociology of Religion,* Boston, 1963.

PARSONS, T., 'On the concept of influence', *Public Opinion Quarterly,* 27, spring 1963, pp. 37-62 (also in: *Sociological Theory and Modern Society,* pp. 355-82, and in *Politics and Social Structure,* pp. 405-29).

PARSONS, T., 'On the concept of political power', *Proceedings of the American Philosophical Society,* 107, 1963, pp. 232-62 (also in: *Sociological Theory and Modern Society,* pp. 297-354, and in *Politics and Social Structure,* pp. 352-404).

PARSONS, T., *Social Structure and Personality,* New York, 1964.

PARSONS, T., 'The ideas of systems, causal explanation and cybernetic control in social science', in D. Lerner, ed., *Cause and Effect,* New York, 1965, pp. 51-73.

PARSONS, T., 'Evolutionary universals in society', *American Sociological Review,* 29, 3, 1964, pp. 339-58 (also in: *Sociological Theory and Modern Society,* pp. 490-520).

PARSONS, T., 'Die jüngsten Entwicklungen in der strukturell-funktionalen Theorie', *Kölner Zeitschrift für Soziologie und Sozialpsychologie,* 16, 1, 1964, pp. 30-49.

PARSONS, T., *Societies; Evolutionary and Comparative Perspectives,* Englewood Cliffs, N.J., 1966.

PARSONS, T., *Sociological Theory and Modern Society,* New York, 1967.

PARSONS, T., 'On the concept of value-commitments', *Sociological Inquiry,* 38, 1968, pp. 135-60 (also in: *Politics and Social Structure,* pp. 439-72).

PARSONS, T., 'Utilitarianism', in *International Encyclopedia of Social Sciences,* New York, 1968.

PARSONS, T., ed., *American Sociology; a collection of essays,* New York, 1968.

PARSONS, T., *Politics and Social Structure,* New York, 1969.

PARSONS, T., 'Some problems of general theory in sociology', in J. McKinney and E. Tiryakian, eds, *Theoretical Sociology; perspectives and developments,* New York, 1970, pp. 29-68.

PARSONS, T., 'On building social system theory, a personal history', *Daedalus,* 99, 4, 1970, pp. 826-81.

PARSONS, T., *The System of Modern Societies,* Englewood Cliffs, N.J., 1971.

PARSONS, T., 'Social structure and the symbolic media of interchange', in P. Blau, ed., *Approaches to the Study of Social Structure,* New York, 1975.

PARSONS, T., BALES, R. E., OLDS, J., ZELDITCH, M. and SLATER, P. E., *Family, Socialization and Interaction Process,* New York, 1955.

PARSONS, T., BALES, R. F. and SHILS, E. A., *Working Papers in the Theory of Action,* New York, 1953.

PARSONS, T. and KROEBER, A. L., 'The concepts of culture and of social system', *American Sociological Review,* 23, 1958, p. 582.

PARSONS, T. and PLATT, G., *The American University,* Cambridge, Mass., 1973.

PARSONS, T. and SHILS, E. A., eds, *Toward a General Theory of Action,* Cambridge, Mass., 1951, New York, 1962.

PARSONS, T., SHILS, E., NAEGELE, K. D. and PITTS, J. R., eds, *Theories of Society,* 2 vols, New York, 1961.

PARSONS, T. and SMELSER, N. J., *Economy and Society,* London, 1956.

POPE, W., 'Classic on classic: Parsons' interpretation of Durkheim', *American Sociological Review,* 38, 1973, pp. 399-415.

POPE, W., 'Parsons on Durkheim, revisited', *American Sociological Review,* 40, 1975, pp. 111-15.

POPE, W., COHEN, J. and HAZELRIGG, L., 'On the divergence of Weber and Durkheim: a critique of Parsons' convergence thesis'. *American Sociological Review,* 40, 1975, pp. 417-27.

POPPER, K., *The Poverty of Historicism,* London, 1960.

POPPER, K., *The Open Society and its Enemies,* 2 vols, London, 1969, rev. ed. (1945).

POPPER, K., *Conjectures and Refutations; the growth of scientific knowledge,* London, 1969, rev. ed. (1963).

POPPER, K., 'Die Logik der Sozialwissenschaften', in T. W. Adorno, *Der Positivismusstreit in der deutschen Soziologie,* Neuwied and Berlin, 1969, pp. 103-23.

REX, J., *Key Problems of Sociological Theory,* London, 1961.

RHOADS, J. K., 'On Gouldner's crisis of western sociology', *American Journal of Sociology*, 78, 1972, pp. 136-54.
RICKERT, H., *Kulturwissenschaft und Naturwissenschaft*, Tübingen, 1926 (1899).
ROCHER, G., *Talcott Parsons et la sociologie américaine*, Paris, 1972; English edition *Talcott Parsons and American Sociology*, London, 1974.
SAHAY, A., *Sociological Analysis*, London, 1972.
SCHUTZ, A., 'The social world and the theory of social action', *Social Research*, 27, 1960, pp. 203-21.
SCHUTZ, A., 'Common sense and scientific interpretation of human action', *Collected Papers*, I, The Hague, 1962, pp. 3-47.
SCOTT, J. F., 'The changing foundations of the Parsonian action schema', *American Sociological Review*, 28, 1963, pp. 716-35.
SIMMEL, G., *The Sociology of Georg Simmel*, ed., with introduction by K. H. Wolff, New York, 1965 (1950).
SIMMEL, G., *Een keuze uit het werk van Georg Simmel*, Deventer, 1976.
SKINNER, B. F., *Science and Human Behavior*, New York, 1965 (1953).
SMELSER, N. J., *Social Change in the Industrial Revolution*, London, 1959.
SMELSER, N. J., 'Epilogue: social structural dimensions of higher education', in T. Parsons and G. Platt, *The American University*, Cambridge, Mass., 1973.
SMELSER, N. J. and PARSONS, T., *Economy and Society*, London, 1956.
SOROKIN, P., *Fads and Foibles in Modern Sociology and Related Sciences*, Chicago, 1956.
SOROKIN, P., *Contemporary Sociological Theories*, New York, 1964 (1928).
SOROKIN, P., *Sociological Theories of Today*, New York, 1966.
STINCHCOMBE, A. L., *Constructing Social Theories*, New York, 1968.
THOMAS, W. I., *The Unadjusted Girl; with cases and standpoints for behavior analysis*, New York, 1967 (1923).
THOMAS, W. I. and ZNANIECKI, F., *The Polish Peasant in Europe and America*, New York, 1974 (1918).
TIMASHEFF, N. S., *Sociological Theory, its nature and growth*, New York, 1955.
TJADEN, K. H., ed., *Soziale Systeme*, Neuwied and Berlin, 1971.
TURNER, J., *The Structure of Sociological Theory*, Homewood, Ill., 1974.
TURNER, J. and BEEGHLEY, L., 'Current folklore in the criticisms of Parsonian action theory', *Sociological Inquiry*, 44, 1974, pp. 47-55.
TURNER, T. S., 'Parsons' concept of generalized media of social interaction and its relevance for social anthropology', *Sociological Inquiry*, 38, spring 1968, pp. 121-34.
URMSON, J. O., 'Utilitarianism', in *International Encyclopedia of the Social Sciences*, vol. 16, New York, 1968.
VEBLEN, T., *The Theory of the Leisure Class: an economic study of institutions*, New York, 1899.
WALLACE, W., *Sociological Theory*, London, 1969.
WEBER, M., *Gesammelte Aufsätze zur Religionssoziologie*, 3 vols, Tübingen, 1956 (1921).
WEBER, M., *Wirtschaft und Gesellschaft; Grundriss der verstehende Soziologie*, Tübingen, 1956 (1921).

WEBER, M., *Gesammelte Aufsätze zur Wissenschaftslehre,* Tübingen, 1968 (1922).
WEBER, M., *The Theory of Social and Economic Organization,* translated by A. M. Henderson and T. Parsons, with an introduction written by Parsons, New York, 1947.
WHITEHEAD, A. N., *Science and the Modern World,* New York, 1925.
WIBIER, M. J., *C. Wright Mills als socioloog en wetenschapstheoreticus,* Deventer, 1976.
WILLIAMS, R., 'The sociological theory of Talcott Parsons', in M. Black, ed., *The Social Theories of Talcott Parsons,* Englewood Cliffs, N.J., 1961.
WRONG, D., 'The oversocialized conception of man in modern sociology', *American Sociological Review,* 26, 1961, pp. 183-93.
ZIJDERVELD, A. C., 'The problem of adequacy', *European Journal of Sociology,* 13, 1972, pp. 176-90.
ZIJDERVELD, A. C., *Over het nut en de zin van de sociologie,* Meppel, 1972.
ZIJDERVELD, A. C., 'Recente inductieve sociologie in Amerika', *Sociale Wetenschappen,* 15, 1972, 1, pp. 26-48.
ZIJDERVELD, A. C., *De theorie van het symbolisch interactionisme,* Meppel, 1973.
ZIJDERVELD, A. C., *De relativiteit van kennis en werkelijkheid,* Meppel, 1974.
ZIJDERVELD, A. C., *Institutionalisering; een studie over het methodologisch dilemma der sociale wetenschappen,* Hilversum, 1966, Meppel, 1974.
ZIJDERVELD, A. C., 'Twee dilemma's, vier denkvormen', *Sociale Wetenschappen,* 17, 1, 1974, pp. 49-66.
ZNANIECKI, F., *Social Relations and Social Roles; the unfinished systematic sociology,* San Francisco, 1965.
ZNANIECKI, F., *Florian Znaniecki on humanistic sociology; selected papers,* ed., with introduction by Robert Bierstedt, Chicago, 1969.
ZOLLSCHAN, G. K. and HIRSCH, W., eds, *Explorations in Social Change,* Boston, 1964.

Index

achievement, 77-8, 181
adaptation, 110-12
adaptive structures, 82
adequacy, 22-3
affect, 148-9
affectivity, affective neutrality, 68-9, 77-8, 207-8
allocation, 78-9
Allport, G., 9, 177
analytical realism, 21-3
anthropocentric postulate, 55, 162
appreciative standards, 62-3
ascription, 77, 181
aspects of theory, 2-6, 10-14, 167, 173-5
authority, 130
axes of differentiation, 109-10

Bales, R. F., 107, 118, 184-5
behavioural system, 116-17, 144
behaviourism, 32, 36, 104, 112-13
Berting, J., 102-3, 184
bipolarity, 90, 99, 101, 104-5
Black, M., 89, 181, 183-4
Blau, P., 102, 186
Boulding, K., 10, 177
Bredemeier, H. C., 183
Brodbeck, M., 183
Buckley, W., 89, 177, 183

Calvinism, 50-1
Cannon, W. B., 71, 181
capitalism, 49-51
cathectic orientation, 62, 180
charismatic leadership, 140
cognitive mapping, 62-3
cognitive orientation, 62

cognitive standards, 63
collectivity orientation, 69, 77
communication, 132-3
compatibility, 81
complementarity, 95, 97-8, 100
Comte, A., 35, 44
conceptual dilemma, 93-106, 164-75
conceptual theory level, 2, 6, 12-13, 58-9, 93-103
conflict, 169
continuity, 174-5
convergence, 33-4
Cooley, C. H., 30, 118, 144
Coser, C. A., 187
Croce, B., 102
cultural system, 73, 91-2, 112-13
cybernetic hierarchy, 141-3, 159-62

Dahrendorf, R., 100, 165, 169-73, 184, 187, 188
definition of the situation, 111, 149
Devereux, E. C., 181
deviance, 85-7
diffuseness, 68-9, 77-8, 108
double bipolarity, 101
Durkheim, E., 11, 19, 28-9, 35, 43, 46-8, 49, 53, 54-7, 161, 166-8, 179-80
dynamic knowledge, 2, 163

economy, 120-6
emergent properties, 60
empiricism, 3, 20-6
empiristic, 11
epistemological theory level, 2-3, 6, 13-14, 58, 95, 168

INDEX

equilibrium, 70-1, 83-5, 170
evaluative orientation, 62

fallacy of misplaced concreteness, 25
Feigl, H., 183
fiduciary system, 120-6
four-function paradigm, 111-15
frame of reference, 12-13
Frankfurt School, 102
Freud, S., 117, 181
function, 70, 111
functional requisites (conditions), 75

Geiger, T., 53
Gemeinschaft, 136-8, 185
Gerstein, D. R., 185
goal attainment, 110-13
Gouldner, A., 89, 164, 169, 182-3, 187-8
Gross, L., 183

Hempel, C., 183
historicism, 14-15
Hobbes, T., 37, 38, 53, 179
Homans, C. G., 98, 102, 118, 171, 184-5, 188
homeostasis, 70-1, 92

ideal type, 16-23
idealism, 3, 33, 48-52
individual positivism, *see* utilitarianism
influence, 135-8
institutional integration, 83-4
institutionalist economic theory, 24-7
integration, 110-13
intelligence, 146-7
interchange paradigm, 111, 117-18
Isajiw, W. W., 183

Kuhn, T., 9, 177

latency, 110-13
Lazarsfeld, P., 19
levels of theory, 2-6, 10-14, 167, 173-5
Lewin, K., 9
Linton, R., 181
Locke, J., 38, 179
Lockwood, D., 169, 187
Lundberg, G. A., 173

McDougall, W., 9
McKinney, J., 184-5, 187
Marshall, A., 19, 43-4, 46, 54
Martindale, D., 99, 100, 162, 165-9, 172, 183-4, 187

Marx, K., 49
mechanical solidarity, 56
mechanism, 84-7
methodological individualism, 28, 54-5
methodological theory level, 2, 6, 13, 31-2, 59, 93-103
middle range theories, 18
Mills, C. W., 165, 169, 172, 183, 187-8
moral standards, 62-3
motivational orientation, 62-3
motivational paradigm, 83

Nagel, E., 183
neo-Kantian epistemology, 21-6
Newton, I., 70, 170
nomological knowledge, 16, 177, 182

objectivism, 3, 33-4, 97, 158-61
ontological knowledge, 182
order, problem of, 38-42, 46, 53-7
orientation, set, 61-5; 98, 108
orthodox economic theory, 24-7

Pareto, V., 19, 28-9, 43-6, 48, 54-5
particularism, 68-70, 77-8, 108-9
pattern variables, 68-70, 76-8, 107-9
patterns of thought, 4, 13, 33-57
performance, capacity, 68-70, 108; 148
personality system, 61, 74, 76, 92-3, 112-13, 143-4
phenomenology, 23
political theory, 156-7
polity, 120-6, 156-7
positivism, 3, 34-57
Platt, G., 157, 185-7
power, 126, 129-35

quality, 68-70, 108

radical, anti-intellectualistic positivism, 41-2
radical rationalistic positivism, 40-2
reification, 25
Rickert, H., 15-16, 20, 23, 154, 177-8
role (-expectation), 75-8, 80
Rosenberg, B., 187

Sartre, J. P., 53
Schutz, A., 23, 178
Shils, E. A., 177, 180-1, 183-4
Sinnzusammenhang, 50-1
situation, 63-4
situation-set, 78, 98, 108

199

INDEX

Smelser, N. J., 119, 185
social behaviourism, 30, 144-5, 162, 185
social control, 85-7
social nominalism/realism, 3, 33-4, 52, 54, 56-7, 91, 99, 161-2, 166
social system, 61, 72-87, 112-13, 118-24
socialization, 85
societal community, 120-5, 141, 185
sociological theory, definition, 29, 171
sociologistic positivism, 47, 56, 168
solidarity, 122
Sombart, W., 49, 51, 178
specificity, 68-9, 77-8, 108-9
Spencer, H., 55
Stinchcombe, A. L., 183
structural analysis, 80-3, 182
structural-functional theory of social system, 72-87
structural-functionalism, 58-115
structural paradigm, 76-80
subjectivism, *see* objectivism
substantive theory level, 2, 6, 11-12
symbolic interactionism, *see* social behaviourism
symbolic medium, 126-41, 145-9
system levels, 117-18, 158-9, 162-3

tendencies, 84-7
theoretical metamorphosis, 166-8, 173
theories of the middle range, 18
theory, concept of, 2, 10-14

Tiryakian, E. A., 185, 187
Tönnies, F., 185

unit act, 59-61, 76, 91, 158
unit of action, 61, 76, 91
universalism, 68-70, 77-8, 108-9
Urmson, J. O., 179
utilitarian dilemma, 41-2, 46
utilitarianism, 36-43, 46-7

value-commitment, 126, 129, 138-41
Veblen, T., 26, 172, 188
voluntarism, 3, 5, 32-57, 58-9, 116, 157-65
voluntary association, 138

Wahlverwandtschaft, 19, 29, 50, 82, 161
Wallace, W., 187-8
Watson, J., 9
Weber, M., 3, 11, 15-24, 28-9, 32-3, 48-53, 57, 82, 119, 129, 140, 148, 152-5, 160-1, 166-8, 173, 177-9, 182
Whitehead, A. N., 179
Wibier, M. J., 188
Winch, P., 102
Wrong, D., 100, 169, 184, 187

zero-sum, 128, 134
Zijderveld, A. C., 4, 23, 53, 57, 94-5, 177-9, 183

Routledge Social Science Series

Routledge & Kegan Paul   London, Henley and Boston

39 Store Street, London WC1E 7DD
Broadway House, Newtown Road,
Henley-on-Thames, Oxon RG9 1EN
9 Park Street, Boston, Mass. 02108

Contents

International Library of Sociology 3
General Sociology 3
Foreign Classics of Sociology 4
Social Structure 4
Sociology and Politics 5
Criminology 5
Social Psychology 6
Sociology of the Family 6
Social Services 7
Sociology of Education 8
Sociology of Culture 8
Sociology of Religion 9
Sociology of Art and Literature 9
Sociology of Knowledge 9
Urban Sociology 10
Rural Sociology 10
Sociology of Industry and Distribution 10
Anthropology 11
Sociology and Philosophy 12
International Library of Anthropology 12
International Library of Social Policy 13
International Library of Welfare and Philosophy 13
Primary Socialization, Language and Education 14
Reports of the Institute of Community Studies 14
Reports of the Institute for Social Studies in Medical Care 15
Medicine, Illness and Society 15
Monographs in Social Theory 15
Routledge Social Science Journals 16
Social and Psychological Aspects of Medical Practice 16

Authors wishing to submit manuscripts for any series in this catalogue should send them to the Social Science Editor, Routledge & Kegan Paul Ltd, 39 Store Street, London WC1E 7DD

●*Books so marked are available in paperback*
All books are in Metric Demy 8vo format (216 × 138mm approx.)

International Library of Sociology

General Editor John Rex

GENERAL SOCIOLOGY

Barnsley, J. H. The Social Reality of Ethics. *464 pp.*
Brown, Robert. Explanation in Social Science. *208 pp.*
● Rules and Laws in Sociology. *192 pp.*
Bruford, W. H. Chekhov and His Russia. *A Sociological Study. 244 pp.*
Burton, F. and **Carlen, P.** Official Discourse. *On Discourse Analysis, Government Publications, Ideology. About 140 pp.*
Cain, Maureen E. Society and the Policeman's Role. *326 pp.*
●**Fletcher, Colin.** Beneath the Surface. *An Account of Three Styles of Sociological Research. 221 pp.*
Gibson, Quentin. The Logic of Social Enquiry. *240 pp.*
Glucksmann, M. Structuralist Analysis in Contemporary Social Thought. *212 pp.*
Gurvitch, Georges. Sociology of Law. *Foreword by Roscoe Pound. 264 pp.*
Hinkle, R. Founding Theory of American Sociology 1883-1915. *About 350 pp.*
Homans, George C. Sentiments and Activities. *336 pp.*
Johnson, Harry M. Sociology: *a Systematic Introduction. Foreword by Robert K. Merton. 710 pp.*
●**Keat, Russell** and **Urry, John.** Social Theory as Science. *278 pp.*
Mannheim, Karl. Essays on Sociology and Social Psychology. *Edited by Paul Kecskemeti. With Editorial Note by Adolph Lowe. 344 pp.*
Martindale, Don. The Nature and Types of Sociological Theory. *292 pp.*
●**Maus, Heinz.** A Short History of Sociology. *234 pp.*
Myrdal, Gunnar. Value in Social Theory: *A Collection of Essays on Methodology. Edited by Paul Streeten. 332 pp.*
Ogburn, William F. and **Nimkoff, Meyer F.** A Handbook of Sociology. *Preface by Karl Mannheim. 656 pp. 46 figures. 35 tables.*
Parsons, Talcott, and **Smelser, Neil J.** Economy and Society: *A Study in the Integration of Economic and Social Theory. 362 pp.*
Podgórecki, Adam. Practical Social Sciences. *About 200 pp.*
Raffel, S. Matters of Fact. *A Sociological Inquiry. 152 pp.*
●**Rex, John.** (Ed.) Approaches to Sociology. *Contributions by Peter Abell, Sociology and the Demystification of the Modern World. 282 pp.*
●**Rex, John** (Ed.) Approaches to Sociology. *Contributions by Peter Abell, Frank Bechhofer, Basil Bernstein, Ronald Fletcher, David Frisby, Miriam Glucksmann, Peter Lassman, Herminio Martins, John Rex, Roland Robertson, John Westergaard and Jock Young. 302 pp.*
Rigby, A. Alternative Realities. *352 pp.*
Roche, M. Phenomenology, Language and the Social Sciences. *374 pp.*
Sahay, A. Sociological Analysis. *220 pp.*

INTERNATIONAL LIBRARY OF SOCIOLOGY

Strasser, Hermann. The Normative Structure of Sociology. *Conservative and Emancipatory Themes in Social Thought. About 340 pp.*
Strong, P. Ceremonial Order of the Clinic. *About 250 pp.*
Urry, John. Reference Groups and the Theory of Revolution. *244 pp.*
Weinberg, E. Development of Sociology in the Soviet Union. *173 pp.*

FOREIGN CLASSICS OF SOCIOLOGY
● **Gerth, H. H.** and **Mills, C. Wright.** From Max Weber: *Essays in Sociology. 502 pp.*
● **Tönnies, Ferdinand.** Community and Association. *(Gemeinschaft and Gesellschaft.) Translated and Supplemented by Charles P. Loomis. Foreword by Pitirim A. Sorokin. 334 pp.*

SOCIAL STRUCTURE
Andreski, Stanislav. Military Organization and Society. *Foreword by Professor A. R. Radcliffe-Brown. 226 pp. 1 folder.*
Carlton, Eric. Ideology and Social Order. *Foreword by Professor Philip Abrahams. About 320 pp.*
Coontz, Sydney H. Population Theories and the Economic Interpretation. *202 pp.*
Coser, Lewis. The Functions of Social Conflict. *204 pp.*
Dickie-Clark, H. F. Marginal Situation: *A Sociological Study of a Coloured Group. 240 pp. 11 tables.*
Giner, S. and **Archer, M. S.** (Eds.). Contemporary Europe. *Social Structures and Cultural Patterns. 336 pp.*
● **Glaser, Barney** and **Strauss, Anselm L.** Status Passage. *A Formal Theory. 212 pp.*
Glass, D. V. (Ed.) Social Mobility in Britain. *Contributions by J. Berent, T. Bottomore, R. C. Chambers, J. Floud, D. V. Glass, J. R. Hall, H. T. Himmelweit, R. K. Kelsall, F. M. Martin, C. A. Moser, R. Mukherjee, and W. Ziegel. 420 pp.*
Kelsall, R. K. Higher Civil Servants in Britain: *From 1870 to the Present Day. 268 pp. 31 tables.*
● **Lawton, Denis.** Social Class, Language and Education. *192 pp.*
McLeish, John. The Theory of Social Change: *Four Views Considered. 128 pp.*
● **Marsh, David C.** The Changing Social Structure of England and Wales, *1871-1961. Revised edition. 288 pp.*
Menzies, Ken. Talcott Parsons and the Social Image of Man. *About 208 pp.*
● **Mouzelis, Nicos.** Organization and Bureaucracy. *An Analysis of Modern Theories. 240 pp.*
Ossowski, Stanislaw. Class Structure in the Social Consciousness. *210 pp.*
● **Podgórecki, Adam.** Law and Society. *302 pp.*
Renner, Karl. Institutions of Private Law and Their Social Functions. *Edited, with an Introduction and Notes, by O. Kahn-Freud. Translated by Agnes Schwarzschild. 316 pp.*

Rex, J. and **Tomlinson**, S. Colonial Immigrants in a British City. *A Class Analysis.* *368 pp.*
Smooha, S. Israel: Pluralism and Conflict. *472 pp.*
Wesolowski, W. Class, Strata and Power. *Trans. and with Introduction by G. Kolankiewicz.* *160 pp.*
Zureik, E. Palestinians in Israel. *A Study in Internal Colonialism.* *264 pp.*

SOCIOLOGY AND POLITICS

Acton, T. A. Gypsy Politics and Social Change. *316 pp.*
Burton, F. Politics of Legitimacy. *Struggles in a Belfast Community.* *250 pp.*
Etzioni-Halevy, E. Political Manipulation and Administrative Power. *A Comparative Study. About 200 pp.*
●**Hechter, Michael.** Internal Colonialism. *The Celtic Fringe in British National Development, 1536–1966.* *380 pp.*
Kornhauser, William. The Politics of Mass Society. *272 pp. 20 tables.*
Korpi, W. The Working Class in Welfare Capitalism. *Work, Unions and Politics in Sweden.* *472 pp.*
Kroes, R. Soldiers and Students. *A Study of Right- and Left-wing Students.* *174 pp.*
Martin, Roderick. Sociology of Power. *About 272 pp.*
Myrdal, Gunnar. The Political Element in the Development of Economic Theory. *Translated from the German by Paul Streeten.* *282 pp.*
Wong, S.-L. Sociology and Socialism in Contemporary China. *160 pp.*
Wootton, Graham. Workers, Unions and the State. *188 pp.*

CRIMINOLOGY

Ancel, Marc. Social Defence: *A Modern Approach to Criminal Problems. Foreword by Leon Radzinowicz.* *240 pp.*
Athens, L. Violent Criminal Acts and Actors. *About 150 pp.*
Cain, Maureen E. Society and the Policeman's Role. *326 pp.*
Cloward, Richard A. and **Ohlin, Lloyd E.** Delinquency and Opportunity: *A Theory of Delinquent Gangs.* *248 pp.*
Downes, David M. The Delinquent Solution. *A Study in Subcultural Theory.* *296 pp.*
Friedlander, Kate. The Psycho-Analytical Approach to Juvenile Delinquency: *Theory, Case Studies, Treatment.* *320 pp.*
Gleuck, Sheldon and **Eleanor.** Family Environment and Delinquency. *With the statistical assistance of Rose W. Kneznek.* *340 pp.*
Lopez-Rey, Manuel. Crime. *An Analytical Appraisal.* *288 pp.*
Mannheim, Hermann. Comparative Criminology: *a Text Book.* *Two volumes. 442 pp. and 380 pp.*
Morris, Terence. The Criminal Area: *A Study in Social Ecology. Foreword by Hermann Mannheim.* *232 pp. 25 tables. 4 maps.*
Podgorecki, A. and **Łos, M.** *Multidimensional Sociology. About 380 pp.*
Rock, Paul. Making People Pay. *338 pp.*

INTERNATIONAL LIBRARY OF SOCIOLOGY

● **Taylor, Ian, Walton, Paul,** and **Young, Jock.** The New Criminology. *For a Social Theory of Deviance. 325 pp.*
● **Taylor, Ian, Walton, Paul** and **Young, Jock.** (Eds) Critical Criminology. *268 pp.*

SOCIAL PSYCHOLOGY

Bagley, Christopher. The Social Psychology of the Epileptic Child. *320 pp.*
Brittan, Arthur. Meanings and Situations. *224 pp.*
Carroll, J. Break-Out from the Crystal Palace. *200 pp.*
● **Fleming, C. M.** Adolescence: Its Social Psychology. *With an Introduction to recent findings from the fields of Anthropology, Physiology, Medicine, Psychometrics and Sociometry. 288 pp.*
● The Social Psychology of Education: *An Introduction and Guide to Its Study. 136 pp.*
Linton, Ralph. The Cultural Background of Personality. *132 pp.*
● **Mayo, Elton.** The Social Problems of an Industrial Civilization. *With an Appendix on the Political Problem. 180 pp.*
Ottaway, A. K. C. Learning Through Group Experience. *176 pp.*
Plummer, Ken. Sexual Stigma. *An Interactionist Account. 254 pp.*
● **Rose, Arnold M.** (Ed.) Human Behaviour and Social Processes: *an Interactionist Approach. Contributions by Arnold M. Rose, Ralph H. Turner, Anselm Strauss, Everett C. Hughes, E. Franklin Frazier, Howard S. Becker et al. 696 pp.*
Smelser, Neil J. Theory of Collective Behaviour. *448 pp.*
Stephenson, Geoffrey M. The Development of Conscience. *128 pp.*
Young, Kimball. Handbook of Social Psychology. *658 pp. 16 figures. 10 tables.*

SOCIOLOGY OF THE FAMILY

Bell, Colin R. Middle Class Families: *Social and Geographical Mobility. 224 pp.*
Burton, Lindy. Vulnerable Children. *272 pp.*
Gavron, Hannah. The Captive Wife: *Conflicts of Household Mothers. 190 pp.*
George, Victor and **Wilding, Paul.** Motherless Families. *248 pp.*
Klein, Josephine. Samples from English Cultures.
  1. Three Preliminary Studies and Aspects of Adult Life in England. *447 pp.*
  2. Child-Rearing Practices and Index. *247 pp.*
Klein, Viola. The Feminine Character. *History of an Ideology. 244 pp.*
McWhinnie, Alexina M. Adopted Children. *How They Grow Up. 304 pp.*
● **Morgan, D. H. J.** Social Theory and the Family. *About 320 pp.*
● **Myrdal, Alva** and **Klein, Viola.** Women's Two Roles: *Home and Work. 238 pp. 27 tables.*

Parsons, Talcott and **Bales, Robert F.** Family: Socialization and Interaction Process. *In collaboration with James Olds, Morris Zelditch and Philip E. Slater.* 456 pp. 50 figures and tables.

SOCIAL SERVICES

Bastide, Roger. The Sociology of Mental Disorder. *Translated from the French by Jean McNeil.* 260 pp.
Carlebach, Julius. Caring For Children in Trouble. 266 pp.
George, Victor. Foster Care. *Theory and Practice.* 234 pp.
    Social Security: *Beveridge and After.* 258 pp.
George, V. and **Wilding, P.** Motherless Families. 248 pp.
● **Goetschius, George W.** Working with Community Groups. 256 pp.
Goetschius, George W. and **Tash, Joan.** Working with Unattached Youth. 416 pp.
Heywood, Jean S. Children in Care. *The Development of the Service for the Deprived Child.* Third revised edition. 284 pp.
King, Roy D., Ranes, Norma V. and **Tizard, Jack.** Patterns of Residential Care. 356 pp.
Leigh, John. Young People and Leisure. 256 pp.
● **Mays, John.** (Ed.) Penelope Hall's Social Services of England and Wales. About 324 pp.
Morris, Mary. Voluntary Work and the Welfare State. 300 pp.
Nokes, P. L. The Professional Task in Welfare Practice. 152 pp.
Timms, Noel. Psychiatric Social Work in Great Britain (1939-1962). 280 pp.
●   Social Casework: *Principles and Practice.* 256 pp.

SOCIOLOGY OF EDUCATION

Banks, Olive. Parity and Prestige in English Secondary Education: a Study in Educational Sociology. 272 pp.
● **Blyth, W. A. L.** English Primary Education. *A Sociological Description.* 2. Background. 168 pp.
Collier, K. G. The Social Purposes of Education: *Personal and Social Values in Education.* 268 pp.
Evans, K. M. Sociometry and Education. 158 pp.
● **Ford, Julienne.** Social Class and the Comprehensive School. 192 pp.
Foster, P. J. Education and Social Change in Ghana. 336 pp. 3 maps.
Fraser, W. R. Education and Society in Modern France. 150 pp.
Grace, Gerald R. Role Conflict and the Teacher. 150 pp.
Hans, Nicholas. New Trends in Education in the Eighteenth Century. 278 pp. 19 tables.
●   Comparative Education: *A Study of Educational Factors and Traditions.* 360 pp.
● **Hargreaves, David.** Interpersonal Relations and Education. 432 pp.
●   Social Relations in a Secondary School. 240 pp.
    School Organization and Pupil Involvement. *A Study of Secondary Schools.*

- **Mannheim, Karl** and **Stewart, W.A.C.** An Introduction to the Sociology of Education. *206 pp.*
- **Musgrove, F.** Youth and the Social Order. *176 pp.*
- **Ottaway, A. K. C.** Education and Society: An Introduction to the Sociology of Education. *With an Introduction by W. O. Lester Smith. 212 pp.*

Peers, Robert. Adult Education: *A Comparative Study. Revised edition. 398 pp.*

Stratta, Erica. The Education of Borstal Boys. *A Study of their Educational Experiences prior to, and during, Borstal Training. 256 pp.*

- **Taylor, P. H., Reid, W. A.** and **Holley, B. J.** The English Sixth Form. *A Case Study in Curriculum Research. 198 pp.*

SOCIOLOGY OF CULTURE

Eppel, E. M. and **M.** Adolescents and Morality: *A Study of some Moral Values and Dilemmas of Working Adolescents in the Context of a changing Climate of Opinion. Foreword by W. J. H. Sprott. 268 pp. 39 tables.*

- **Fromm, Erich.** The Fear of Freedom. *286 pp.*
- The Sane Society. *400 pp.*

Johnson, L. The Cultural Critics. *From Matthew Arnold to Raymond Williams. 233 pp.*

Mannheim, Karl. Essays on the Sociology of Culture. *Edited by Ernst Mannheim in co-operation with Paul Kecskemeti. Editorial Note by Adolph Lowe. 280 pp.*

Zijderfeld, A. C. On Clichés. *The Supersedure of Meaning by Function in Modernity. About 132 pp.*

SOCIOLOGY OF RELIGION

Argyle, Michael and **Beit-Hallahmi, Benjamin.** The Social Psychology of Religion. *About 256 pp.*

Glasner, Peter E. The Sociology of Secularisation. *A Critique of a Concept. About 180 pp.*

Hall, J. R. The Ways Out. *Utopian Communal Groups in an Age of Babylon. 280 pp.*

Ranson, S., Hinings, B. and **Bryman, A.** Clergy, Ministers and Priests. *216 pp.*

Stark, Werner. The Sociology of Religion. *A Study of Christendom.*
Volume II. *Sectarian Religion. 368 pp.*
Volume III. *The Universal Church. 464 pp.*
Volume IV. *Types of Religious Man. 352 pp.*
Volume V. *Types of Religious Culture. 464 pp.*

Turner, B. S. Weber and Islam. *216 pp.*

Watt, W. Montgomery. Islam and the Integration of Society. *320 pp.*

SOCIOLOGY OF ART AND LITERATURE

Jarvie, Ian C. Towards a Sociology of the Cinema. *A Comparative Essay on the Structure and Functioning of a Major Entertainment Industry.* 405 pp.

Rust, Frances S. Dance in Society. *An Analysis of the Relationships between the Social Dance and Society in England from the Middle Ages to the Present Day.* 256 pp. 8 pp. of plates.

Schücking, L. L. The Sociology of Literary Taste. *112 pp.*

Wolff, Janet. Hermeneutic Philosophy and the Sociology of Art. *150 pp.*

SOCIOLOGY OF KNOWLEDGE

Diesing, P. Patterns of Discovery in the Social Sciences. *262 pp.*

● **Douglas, J. D.** (Ed.) Understanding Everyday Life. *370 pp.*

Glasner, B. Essential Interactionism. *About 220 pp.*

● **Hamilton, P.** Knowledge and Social Structure. *174 pp.*

Jarvie, I. C. Concepts and Society. *232 pp.*

Mannheim, Karl. Essays on the Sociology of Knowledge. *Edited by Paul Kecskemeti. Editorial Note by Adolph Lowe.* 353 pp.

Remmling, Gunter W. The Sociology of Karl Mannheim. *With a Bibliographical Guide to the Sociology of Knowledge, Ideological Analysis, and Social Planning.* 255 pp.

Remmling, Gunter W. (Ed.) Towards the Sociology of Knowledge. *Origin and Development of a Sociological Thought Style.* 463 pp.

URBAN SOCIOLOGY

Aldridge, M. The British New Towns. *A Programme Without a Policy.* About 250 pp.

Ashworth, William. The Genesis of Modern British Town Planning: *A Study in Economic and Social History of the Nineteenth and Twentieth Centuries.* 288 pp.

Brittan, A. The Privatised World. *196 pp.*

Cullingworth, J. B. Housing Needs and Planning Policy: *A Restatement of the Problems of Housing Need and 'Overspill' in England and Wales.* 232 pp. 44 tables. 8 maps.

Dickinson, Robert E. City and Region: *A Geographical Interpretation.* 608 pp. 125 figures.

The West European City: *A Geographical Interpretation.* 600 pp. 129 maps. 29 plates.

Humphreys, Alexander J. New Dubliners: *Urbanization and the Irish Family. Foreword by George C. Homans.* 304 pp.

Jackson, Brian. Working Class Community: *Some General Notions raised by a Series of Studies in Northern England.* 192 pp.

● **Mann, P. H.** An Approach to Urban Sociology. *240 pp.*

Mellor, J. R. Urban Sociology in an Urbanized Society. *326 pp.*

Morris, R. N. and **Mogey, J.** The Sociology of Housing. *Studies at Berinsfield.* 232 pp. 4 pp. plates.

Rosser, C. and Harris, C. The Family and Social Change. *A Study of Family and Kinship in a South Wales Town.* 352 pp. 8 maps.
● Stacey, Margaret, Batsone, Eric, Bell, Colin and Thurcott, Anne. Power, Persistence and Change. *A Second Study of Banbury.* 196 pp.

RURAL SOCIOLOGY

Mayer, Adrian C. Peasants in the Pacific. *A Study of Fiji Indian Rural Society.* 248 pp. 20 plates.
Williams, W. M. The Sociology of an English Village: *Gosforth.* 272 pp. 12 figures. 13 tables.

SOCIOLOGY OF INDUSTRY AND DISTRIBUTION

Dunkerley, David. The Foreman. *Aspects of Task and Structure.* 192 pp.
Eldridge, J. E. T. Industrial Disputes. *Essays in the Sociology of Industrial Relations.* 288 pp.
Hollowell, Peter G. The Lorry Driver. 272 pp.
● Oxaal, I., Barnett, T. and Booth, D. (Eds) Beyond the Sociology of Development. *Economy and Society in Latin America and Africa.* 295 pp.
Smelser, Neil J. Social Change in the Industrial Revolution: *An Application of Theory to the Lancashire Cotton Industry, 1770–1840.* 468 pp. 12 figures. 14 tables.
Watson, T. J. The Personnel Managers. *A Study in the Sociology of Work and Employment.* 262 pp.

ANTHROPOLOGY

Brandel-Syrier, Mia. Reeftown Elite. *A Study of Social Mobility in a Modern African Community on the Reef.* 376 pp.
Dickie-Clark, H. F. The Marginal Situation. *A Sociological Study of a Coloured Group.* 236 pp.
Dube, S. C. Indian Village. *Foreword by Morris Edward Opler.* 276 pp. 4 plates.
    India's Changing Villages: *Human Factors in Community Development.* 260 pp. 8 plates. 1 map.
Firth, Raymond. Malay Fishermen. *Their Peasant Economy.* 420 pp. 17 pp. plates.
Gulliver, P. H. Social Control in an African Society: a Study of the Arusha, Agricultural Masai of Northern Tanganyika. 320 pp. 8 plates. 10 figures.
    Family Herds. 288 pp.
Jarvie, Ian C. The Revolution in Anthropology. 268 pp.
Little, Kenneth L. Mende of Sierra Leone. 308 pp. *and folder.*
    Negroes in Britain. *With a New Introduction and Contemporary Study by Leonard Bloom.* 320 pp.

Madan, G. R. Western Sociologists on Indian Society. *Marx, Spencer, Weber, Durkheim, Pareto. 384 pp.*
Mayer, A. C. Peasants in the Pacific. *A Study of Fiji Indian Rural Society. 248 pp.*
Meer, Fatima. Race and Suicide in South Africa. *325 pp.*
Smith, Raymond T. The Negro Family in British Guiana: *Family Structure and Social Status in the Villages. With a Foreword by Meyer Fortes. 314 pp. 8 plates. 1 figure. 4 maps.*

SOCIOLOGY AND PHILOSOPHY

Barnsley, John H. The Social Reality of Ethics. *A Comparative Analysis of Moral Codes. 448 pp.*
Diesing, Paul. Patterns of Discovery in the Social Sciences. *362 pp.*
● **Douglas, Jack D.** (Ed.) Understanding Everyday Life. *Toward the Reconstruction of Sociological Knowledge. Contributions by Alan F. Blum, Aaron W. Cicourel, Norman K. Denzin, Jack D. Douglas, John Heeren, Peter McHugh, Peter K. Manning, Melvin Power, Matthew Speier, Roy Turner, D. Lawrence Wieder, Thomas P. Wilson and Don H. Zimmerman. 370 pp.*
Gorman, Robert A. The Dual Vision. *Alfred Schutz and the Myth of Phenomenological Social Science. About 300 pp.*
Jarvie, Ian C. Concepts and Society. *216 pp.*
Kilminster, R. Praxis and Method. *A Sociological Dialogue with Lukács, Gramsci and the early Frankfurt School. About 304 pp.*
● **Pelz, Werner.** The Scope of Understanding in Sociology. *Towards a More Radical Reorientation in the Social Humanistic Sciences. 283 pp.*
Roche, Maurice. Phenomenology, Language and the Social Sciences. *371 pp.*
Sahay, Arun. Sociological Analysis. *212 pp.*
Slater, P. Origin and Significance of the Frankfurt School. *A Marxist Perspective. About 192 pp.*
Spurling, L. Phenomenology and the Social World. *The Philosophy of Merleau-Ponty and its Relation to the Social Sciences. 222 pp.*
Wilson, H. T. The American Ideology. *Science, Technology and Organization as Modes of Rationality. 368 pp.*

International Library of Anthropology

General Editor Adam Kuper

Ahmed, A. S. Millenium and Charisma Among Pathans. *A Critical Essay in Social Anthropology. 192 pp.*
  Pukhtun Economy and Society. *About 360 pp.*

Brown, Paula. The Chimbu. *A Study of Change in the New Guinea Highlands. 151 pp.*
Foner, N. Jamaica Farewell. *200 pp.*
Gudeman, Stephen. Relationships, Residence and the Individual. *A Rural Panamanian Community. 288 pp. 11 plates, 5 figures, 2 maps, 10 tables.*
 The Demise of a Rural Economy. *From Subsistence to Capitalism in a Latin American Village. 160 pp.*
Hamnett, Ian. Chieftainship and Legitimacy. *An Anthropological Study of Executive Law in Lesotho. 163 pp.*
Hanson, F. Allan. Meaning in Culture. *127 pp.*
Humphreys, S. C. Anthropology and the Greeks. *288 pp.*
Karp, I. Fields of Change Among the Iteso of Kenya. *140 pp.*
Lloyd, P. C. Power and Independence. *Urban Africans' Perception of Social Inequality. 264 pp.*
Parry, J. P. Caste and Kinship in Kangra. *352 pp. Illustrated.*
Pettigrew, Joyce. Robber Noblemen. *A Study of the Political System of the Sikh Jats. 284 pp.*
Street, Brian V. The Savage in Literature. *Representations of 'Primitive' Society in English Fiction, 1858–1920. 207 pp.*
Van Den Berghe, Pierre L. Power and Privilege at an African University. *278 pp.*

International Library of Social Policy

General Editor Kathleen Jones

Bayley, M. Mental Handicap and Community Care. *426 pp.*
Bottoms, A. E. and **McClean, J. D.** Defendants in the Criminal Process. *284 pp.*
Butler, J. R. Family Doctors and Public Policy. *208 pp.*
Davies, Martin. Prisoners of Society. *Attitudes and Aftercare. 204 pp.*
Gittus, Elizabeth. Flats, Families and the Under-Fives. *285 pp.*
Holman, Robert. Trading in Children. *A Study of Private Fostering. 355 pp.*
Jeffs, A. Young People and the Youth Service. *About 180 pp.*
Jones, Howard, and **Cornes, Paul.** Open Prisons. *288 pp.*
Jones, Kathleen. History of the Mental Health Service. *428 pp.*
Jones, Kathleen, with **Brown, John, Cunningham, W. J., Roberts, Julian** and **Williams, Peter.** Opening the Door. *A Study of New Policies for the Mentally Handicapped. 278 pp.*
Karn, Valerie. Retiring to the Seaside. *About 280 pp. 2 maps. Numerous tables.*
King, R. D. and **Elliot, K. W.** Albany: Birth of a Prison—End of an Era. *394 pp.*

Thomas, J. E. The English Prison Officer since 1850: *A Study in Conflict.* 258 pp.
Walton, R. G. Women in Social Work. *303 pp.*
● **Woodward, J.** To Do the Sick No Harm. *A Study of the British Voluntary Hospital System to 1875. 234 pp.*

International Library of Welfare and Philosophy

General Editors Noel Timms and David Watson

● **McDermott, F. E.** (Ed.) Self-Determination in Social Work. *A Collection of Essays on Self-determination and Related Concepts by Philosophers and Social Work Theorists. Contributors: F. B. Biestek, S. Bernstein, A. Keith-Lucas, D. Sayer, H. H. Perelman, C. Whittington, R. F. Stalley, F. E. McDermott, I. Berlin, H. J. McCloskey, H. L. A. Hart, J. Wilson, A. I. Melden, S. I. Benn. 254 pp.*
● **Plant, Raymond.** Community and Ideology. *104 pp.*
Ragg, Nicholas M. People Not Cases. *A Philosophical Approach to Social Work. About 250 pp.*
● **Timms, Noel** and **Watson, David.** (Eds) Talking About Welfare. *Readings in Philosophy and Social Policy. Contributors: T. H. Marshall, R. B. Brandt, G. H. von Wright, K. Nielsen, M. Cranston, R. M. Titmuss, R. S. Downie, E. Telfer, D. Donnison, J. Benson, P. Leonard, A. Keith-Lucas, D. Walsh, I. T. Ramsey. 320 pp.*
● (Eds). Philosophy in Social Work. *250 pp.*
● **Weale, A.** Equality and Social Policy. *164 pp.*

Primary Socialization, Language and Education

General Editor Basil Bernstein

Adlam, Diana S., with the assistance of Geoffrey Turner and Lesley Lineker. Code in Context. *About 272 pp.*
Bernstein, Basil. Class, Codes and Control. *3 volumes.*
● 1. Theoretical Studies Towards a Sociology of Language. *254 pp.*
2. Applied Studies Towards a Sociology of Language. *377 pp.*
● 3. Towards a Theory of Educational Transmission. *167 pp.*
Brandis, W. and **Bernstein, B.** Selection and Control. *176 pp.*

Brandis, Walter and **Henderson, Dorothy.** Social Class, Language and Communication. *288 pp.*
Cook-Gumperz, Jenny. Social Control and Socialization. *A Study of Class Differences in the Language of Maternal Control. 290 pp.*
● **Gahagan, D. M** and **G. A.** Talk Reform. *Exploration in Language for Infant School Children. 160 pp.*
Hawkins, P. R. Social Class, the Nominal Group and Verbal Strategies. *About 220 pp.*
Robinson, W. P. and **Rackstraw, Susan D. A.** A Question of Answers. *2 volumes. 192 pp. and 180 pp.*
Turner, Geoffrey J. and **Mohan, Bernard A.** A Linguistic Description and Computer Programme for Children's Speech. *208 pp.*

Reports of the Institute of Community Studies

Baker, J. The Neighbourhood Advice Centre. A Community Project in Camden. *320 pp.*
● **Cartwright, Ann.** Patients and their Doctors. *A Study of General Practice. 304 pp.*
Dench, Geoff. Maltese in London. *A Case-study in the Erosion of Ethnic Consciousness. 302 pp.*
Jackson, Brian and **Marsden, Dennis.** Education and the Working Class: *Some General Themes raised by a Study of 88 Working-class Children in a Northern Industrial City. 268 pp. 2 folders.*
Marris, Peter. The Experience of Higher Education. *232 pp. 27 tables.*
● Loss and Change. *192 pp.*
Marris, Peter and **Rein, Martin.** Dilemmas of Social Reform. *Poverty and Community Action in the United States. 256 pp.*
Marris, Peter and **Somerset, Anthony.** African Businessmen. *A Study of Entrepreneurship and Development in Keyna. 256 pp.*
Mills, Richard. Young Outsiders: *a Study in Alternative Communities. 216 pp.*
Runciman, W. G. Relative Deprivation and Social Justice. *A Study of Attitudes to Social Inequality in Twentieth-Century England. 352 pp.*
Willmott, Peter. Adolescent Boys in East London. *230 pp.*
Willmott, Peter and **Young, Michael.** Family and Class in a London Suburb. *202 pp. 47 tables.*
Young, Michael and **McGeeney, Patrick.** Learning Begins at Home. *A Study of a Junior School and its Parents. 128 pp.*
Young, Michael and **Willmott, Peter.** Family and Kinship in East London. *Foreword by Richard M. Titmuss. 252 pp. 39 tables.*
The Symmetrical Family. *410 pp.*

Reports of the Institute for Social Studies in Medical Care

Cartwright, Ann, Hockey, Lisbeth and Anderson, John J. Life Before Death. *310 pp.*
Dunnell, Karen and Cartwright, Ann. Medicine Takers, Prescribers and Hoarders. *190 pp.*
Farrell, C. My Mother Said. . . . *A Study of the Way Young People Learned About Sex and Birth Control.* 200 pp.

Medicine, Illness and Society

General Editor W. M. Williams

Hall, David J. Social Relations & Innovation. *Changing the State of Play in Hospitals.* 232 pp.
Hall, David J., and Stacey, M. (Eds) Beyond Separation. *234 pp.*
Robinson, David. The Process of Becoming Ill. *142 pp.*
Stacey, Margaret *et al.* Hospitals, Children and Their Families. *The Report of a Pilot Study.* 202 pp.
Stimson G. V. and Webb, B. Going to See the Doctor. *The Consultation Process in General Practice.* 155 pp.

Monographs in Social Theory

General Editor Arthur Brittan

● Barnes, B. Scientific Knowledge and Sociological Theory. *192 pp.*
Bauman, Zygmunt. Culture as Praxis. *204 pp.*
● Dixon, Keith. Sociological Theory. *Pretence and Possibility.* 142 pp.
Meltzer, B. N., Petras, J. W. and Reynolds, L. T. Symbolic Interactionism. *Genesis, Varieties and Criticisms.* 144 pp.
● Smith, Anthony D. The Concept of Social Change. *A Critique of the Functionalist Theory of Social Change.* 208 pp.

Routledge Social Science Journals

The British Journal of Sociology. *Editor – Angus Stewart; Associate Editor – Leslie Sklair. Vol. 1, No. 1 – March 1950 and Quarterly. Roy. 8vo. All back issues available. An international journal publishing original papers in the field of sociology and related areas.*

ROUTLEDGE SOCIAL SCIENCE JOURNALS

Community Work. *Edited by David Jones and Marjorie Mayo. 1973. Published annually.*

Economy and Society. *Vol. 1, No. 1. February 1972 and Quarterly. Metric Roy. 8vo. A journal for all social scientists covering sociology, philosophy, anthropology, economics and history. All back numbers available.*

Ethnic and Racial Studies. *Editor – John Stone. Vol. 1 – 1978. Published quarterly.*

Religion. *Journal of Religion and Religions. Chairman of Editorial Board, Ninian Smart. Vol. 1, No. 1, Spring 1971. A journal with an interdisciplinary approach to the study of the phenomena of religion. All back numbers available.*

Sociology of Health and Illness. *A Journal of Medical Sociology. Editor – Alan Davies; Associate Editor – Ray Jobling. Vol. 1, Spring 1979. Published 3 times per annum.*

Year Book of Social Policy in Britain, The. *Edited by Kathleen Jones. 1971. Published annually.*

Social and Psychological Aspects of Medical Practice

Editor Trevor Silverstone

Lader, Malcolm. Psychophysiology of Mental Illness. *280 pp.*
● **Silverstone, Trevor** and **Turner, Paul.** Drug Treatment in Psychiatry. *Revised edition. 256 pp.*
Whiteley, J. S. and **Gordon, J.** Group Approaches in Psychiatry. *256 pp.*